CASE STUDIES IN

Intercultural Dialogue

Nazan Haydari
Prue Holmes
EDITORS

Kendall Hunt
publishing company

Cover image courtesy of Nevin Hirik

Kendall Hunt
publishing company

www.kendallhunt.com
Send all inquiries to:
4050 Westmark Drive
Dubuque, IA 52004-1840

Printed in the United States of America

CONTENTS

FOREWORD

Creating Spaces for Intercultural Dialogue

Wendy Leeds-Hurwitz

In a world where members of different cultural groups find it hard to avoid contact, intercultural dialogue is essential. As a result, politicians and diplomats frequently call for intercultural dialogue, naming this as the way the world will avoid conflict and achieve peace between the many neighboring cultural groups. Yet there have been surprisingly few academic studies of intercultural dialogue: what it is, what aspects are essential, whether and how these can be taught, how can dialogues be started, and how can they impact a larger group than only those who participate. We need to know how to create a space within which intercultural dialogue can be established, where it will flourish, and how it can have an impact on participants. Too often, the scholars have left intercultural dialogue to the practitioners, as if it were none of their concern. This book makes a substantial contribution to the scholarly conversation. Much more remains to be done, of course, as might be expected with such a potentially large and significant topic, but this book provides a strong starting point.

Several facts are noteworthy in this collection in addition to the focus on intercultural dialogue as a topic. First, these are case studies. That means they are concrete, examining particular examples of intercultural dialogue in order to document what happened and analyze what might be learned from each case. Second, the authors are an international and interdisciplinary group, so they bring a wide range of perspectives, theories, and methods to bear on the various cases they examine. The result is a book covering an uncommon scope geographically, topically, and contextually. Given that any dialogue requires communication, many of the authors have academic homes within Communication. Traditionally this discipline has rarely addressed the topic of dialogue, so it is exciting to see so many take the topic under consideration. Third, while interaction is most often the focus, media, the arts, and new information technologies are also analyzed. Fourth, multiple suggestions are made for how to apply theory to practice, whether within educational contexts or other organizations such as non-profits.

The result is a good start on opening up the topic of intercultural dialogue to careful study. It is to be hoped that other volumes examining intercultural dialogue in even more places and contexts will follow. By definition case studies rarely exhaust a topic, but they serve especially well to open up a new topic for examination, and as such are particularly appropriate for the study of intercultural dialogue at this point in time.

ACKNOWLEDGMENTS

This collection of case studies is the product of a long journey that has itself involved enriching practices of intercultural dialogue. We would like to thank all of the contributors for their invaluable work and generous commitment to this book. Collaborating with every one of them was a privilege and we are sincerely grateful for all the effort, energy, and ideas they each brought to this collection. We are sincerely grateful to Wendy Leeds-Hurwitz for being a brilliant mentor at every stage. The idea of this book emerged from the National Communication Association Summer Conference on Intercultural Dialogue, 2009, at Maltepe University, Istanbul, which Wendy chaired. We thank her for enthusiastically supporting us and for being there whenever we needed her input and guidance. Our particular appreciation goes to Dawn O. Braithwaite for putting faith in us and in the idea behind this collection, and for initiating the contacts for the publication of this book. We are thankful to Chuck Braithwaite for helping us define the scope of the collection

We would like to acknowledge the great contribution of Nevin Hirik for sharing without hesitation her beautiful painting, *Praying,* as the cover for a book "dealing with the beautiful topic of intercultural dialogue," as she commented.

Finally, many thanks to Angela Willenbring, our development editor, Paul B. Carty, Director of Publishing Partnership, at Kendall Hunt Publishing Company, and Karen Fleckenstein, our compositor, for their support, and belief in this collection.

Nazan Haydari and Prue Holmes
March 2014

NOTES ON CONTRIBUTORS

About the Editors

Nazan Haydari is Associate Professor of Media School, Faculty of Communication at Istanbul Bilgi University, Turkey. Previously, she worked at Maltepe University, Istanbul for eight years and at Foothill Community College, California for four years. Her research interests are on alternative media studies, feminist media, use of various media forms for the development of critical pedagogy and intercultural dialogue, and radio studies. She is a Board Member of Research and Implementation Center on Street Children (SOYAÇ) at Maltepe University (and Advisory Board Member of Center for Intercultural Dialogue (http://centerforinterculturaldialogue.org/). Haydari is involved in the development of various media projects with street-involved children and youngsters. Her recent publications appear in *Innovations in Education and Teaching International Journal, New Public Spheres: Recontextualizing the Intellectual* (Edited by Thijssen et al., Ashgate Publications, 2013); and *The Social Dimension of the Economic Crisis in Europe: Social Work in European and Transnational Context (Ed.* Steph-Fine Schibri- Verlag Publications, 2013). Nazan holds a Ph.D. in Communications and MAIA in Communication and Development from Ohio University, USA.

Prue Holmes is Reader in Intercultural Education in the School of Education, Durham University, where she teaches an MA in Intercultural Communication and Education, and Adjunct Professor, Department of Teacher Education, University of Helsinki, Finland. She has a Ph.D. and M.MS from the University of Waikato, New Zealand, and an M.Ed. from Hong Kong University. She has taught intercultural communication at the University of Waikato, New Zealand, and English as a Foreign Language and English language teacher education in Italy, China, and Hong Kong. Prue supervises post-graduate theses and dissertations in intercultural communication, identity, and competence; international and intercultural education; English and foreign language education; and student mobility experiences. Prue has led the AHRC-funded "Researching Multilingually" project (http://researching-multilingually-at-borders.com/) on the complexities and possibilities of researching in contexts where more than one language is at play. This research is now embedded in the larger AHRC-funded project "Researching Multilingually at the Borders of Language, the Body, Law and the State" led by Professor Alison Phipps http://gramnet.wordpress.com/2013/09/18/research ing-multilingually-at-the-borders-of-language-the-body-law-and-the-state/. She is a partner in the European multilateral Erasmus project entitled "Intercultural Education Resources for Erasmus Students and their Teachers" (IEREST http://ierest-project.eu/), and received funding from HEA/UKCISA on internationalisation and the student experience. Other current research includes intercultural dialogue; the cultural and intercultural dimensions of language education and lingua francas. She has published extensively on intercultural encounters, intercultural dialogue, communication and learning experiences of international and Chinese students, intercultural competence, immigrant communication experiences, and intercultural education. She has received further research commissions from UNESCO (Paris), Education New Zealand, and the Ministry of Education (International), New Zealand. Prue chairs the International Association of Language and Intercultural Communication (IALIC) http://ialic.net/?page_id=2.

About the Contributors

Farshad Aminian-Tankei is Associate Professor in the Department of Communication and Philosophy at Florida Gulf Coast University. He teaches new Iranian cinema, Third World cinema, science and technology in cinema, classical Japanese cinema, foundations of civic engagement, film production and studies. His current research focuses on co-producing six short environmental fable films on stewardship, justice, and spirit. His recently contributed entry is on Iranian cinema and politics to the *Historical Dictionary of Middle Eastern Cinema.*

Jolanta Aritz is Associate Professor of Clinical Management Communication at the Center for Management Communication, Marshall School of Business at the University of Southern California. Aritz conducts research on small group communication, cross-cultural issues, leadership, and business discourse. She has published in the Journal of Intercultural Communication Research, Journal of Business Communication, and Journal of Asian Pacific Communication. She is co-editor of a research volume Discourse Perspectives on Organizational Communication that received The Association for Business Communication Award for Distinguished Publication in Business Communication (2012). She is also co-author of *Leadership Talk: A Discourse Approach to Leader Emergence* (2014).

Cigdem Bozdağ is Assistant Professor at New Media Department, Kadir Has University, Istanbul, Turkey. She was a postdoctoral researcher at Mercator–IPC fellow in the field of educaton at the Istanbul Policy Center of Sabanci University, Turkey between 2013 and 2014. Bozdağ is carrying out a research project on intercultural networks in schools through information and communication technologies. She has a Ph.D. degree in communication and media studies at the University of Bremen where she also worked as a lecturer. She was involved in the research project "Communicative connectivity of ethnic minorities, the integrative and segregative potential of digital media for diasporas" funded by the DFG (German Research Foundation), and in the EU-funded research project "ICT and Cultural Diversity, the potential of Information and Communication Technologies (ICT) for the promotion of cultural diversity in the EU." Bozdağ's main research and teaching areas are intercultural communication, globalization, education, new media, and migration studies. She has been teaching courses on similar topics at the University of Bremen and at Kadir Has University, Istanbul. Bozdağ received her M.A. degree from the University of Bremen, in the field of media culture. Her bachelor degree is from Boğaziçi University, in the field of political science and international relations.

Benjamin Broome is Professor in the Hugh Downs School of Human Communication at Arizona State University, USA. His teaching, research, and practice focus on intercultural dialogue, peacebuilding, facilitation processes, and relational empathy. He has facilitated intercultural dialogue with community and professional organizations, civil-society groups, indigenous/tribal groups, corporations, and academic and governmental institutions around the world, including the eastern Mediterranean, Western Europe, North America, and the southern Pacific. He has been involved with peacebuilding efforts in the eastern Mediterranean for over two decades, working closely with civil-society actors and the diplomatic community, designing and facilitating dialogue processes that allow sustained contact and joint projects aimed at creating a shared future. His book on peacebuilding efforts in Cyprus, *Building Bridges Across the Green Line*, can be downloaded from the United Nations Development Projects (UNDP) Action for Cooperation Trust in Cyprus.

Christine Develotte is Professor of Communication and Applied Linguistics at the École Normale Supérieure de Lyon. Her main research interests are Computer-Mediated Communication (CMC) and Intercultural Communication. She teaches on the graduate level and directs doctoral dissertations in these domains. She initiated the international project "Le français en (première) ligne" in 2001 when she was Lecturer at the University of Sydney in Australia. Her recent books are: *Décrire la conversation en ligne* (in collaboration with Kern & Lamy, 2011) and *L'éducation à l'heure du numérique: état des lieux, enjeux et perspectives* (with Poyet 2011).

David M. Duty is Adjunct Assistant Professor of communication at the University of Central Oklahoma located in Edmond, Oklahoma. His scholarly efforts in intercultural communication have focused on cross-cultural adaptation. His article for this edition originates from his dissertation which studied the perceptions of language, identity, and ethnicity among Hispanic emerging adults. He has presented conference papers related to his dissertation research at the International Communication Association and the National Communication Association conferences. Duty's research area is on ethnic identity formation among bi-ethnic (or mixed parentage) Hispanic emerging adults.

Susana Gonçalves is Coordinator Professor at the Polytechnic of Coimbra/Department of Education and Director of the Centre for the Study and Advancement of Pedagogy in Higher Education (CINEP)/ Polytechnic Institute of Coimbra (IPC). She is a researcher at the Research Unit for Education and Training (University of Lisbon) and teaches in the area of Psychology and Intercultural Communication/Education. She is a founding member of the European Association CiCea and an active member of the academic European Erasmus network CICE (Children's Identity and Citizenship in Europe), where she has served as Secretary General since 2007. Some of her most recent works are the edited books *The Challenges of Diversity and Intercultural Encounters* (2013, Routledge) and *Intercultural Policies and Education* (2011, Peter Lang).

David Gunn is Founding Director of Incidental, an organization specializing in cross-disciplinary creative practice that explores notions of identity and place. Gunn has led a variety of projects in the UK, Europe, Asia, and the US, with a diverse output including websites, live performances, installations, software design, and site-specific interventions in Europe, US, and Asia. An ongoing strand of David's work for Incidental focuses upon collaborations with communities and artists in Phnom Penh, Cambodia, exploring contemporary approaches to Khmer culture. His work has been commissioned by organizations including the Foreign and Commonwealth Office, Opera North, Futuresonic Festival, Arnolfini, Kings Place London, Manchester International Festival, Fundacao Serralves, and The New York Lower East Side Tenement Museum, and has been featured extensively in press including The Wire, The Guardian, Time Out, BBC, Wired Magazine, Voice of America, and numerous online publications. In 2011 David was invited to speak at the UN Social Forum on the Right to Development, exploring the role of contemporary culture in both informing and critiquing forms of international development.

Erika Hepple is Assistant Professor specialising in intercultural communication and international teacher education in the School of Cultural and Professional Learning, Queensland University of Technology, Australia. Erika has taught in a range of tertiary contexts, including in Saudi Arabia, Hong Kong, and Singapore. A central focus of her teaching and research is dialogue as pedagogy, in particular, exploring how intercultural dialogue can be a catalyst for transformative learning in teacher education. Erika's current research interests include intercultural learning through professional practice, and social constructions of identity and pedagogy in international teacher education. She is reviewer for the *Journal of International and Intercultural Communication; The Australian Education Researcher;* and the *International Education Journal: Comparative Perspectives.*

Tabassum "Ruhi" Khan is Assistant Professor in the Department of Media and Cultural Studies at University of California, Riverside. She received her Ph.D. from Ohio University in June 2009 and a Masters degree from Syracuse University in 1998. She teaches courses analyzing intersections of media and popular culture within neoliberal globalized contexts, and investigating influence of political-economy of media on media content. Her research interests include a focus on minority and marginalized identities in interconnected and mediated worlds and on possibilities for participation and assertion of citizenship rights afforded by digital interactive spheres of Internet and social-networking platforms. Specifically, she focuses on emerging minority Muslim identity in globalized India. Prior to pursuing an academic career, Dr. Khan worked as a film maker and channel manager with the Discovery Channels International, National Geographic Channel, and STAR TV, in Washington DC, New Delhi, and Hong Kong.

Wendy Leeds-Hurwitz is the Harron Family Endowed Chair in Communication at Villanova University, Director of the Center for Intercultural Dialogue, and Professor Emerita of Communication at the University of Wisconsin-Parkside. In addition to having chaired the International and Intercultural Communication Division of the National Communication Association, and the Language and Social Interaction Division of the International Communication Association, she has served as an expert for UNESCO's Division of Cultural Policies and Intercultural Dialogue, and as Fulbright Senior Specialist at the Instituto Politécnico de Coimbra in Portugal. She has been Invited Scholar at the École Normale Supérieure de Lyon, Senior Fellow at the Collegium de Lyon Institute for Advanced Studies (both in France), and Fellow at the Center for Twentieth Century Studies (in the US). Among her books are: *From Generation to Generation: Maintaining Cultural Identity over Time* (edited in 2005) and *Wedding as Text: Communicating Cultural Identities through Ritual* (2002).

Maria Flora Mangano is Invited Professor of Dialogue among Cultures in St. Peter's Philosophical-Theological Institute of Viterbo, Italy, and freelance lecturer of communication of scientific research to Ph.D. students and post-doctoral fellows of some Italian faculties. She has a scientific and humanistic background, and her focus on research and academic teaching is the idea of dialogue as a space of relationship between, across, and beyond cultures and disciplines. Her recent contribution on intercultural communication is *When Dialogue between Cultures is the Basis of Dialogue between Disciplines: Experiments of Transcultural Dialogue in a Faculty of Philosophy-Theology in Italy.* In: Z. Karahan Uslu, & C. Bilgili (Eds.). *Media Critiques 2011—Broken Grounds 2: Intercultural Communication, Multiculturalism.* Istanbul, Turkey: Beta Publishing House (2010, in Turkish); Marin Drinov Academic Publishing House, Sophia (2011, in English).

Eddah Mbula Mutua is Associate Professor of communication studies at St. Cloud State University, Minnesota. She teaches in the area of intercultural communication. Her research focuses on peace communication in post-conflict societies in Eastern Africa with a special interest in the role of women in post-genocide Rwanda. In the US, her areas of research include East African refugee and host communities' interactions in Central Minnesota, critical service-learning as a pedagogical practice in peace education, and African and African-Americans relations. Her publications appear in Qualitative Inquiry, Africa Media Review, African Yearbook of Rhetoric, Women and Language and several edited books.

Sandra L. Pensoneau-Conway is Assistant Professor in the Department of Communication Studies at Southern Illinois University Carbondale. She teaches critical communication pedagogy, intercultural communication, and the social construction of identity, using critical qualitative methods. Her current areas of research include the politics of grading in higher education, dialogue as a pedagogical philosophy, and automethodological approaches to cultural identity. Her recent publications appear in *Cultural Studies; Critical Methodologies; Handbook of Autoethnography; International Journal of Qualitative Methods; Identity and Communication Research: Intercultural Reflections and Future Directions.*

Ruma Sen has a Ph.D. in Communication Studies and an MA in International Studies from Ohio University, and an MA in Communication from the University of Delaware. Her teaching and research have been in the areas of communication and media studies, and she brings with her over eighteen years of academic and professional experience. Most recently she has taught at the Mudra Institute of Communication, Ahmedabad, India, and is a full-time tenured faculty member at Ramapo College of New Jersey, USA. Professor Sen has worked in a range of professional fields including news reporting, advertising, women's empowerment, rural development, and consulting for international development funding agencies. She is a feminist ethnographer whose research areas include globalization and transnational migration, popular culture, and the impact of race, class, and ethnicity on identity construc- tions. Her recent publications focus on re-reading race, nation, and masculinity in the South Asian diaspora in the United States and the impact of globalization on Indian culture and media.

Sachiko Tankei-Aminian is Assistant Professor in the Department of Communication and Philosophy at Florida Gulf Coast University. She teaches and studies intercultural and interracial communication and Japanese pop culture from interpretive and critical perspectives. She uses various methods in her scholarly work, such as autoethnography, performance, and filmmaking. Her current areas of research include relational ethics in autoethnography, the contextual nature of privilege, intercultural identity, and anti-war education. Her recent publication appears in *A Forum on Language and Communication* and *Liminalities*: *A Journal of Performance Studies.*

Gertrud Tarp received her Ph.D. in Intercultural Learning at the Department of Learning and Philosophy, Aalborg University, Denmark. Her field of work is secondary and tertiary language education, and her international experience includes teaching at an American high school as a Fulbright teacher and supervising internationalization projects. She is a reviewer of British research journals, and her current research focus is student voices in intercultural classroom communication. She has published articles and books on agent agendas, intercultural learning, linguistics, research methodology, and student voices. Her recent book is *Agent Agendas in Student Exchanges: A Grounded Theory Study* (2011).

Satoshi Toyosaki is Associate Professor in the Department of Communication Studies at Southern Illinois University Carbondale. He researches and teaches international and intercultural communication from interpretive and critical perspectives. He employs various ethnographic methods, particularly autoethnography, in his research. His recent publications appear in *Identity and Communication Research: Intercultural Reflections and Future Directions*, *International Journal of Qualitative Methods*, and *Journal of International and Intercultural Communication*.

Robyn C. Walker is Associate Professor of Clinical Management Communication at the Center for Management Communication, Marshall School of Business at the University of Southern California. She is the author of the textbook *Strategic Management Communication for Leaders* (3rd edition) and editor of *BCOM* (1st, 2nd, 3rd, 4th, 5th, and 6th editions), (both published by Cengage). She is editor of the *International Journal of Business Communication* and co-editor of a volume of research, *Discourse Perspectives on Organizational Communication* (2012) that received The Association for Business Communication Award for Distinguished Publication in Business Communication (2012). She is also a co-author of the book *Leadership Talk: A Discourse Approach to Leader Emergence* (2014).

About the Cover Artist

Nevin Hirik is an artist, who was born in Turkey, and now lives in Melbourne, Australia. For Nevin, the female figure represents the focal point of the environment created around it. Her female figures are gentle, airily translucent, and emotional. The figures are stripped back from the human to the energy of a soul. That soul orchestrates a mood, which dictates the observer's response to the image in view. Paintings, which engage an image, usually of a young female, are totally subjected to a background defining a mood. Hirik's quirky, angular figures are profiled against the velvety darkness of night. Tough, young, and vivacious they seem like metaphors for the artist herself, who emphatically states: *"My work is my philosophy, it is my life, it is me. It is my experiences, my passion, and my desire. I can not separate it from my life as it is what I am. All of the pain, the happiness, the love, and my emotions escape from my body and are splashed over my canvas for all to see, for all to feel. Nothing is hidden, there are no secrets, you just have to look and you will see all . . ."*

The painting used for the cover of this book is from *"praying series"* 2010 Acrylic on linen 91.5 × 91.5 cm (http://nevinhirik.com/)

INTRODUCTION

Contextualizing 'Intercultural Dialogue' and the 'Case Study'

Nazan Haydari and Prue Holmes

The oft-cited definition of intercultural dialogue as "*a process that comprises an **open** and **respectful** exchange or interaction between individuals, groups and organizations with different cultural backgrounds or world views*" (Council of Europe 2008, 10) is often perceived as the starting point for thinking about the communication that takes place when people—whether individually, or as members of groups and organizations—from similar and different horizons meet. While this description underlines the significant aspects of building and maintaining dialogue such as exchange, openness, and respect, as well as difference, it does not fully reflect the complexity of dialogue as a process within its own context. For example, what potential does intercultural dialogue offer vis-a-vis disagreement and conflict? How might it lead to resolution, reconciliation, and reconstruction of human engagement and relationships? And how do the complex dynamics and interplay of history, culture, power, and agency influence intercultural dialogic processes? We offer a collection of case studies that invite possibilities for theoretical, methodological, and practical ways of reconceptualizing and reconsidering the process of "dialogue" to offer a fresh point of entry into intercultural communication.

Recently, consecutive events that have taken place globally and the spaces of interactions these events have engendered help us to frame the rationale for this book. The plan of the Turkish state to demolish Taksim Gezi Park, one of the few green and non-commercial spaces in the capital, sparked protests all over the country. The rise in public transportation fares in Brazil mobilized people within the country's biggest cities to protest over the destruction of public services, like health care, education, and transportation, and the high costs of the 2014 World Cup. The closure of the national radio and television broadcaster in

Greece was followed by protests all over the country. And ongoing protests in Ukraine, following on from multiple Arab Spring uprisings, signpost people's resistance to political silencing and dictatorial interventions by autocratic states and their leaders. These global uprisings are characterized by their multiplicity of participants, ideologies, political views, and forms of actions; as well as the role of the new information technologies and social media. Solidarity groups within and across countries have been formed to react, resist, and change. While collaboration and dialogue embody everyday interactions and social media conversations, governmental and various other control mechanisms present a more complex picture, revealing the complex relationships between history, power, and various political, economic, and media institutions and grassroots groups. The collection of case studies we present here focus on the significance of intercultural dialogue in these various contexts, illustrating its potential, possibilities, and limits for deeper human engagement and understanding in a range of contexts and at varying levels of complexity.

Dialogue is often perceived as a critical point of entry into intercultural communication where tensions emerge from differences: dialogue invites us to reconsider our positions to understand, accept, and communicate through these differences. Intercultural dialogue is, without any doubt, an important step in overcoming the boundaries that separate people; yet we need spaces to go beyond dialogues of differences to locate positions of similarity, to explore understandings and meanings of dialogic processes and their related—and varying—concepts, and to reconsider the changes that globalization and new technologies bring to interactions among groups, cultures, and individuals. These experiences exist in the theory of understanding commonalities as well as differences.

By bringing a variety of theoretical and methodological approaches applied to different settings together in this collection, we aim to contribute to the shifting common understanding of intercultural communication, not as a process occurring between two cultures, but as a more complex account of the role of individual agency. Our intention is not to suggest resolutions to any sort of intercultural conflict or misunderstanding, but rather, in more general terms, to reveal the multiplicity of actors and the complexity of processes at play in dialogue by emphasizing that dialogue requires close attention and adjustment to power shifts at various levels: in interpersonal organizational relations, and across the hegemonic structures of society that seek to constrain dialogue. From this angle, the case studies we present form spaces of discussion for a more context-based understanding of the situations described by the authors.

Significance of the 'Case Study' Approach for Intercultural Dialogue

Despite the fact that the term "case study" is widely applied and referred to within social research, the question of whether it is a methodology, a strategy, a design, or an approach continues to remain under discussion. While case studies are often criticized as weak strategies to support existing theories, due to the fact that they provide an incomplete basis for generalization, they are seen as the ideal research strategy to cast doubt on theoretical claims (Tight 2010; Polletta & Amenta 2001; Yin 1994). A case study has the potential to reveal the complexity of a single situation within a larger context, thus making it a valuable approach, especially for studying unfamiliar phenomena in various contexts. It is within and in relation to this complexity that the significance of cases for studying and teaching intercultural dialogue becomes clear.

In this collection, "case study" is defined as an approach and a conscious strategy to draw out the "context" of particular dialogic situations; to emphasize dialogue, and to suggest an understanding and potential of intercultural dialogue within its complexity. "Context" is considered as a building block of intercultural communication, along with culture, communication, and power (Martin & Nakayama 2001), and refers to the physical, cultural, historical, political, and social situation in which the communication and dialogue take place. Relevant situations can range from conversations to curricular classroom activities, from a series of community activities to biographical accounts, and from forms of representation or organizational structures to online activities.

Mohanty (1991) defines context-based thinking to be against generalization by suggesting that it is through understanding the intersections among the historically specific systems of domination and dynamic oppositional agency that "we can attempt to explore questions of agency and consciousness without naturalizing either individuals or structures" (13). The main premise of context-based thinking is on "relationality," but not on cultural relativism. It focuses on the "micro politics of context, subjectivity and struggle" as well as "macro politics of global economic and political systems and processes" (13). It illuminates the universal and global by creating context and understanding of the particular. The case studies in this collection are examples of particular sites of dialogue, and thus, invite readers to transfer their analyses to other similar or shared historical, social, political contexts of dialogic interaction.

The case study approach also creates opportunities for the theorization and conceptualization of areas that have been under-investigated by scholars by creating a bridge between research and actual lived experiences. There are now, for example, countless "dialogue building" projects at the local, national, international, and global levels addressing various issues from grassroots rights to leadership level. They all share the aim of trying to resolve, settle, or moderate conflicts for the purpose of promoting understanding and dialogue. The impetus for much of this activity has been generated by the 2008 "Year of Intercultural Dialogue." Yet current scholarship has fallen behind in addressing the diversifying and changing agenda of these activities, struggles, and actions. Considering the politics involved in the processes of building dialogue to promote peace and understanding, intercultural communication research should be in a continuous search for methods and approaches which can be effective in the theorization of the dynamic realities of culture and communication. Paulo Freire (1998) points out that critical praxis "involves a dynamic and dialectic movement between 'doing' and 'reflecting on doing'" (43). Mohanty (1991) reflects on the relationship that should be established between theory and practice: that "it is the practice within movements that anchors the theory, the analysis is undertaken to improve the practice" (13). Further, Cronen (1995) and Craig and Tracy (1995) have strongly argued the need for "practical theory." Case studies as examples drawn from everyday experiences and observations therefore are particularly important to creating an active dialogic relationship between scholarship/analysis and communities/movements.

Positionality refers to one's own location at the intersections of various dimensions such as past experiences, race, class, gender, religion, nationality, sexual orientation to name a few. Closely related to feminist standpoint theory, positionality places an epistemological significance upon the social position of the researcher in the process of knowledge production by suggesting that knowledge is not neutral or abstract but embodied materially in lived experiences. Standpoint theory, combined with understandings of various positionalities, offers a powerful lens through which to make sense of, address, and act upon issues and challenges in intercultural communication. Such an approach also helps to avoid ethnocentrism which is the idea that one's own group's way of acting, living, thinking in the world is superior to others; such thinking can easily result in discrimination, conflict, violence, and justification and normalization of certain power relations such as imperialism, colonization, oppression, war, and ethnic cleansing (Sorrels 2013). A corollary of standpoint theory within intercultural communication is the suggestion that Afrocentric and Asiacentric approaches need to be included, rather than always taking a Eurocentric position as the obvious baseline (Asante & Miike 2013). Any research in intercultural communication should challenge and question our assumptions of others and ourselves and be in search of spaces of dialogue and peace. The case study approach forms a powerful tool for researchers to define and question their own location in the process of knowledge production.

Aims and Content

The case studies presented in this collection, with their focus on intercultural dialogue, illustrate the current status of intercultural communication in various contexts, and how misunderstandings and conflict, emergent during intercultural communication and dialogue, can be theorized and conceptualized. Overall, the format of the collection aims to create engagement in discussion from different perspectives and through various theoretical and methodological approaches to opportunities, possibilities, challenges, and ethical issues of intercultural communication and dialogue. The cases aim to open a space to consider the specifics of our own lives and perceive ourselves as the agents of the communication process promoting intercultural dialogue.

At the same time, recent investigations show that "intercultural dialogue" is not a panacea or salvation. A recent special issue on intercultural dialogue provides a collection of studies that show the optimism and scope of the concept, but also a disease, highlighting its challenges and limitations (Holmes 2014). For example, Phipps (2014) concludes that the concept "is at best problematic and largely inoperable under present conditions of globalization" where there is "conflict, vulnerability, insecurity and aggression" (113). Instead, she argues, models that are designed for "depoliticised and normatively conservative conditions" (122) need to be replaced by "models of creative practice and transformation." Ganesh and Holmes (2011) address the need for more intercultural dialogue research engaging multiple areas of communication inquiry. Furthermore, Holmes (2014) suggests that the related concepts of interculturality, capability, responsibility, ethics, interreligious dialogue, and conflict transformation (theorized and discussed within the articles in the 2014 special issue) open up possibilities for new lines of inquiry which invite further theorizing of intercultural dialogic communication. The studies within the pedagogic section also highlight the importance of educational programmes and pedagogic methods that provide foundations of intercultural understanding among students, young people, and the wider community.

The interdisciplinary and multidisciplinary nature of the case studies of intercultural communication presented in this collection begin to address these needs by expanding the scope of "dialogue on dialogue" (Ganesh & Holmes 2011, 85) in various disciplines including anthropology, education, linguistics, organization, intergroup and interpersonal communication; film and media studies; intercultural communication; management and leadership; new communication technologies; peace studies, and performance arts. A variety of theoretical approaches—situational and interactive models, grounded theories, standpoint theories, Bakhtinian dialogism, transdisciplinarity, community driven approaches, and interpretive and critical/cultural approaches are applied across the papers. Similarly, a wide selection of methodological approaches is represented, including ethnography, community autoethnography, conversation analysis, speech analysis, in-depth interviews, fieldwork, action research, organizational analysis, discourse analysis, textual analysis, and thematic analysis. Various concepts, such as spaces of dialogue, peaceful co-existence, reconciliation, peacebuilding, contact zone, intercultural contact, philosophy of dialogue, space of interaction, intersubjectivity, intercultural competence, collaboration, synchronous communication, multimodal communication, transcultural communication, and intercultural relationship are integrated into discussions to challenge, expand, reconceptualize, or redefine already established definitions of intercultural dialogue.

The discussion points in the case studies further illustrate the diversity and complexity of intercultural dialogue: for example, the potential of information and communication technologies (ICTs) as new "contact zones" where cultures meet; language learning; leadership in intercultural dialogue; the potential of communicative practices in enabling and constraining intercultural dialogue at the organizational level; the role of language in fostering dialogue between the members of ethnic groups and the dominant society; the formative nature of intercultural relationships in defining identities at the complex intersections of cultural, national, ideological, linguistics, and historical politics; the conceptualization of intercultural creative experiences that resist conventional models of communicative exchange; the consumption of popular culture within the global media economy; the creative processes of entertainment/education production; the theorization of Internet culture and intercultural dialogue; the politics of education in promoting intercultural sensibility and competence; the potential of community driven approaches in engendering collective action toward reconstruction, reconciliation, and co-existence; and facilitating dialogue through innovative conference design.

The presented issues are discussed across a diverse selection of contexts, such as French language learners in Australia and the United States, Moroccan and Turkish diasporas in Germany, non-governmental organizations serving the adaptation/adjustment needs of migrants and refugees in New Zealand, Hispanic communities in New Mexico and Oklahoma, Bollywood in America, Khmer musicians in Cambodia, the intercultural interaction of Australian and Hong Kong trainee teachers, teaching transcultural and transdisciplinary communication lectures in an Italian university, teaching intercultural education courses in Portugal, Turkish-Cypriot, and Greek-Cypriot communities, post-genocide Rwanda, and an intercultural dialogue conference in Turkey. The majority of the authors write their chapters from the position of an active participant, observer, and/or activist directly involved in the process (and who specify the level of their involvement in the case studies they discuss).

Organization of the Book

The case studies are structured around the idea that intercultural dialogue is an important component of everyday life, one that may and should be practiced at various levels—from the spaces aiming to build dialogue, to peacebuilding and reconciliation, education, the arts and media, everyday communication and relationships, institutional and organizational engagement, and in and through new communication technologies. Accordingly, the case studies have been organized into six parts, all with "building dialogue" as their focus.

Part I: Building Spaces for Dialogue

Our inspiration in bringing together this edited collection of case studies emerged as an outcome of a very successful international conference, the National Communication Association Summer Conference on Intercultural Dialogue, convened by Wendy Leeds-Hurwitz and hosted by Maltepe University in Istanbul in 2009. The interactive nature of the conference itself was designed to create a space for dialogue between the participants. The first case study of this collection, "Facilitating Intercultural Dialogue through Innovative Conference Design" by Wendy Leeds-Hurwitz, sets an example for the significance of *building spaces for dialogue* as the main contribution of Part I. Conferences are significant spaces of knowledge production and exchange as well as interactions and relationship among people with different backgrounds, disciplines, and theoretical and methodological approaches. Leeds-Hurwitz reports on the innovative design developed for a small conference with the deliberate intent to permit and encourage dialogue among an international group of scholars studying the topic of intercultural dialogue. She argues that a more interactive and dialogic conference format creates a space for different voices and experiences to be heard, permitting the emergence of long-term networking, friendships, and continued collaborations. Such interaction carries further significance in the field of intercultural dialogue not only by challenging and questioning established dominant paradigms and concepts through the theorization of marginalized voices and experiences, but also through developing collaborative projects growing out of dialogic relationships where the distinction between the self and the other becomes less critical.

Part II: Dialogue for Peacebuilding and Reconciliation

As the issues around peacebuilding, conflict resolution, reconciliation, promoting nonviolent communication, negotiation, and mediation are widely integrated in the activities of various organizations—governmental and nongovernmental institutions, those in civil society, international agencies, and other collaborative efforts, this section aims to highlight the concept of peacebuilding for the theorization of intercultural dialogue. "Community Driven Peacebuilding Approaches: The Case of Post-Genocide Rwanda" by Eddah Mbula Mutua addresses peacebuilding initiatives that privilege the community sphere as a transformative space for peace. The argument presented by Mbula Mutua challenges the dominant peacebuilding discourses and agendas where there is a global-local dichotomy; the "local" is reproduced through the lens of the universal, and an appreciation of post-colonial hybrid forms of peacebuilding approaches is prevented. What Rwandan communities do as mutual bodies to articulate and defend collective interests and goals makes a significant contribution to understanding peacebuilding in a post-genocide context. In Rwanda, localized efforts work because they prioritize locally available resources manifested in cultural traditions, local ways of knowing and communities' urgency.

In "Dialogue across the Divide: Bridging the Separation in Cyprus," Benjamin Broome draws on the dialogic activities of a small group of civil-society actors to bring Greek Cypriots and Turkish Cypriots together across the buffer zone separating the two communities since 1974. In spite of the many unknowns about the effects of dialogue and numerous challenges that limit the overall impact of dialogue, Broome argues that societies such as Cyprus can develop a culture in which dialogue is viewed as the means for dealing with differences and settling the disputes that arise from them. By utilizing a dialogic framework based on contact theory, concepts of reconciliation and conflict transformation, and research on cooperative/constructive approaches to conflict, this case study underlines the significance of dialogue in contributing to sustainable peace in five interrelated ways: enabling sustained contact, reducing deep-seated hostility, nurturing greater respect for the other, developing a narrative of peace and hope, and establishing a stronger basis for cooperation.

Part III: Building Dialogue in/for Education

Education and classroom settings always come with a potential to initiate change, and promote cultural sensitivity and ethical understanding. The result is that education is frequently considered an obvious context for establishing the basics of intercultural dialogue (i.e., Bergan & Restoueix 2009). Thus there is substantial need for the systematic critique of education systems, as well as the theorization of the cases that address the politics and potential of education in dialogue building. Part III, *Building Dialogue in/for Education,* addresses the significance of the concept of dialogue in education and the potential of curricular in promoting and facilitating dialogue. In "Multiculturalism, Contact Zones, and the Political Core of Intercultural Education," Susana Gonçalves foregrounds the politics involved in education by exploring how teaching and learning can be structured to foster the sort of intercultural sensitivity and active citizenship that imply respect and appreciation for diversity in society. Gonçalves describes various strategies she used in teaching an Intercultural Education course at the College of Education of the Polytechnic of Coimbra in Portugal to foster students' awareness and develop their ability to cooperate across cultural and national borders. She discusses the significance of integrating case studies, storytelling, guest speakers, Socratic dialogue, and community projects into the curriculum.

Transcultural and transdisciplinary approaches to dialogue appear to be little investigated within the intersecting areas of education and intercultural dialogue. By generating a discussion in this area, "Dialogue, a Space *Between*, *Across*, and *Beyond* Cultures and Disciplines: A Case Study of Lectures in Transcultural and Transdisciplinary Communication" by Maria Flora Mangano, proposes a philosophical approach to dialogue by exploring the relationship between, among, and beyond cultures and disciplines. This understanding implies a call for a dialogue as a "lifestyle," an attempt to apply this approach in everyday life, and in teaching and research on intercultural dialogue. Drawing from two courses of transcultural dialogue in an Italian Philosophical-Theological Faculty and three intensive Schools of communication of scientific research for young researchers, Mangano underlines students' developing awareness of the meaning of dialogue among cultures and disciplines, and as an opportunity to meet the Other.

Erika Hepple, in "Developing *Cosmopolitan* Professional Identities: Engaging Australian and Hong Kong Trainee Teachers in Intercultural Conversations," argues for the priority for teacher education programs to assist trainee teachers to engage productively with increasing cultural and linguistic diversity in school classrooms. Hepple describes a curriculum intervention that brings together trainee teachers from Australia and Hong Kong in intercultural conversations. The program aims to develop in teachers a more *cosmopolitan* teacher identity, thus enabling teachers to interact more empathetically with student diversity. The chapter outlines the structuring of these conversations and explores the trainees' reflections on their participation in intercultural dialogues. This chapter highlights the reciprocal nature of intercultural communication, indicating how both domestic and international trainees have much to gain by engaging in substantive conversations which can strengthen their intercultural communication knowledge and skills and help them to develop as more cosmopolitan professionals.

"Challenges in International Baccalaureate Students' Intercultural Dialogue" by Gertrud Tarp, is an attempt to understand the intercultural dialogic experiences of students in an international baccalaureate (IB) educational context. The method applied is grounded theory, i.e., a multi-faceted approach comprising semi-structured written narratives, retrospective questionnaires with student statements, and semi-structured focus group interviews. The study documents two educational spaces of interaction: in class and outside class. Tarp argues that International Baccalaureate students develop competence in the two spaces depending on their ability to build up academic and linguistic knowledge and to take part in intercultural dialogue with the purpose of creating an international friendship.

Part IV: Building Dialogue through Arts and Media

Various forms of media and arts from radio, television, short film; photography to puppet theatre, street art or graffiti are widely used in building intercultural dialogue. While the process of media and art production form powerful spaces for facilitating interaction, collaboration, exchange, and participation; the outcomes of such process carry the potential of challenging established forms of representations. The chapters here present a critical understanding of intercultural dialogue by challenging established definitions of intercultural dialogue in media and arts. "Bollywood in the City: Can the Consumption of Bollywood Cinema Serve as a Site for Intercultural Discovery and Dialogue?" by Ruma Sen explores the transcultural consumption of Bollywood cinema across global urban spaces like the New York metropolitan area. Bollywood acts as a site for intercultural dialogue by providing the possibility of learning, exchange, and consumption of culture. As Bollywood gets more involved in the production of content that caters to western audiences, and as mainstream western audiences are drawn to watch these films, Bollywood and its associated cultural artifacts become convenient vehicles and sites for intercultural exchange. This leads in turn to a mainstreaming of Indian identity that is inherently apolitical, and readily consumable by western audiences. As such, consumption gains ground, and overarching issues of contemporary, postcolonial India, for example, the politics of visibility (of what constitutes Indian culture in global urban spaces), remain unexplored. This study therefore questions the viability of authentic intercultural dialogue within such contexts, and suggests that cultural contact mediated through Bollywood films remains at the superficial level of consumption and global capital flows.

In "Storms, Lies, and Silence: Notes toward a Non-Dialogic Mode of Intercultural Contact," David Gunn considers the ways in which processes of intercultural dialogue and exchange operate within contemporary creative practice. Commencing with an examination of the notion of intercultural dialogue, Gunn explores how linguistic models of dialogue and communicative exchange are commonly used to both frame and evaluate experiences of intercultural contact. Drawing from the author's own experiences of running intercultural projects, the paper then explores aspects of intercultural contact that may be excluded or distorted by models based exclusively upon language. Exploring moments of intercultural contact where language breaks down into misunderstanding, or where participants themselves seek to destabilize the viability of communication, Gunn argues that such moments should not only be understood as an impoverished dialogue, but rather, a fundamentally different kind of intercultural experience.

Part V: Building Dialogue in/through Research

This part of the collection starts from the discipline of anthropology by providing a space to reflect on the positionality of the researchers in the process of knowledge production. As anthropology carries significant weight in defining culture and identity, it is crucial researchers follow a critical and reflective approach to power relations and their own roles in the construction of knowledge about certain cultures and perspectives. In "Anthropology as Intercultural Critique: Challenging the Singularity of Islamic Identity," Ruhi Khan draws from her own research experience as a Muslim woman to question her assumptions and authority among her informants—young Muslim women residents of an exclusive Muslim enclave in New Delhi, India. Her case study describes the performance of a religious ritual constructing the core of Islamic identity to show the diversity in the internalizations of religiosity, and to argue that native ethnographers, in overlooking the complex layers of experiences shaping a religious identity, can also be guilty of perpetuating homogenizing and totalizing narratives.

The collaborative narration of Sandra L. Pensoneau-Conway, Satoshi Toyosaki, Sachiko Tankei-Aminian, and Farshad Aminian-Tankei on "Community Autoethnography: A Critical Visceral Way of "Doing" Intercultural Relationships" presents a relational research practice by challenging us to put individual autoethnographic investigations into dialogical relations with those of others. Community autoethnography denies that our subjectivities are private and equips us to capture them in relation to our intercultural relationship partners. Using community autoethnography, one of the narrators starts the process by writing a short piece about his or her lived experience of cultural issues in the course of relationships. Then, the writer shares the narrative with the rest of the group. The one who finds some theoretical, conceptual, critical, and/or performative connection with the original piece responds with a thematically connected narrative, thus eventually developing a collective autoethnographic investigation. The community autoethnography presented in this chapter is simultaneously research data, research methodology, nuanced theorization, and cultural criticism of the authors' own intercultural relationships. Intercultural topics included in the process consist of postcolonialism, globalization, media, relational dialogic competence, conflict, caring, and love.

Part VI: Building Dialogue in Everyday Interactions

In "The Fusion of Language and Ethnic Identity: The Voices of Hispanic Emerging Adults in New Mexico and Oklahoma," David Duty not only provides fundamental information about emerging adults from the largest ethnic minority in the United States, but also advances our understanding of the connection between language, identity, and intercultural dialogue. By utilizing Communication Accommodation Theory and Co-Cultural Theory, Duty draws from the case of Hispanic emerging adults in two distinct environments—the metropolitan areas of Albuquerque, New Mexico, and Oklahoma City, Oklahoma. The former offers a unique history of Hispanic influence and the latter recently has found its Hispanic population on the rise. Hispanic emerging adults in this study present a wide-ranging ethnic identity orientation, from cultural fusion to ethnic identity achievement. This varied ethnic identity orientation is not unusual, as emerging adulthood is a distinct period of life described as the age of identity explorations. The language practices of the emerging adults in this study also vary. The New Mexico participants are English monolinguals while the participants from Oklahoma are generally bilingual. The New Mexican population do not appear to reveal any loss of culture, self, or pride as previous scholarship indicates. The Oklahoma population engages in code switching and appears to implement a convergence speaker strategy in interactions with others. The environmental composition of the United States will inevitably change as Hispanic emerging adults become new social actors, thus warranting greater avenues of dialogue between and among this emergent group and the dominant society.

Part VII: Building Dialogue at the Institutional/Organizational Level

In "'Why Did it All Go So Horribly Wrong?': Intercultural Conflict in an NGO in New Zealand," Prue Holmes documents intercultural conflict in a small, non-governmental organization, a migrant community center (MCC), in a New Zealand city. The case describes three critical incidents of unsuccessful intercultural dialogue as perceived by Ian, a white New Zealander and the MCC manager, and his Chinese employee, Felix. The once amicable relationship between the two turned hostile when the rolling contract for Felix's work expired and Ian was obliged to terminate Felix's employment. The conflict led to mediation, formalizing the completion of Felix's contract, but failing to resolve the conflict between the one-time friends. The case describes the communication events that led to mediation. The analysis draws on intercultural conflict theory, Chinese communication styles, culturally informed relationship practices, and power in an attempt to make sense of the (mis)communication, and participant interactions. The characters and events in the case are all fictitious, representing a reconstruction of a number of scenarios and intercultural communication exchanges Holmes encountered in her research, consultancy, and service within the migrant/refugee community sector over several years. In the style of Van Maanen's "impressionist tales" (1988), Holmes uses this technique to explore complex intercultural relations in an ethical way that protects the identities of immigrants as a potentially vulnerable group, yet at the same time underscoring the need for studies that reveal the inexplicable—and thus, the limits and impossibilities of—dialogue.

In "Leadership in Intercultural Dialogue: A Discursive Approach," Aritz and Walker contribute to the concept of intercultural dialogue by examining the construct of leadership as central in accomplishing the goal of fostering mutual respect, advancing dialogue, including different perspectives, and avoiding unilateral decision-making. By examining leadership as a dialogic, skill-based phenomenon grounded in intercultural competence, the study uses a situational and interactive model developed by Gumperz that underscores the importance of cultural norms and socio-cultural knowledge. Individuals from different cultures often learn the other's language but apply their own discourse conventions when using it. They analyze conversational interaction to examine different leadership styles and team dynamics. Excerpts from three decision-making meetings are used to analyze the emergence of leadership in intercultural teams and to identify different leadership styles. The analysis illustrates two styles of leadership—autocratic and collaborative—and their effects on other team members, particularly in terms of whether they come from individualist or collectivist cultures. A more collaborative leadership style was found to lead to more balanced contribution and participation of all members in intercultural groups. The study also illustrates how context, including the cultural backgrounds of team members, affects which leadership style may be recognized and adapted by group members.

Part VIII: Building Dialogue through New Information Technologies

Despite the existing digital and information divides in the world, new information technologies have drastically transformed the communication space by permitting the construction of intercultural dialogues across geographic distance and even international borders, simultaneously creating an excellent resource for learning about other cultures, one far less superficial than many alternatives. In "*Le Francais en (Première) Ligne*: Creating Contexts for Intercultural Dialogue in the Classroom," Christine Develotte and Wendy Leeds-Hurwitz document a case study of teaching French online, focusing on the ways in which readily available technologies can be used to create a sense of community through synchronous online communication and encourage intercultural dialogues among participants. This study incorporates two populations in an uncommon way, with the result that each gains something different from the experience: French graduate students learning to become language teachers gain practice in teaching, while US undergraduates expand their knowledge of grammar and gain intercultural communicative competence. The chapter provides extensive examples of successful collaboration leading to intercultural dialogues, as well as sufficient details so others may design comparable projects.

In conclusion, taking action to build a more peaceful and socially just environment and relationship is an important aspect of intercultural communication. We hope that the case studies presented in this collection can open up spaces for the development of similar situations, projects, and actions. We also hope that "case studies," as an approach, can be more strategically integrated into intercultural communication research to challenge already established views of culture, identity, and power, to emphasize the agency and relationality of individuals and communities in the process of dialogue building, and to encourage the theorization of everyday experiences and practices for the purpose of integrating the concept of intercultural dialogue into research within other topics.

References

Asante, M. K., & Miike, Y. (2013). Paradigmatic issues in intercultural communication studies: An Afrocentric–Asiacentric dialogue. *China Media Research, 9*(3), 1–19.

Bergan, S., & Restoueix, J.-P. (Eds.). (2009). *Intercultural dialogue on campus*. Strasbourg: Council of Europe Publishing.

Council of Europe. (2008). *White paper on intercultural dialogue: "Living together as equals in dignity."* Retrieved from http://www.coe.int/t/dg4/intercultural/concept_EN.asp

Craig, R. T., & Tracy, K. (1995). Grounded practical theory: The case of intellectual discussion. *Communication Theory, 5*(3), 248–272.

Cronen, V. E. (1995). Practical theory and the tasks ahead for social approaches to communication. In W. Leeds-Hurwitz (Ed.), *Social approaches to communication* (pp. 217–242). New York: Guilford Press.

Freire, P. (1998). *Pedagogy of freedom: Ethics, democracy, and civic courage*. Lanham, MD: Rowman & Littlefield.

Ganesh, S., & Holmes, P. (2011). Positioning intercultural dialogue—Theories, pragmatics, and an agenda. *Special issue on intercultural dialogue. Journal of International and Intercultural Communication, 4*(2), 81–86.

Holmes, P. (2014). Intercultural dialogue: Challenges to theory, practice, and research. *Language and Intercultural Communication, 14*(1), 1–6.

Martin, J. N., & Nakayama, T. K. (2001). *Experiencing intercultural communication: An Introduction*. Mountain View, CA: MayField Publishing Company.

Mohanty, C. T. (1991). Introduction: Cartographies of struggle: Third World Women and the politics of feminism. In C. T. Mohanty, A. Russo, & L. Torres (Eds.), *Third World Women and the Politics of Feminism* (pp. 1–57). Bloomington: Indiana University Press.

Phipps, A. (2014). 'They are bombing now': 'Intercultural Dialogue' in times of conflict. *Language and Intercultural Communication, 14*(1), 108–124.

Polletta, F., & Amenta, E. (2001) Second that emotion? Lessons from once-novel concepts in movement research. In Goodwin, J., Jasper, J., & Polletta, F. (Eds.), *Passionate politics: Emotions and social movements* (pp. 303–316). Chicago: University of Chicago Press.

Sorrels, K. (2013). *Intercultural communication: Globalization and social justice*. Thousand Oaks, CA: Sage Publications.

Tight, M. (2010). The curious case of case study: a viewpoint. *International Journal of Social Research Methodology, 13*(4), 329–339.

Van Maanen, J. (1988). *On writing ethnography: Tales of the field*. Chiaco: Chigaco University Press.

Yin, R. K. (1994). *Case study research: Design and methods*. (2nd ed.). Thousand Oaks, CA: Sage Publishing.

PART I

Building Spaces for Dialogue

1

Facilitating Intercultural Dialogue through Innovative Conference Design

Wendy Leeds-Hurwitz

Key Words

- ► Dialogue facilitation
- ► Innovative conference design
- ► International conference

1. Introduction

This chapter reports on the innovative design developed for a small conference intended to permit and encourage intercultural dialogues among an international group of scholars studying the topic of intercultural dialogue. It is argued that a more interactive and dialogic conference format creates a space for different voices and experiences to be heard, permitting the emergence of long-term networking and friendships. Such interaction carries further significance in the field of intercultural dialogue not only by challenging and questioning established dominant paradigms and concepts through the theorization of marginalized voices and experiences, but also through developing collaborative projects growing out of dialogic relationships where the distinction between the self and the other becomes less critical.

2. Innovative Conference Design

National and international conferences today generally range from large (with hundreds of participants) to enormous (thousands). Most entail numerous brief formal presentations, typically organized into sets of four or five as panels, with an assigned chair and respondent.[1] Large conferences serve the best interests of sponsoring organizations as a source of income generation, but are not always in the best interests of participants, who complain about the limited time available for considered exchange of ideas, and the difficulty of actually meeting senior colleagues whose work they have read, or picking out new junior colleagues with overlapping interests. Perhaps major revisions to the format of large conferences actually are impossible, given their many goals and constraints, but small conferences appear far more amenable to revision.

In 1968, Margaret Mead concluded that

> the small conference is a new and powerful communication form...The small substantive conference is, in fact, a new social invention...a new kind of communication suitable for the mid-twentieth century demands for rapid communication among individuals of very different academic, social, national, cultural, and ideological orientations. (1968a, v)

Many of the small conferences held in the forty years since her comments have been merely miniatures of typical large conferences, resolving some issues, but not all. Mead's "new social invention" of "a new kind of communication" merits more attention than received to date, and small conferences must evolve further to better fit with participants' needs.

Mead went on to argue for "the conference process as a unique form of communication characterized by continuous, simultaneous multi-model communication from many-to-many in the pursuit of an intellectual goal" (1968b, 14). In keeping with the shifts now taken for granted from one-to-many/single channel communication to many-to-many/multimodal communication in other contexts, conferences have greatest value to the largest number of participants when providing an opportunity "to come together, *informally*, to exchange information and explore new ideas" (Reid 1992, 391, emphasis added). If the goal were merely to present new ideas, there would be little justification for everyone traveling to a common destination, and reading publications could adequately substitute for conference attendance. Making everyone take the trouble to travel to a joint site requires that the interactions available at the conference adequately repay the cost in time and funds.

Just as student-centered learning requires actively involving students in their own education, increasing involvement of conference participants similarly increases their learning of new ideas presented (Ravn & Elsborg 2007, 2011). Among other issues, Ravn and Elsborg argue specifically that standard conference design incorporates "too much lecturing, too little learning" (2007, 4). That sounds a lot like typical complaints about large introductory lecture courses. Both use the old one-to-many structure despite that no longer being the only available model, and clearly not the only appropriate model for all occasions. A wide range of innovations have been introduced over the past decade or two, ranging from entire "unconferences" to the introduction of a few fishbowls or world cafes into an otherwise unchanged conference design.[2]

3.   NCA Summer Conference on Intercultural Dialogue

The innovative design described here was prepared for and implemented during the National Communication Association Summer Conference on Intercultural Dialogue, held July 22–26, 2009, at Maltepe University in Istanbul, Turkey. Conference papers were solicited, subjected to blind peer review, and either accepted or rejected, partially due to NCA sponsorship since these remain key elements of NCA conferences, and partially because having papers accepted through a process of peer review permitted most attendees to obtain funding for their travel.[3] But rather than organize accepted papers into formal panels, conference planners took advantage of the small size of the group to make this a working conference. Several of Ravn and Elsborg's proposals for innovative design were incorporated, specifically that time be explicitly devoted to networking and knowledge sharing, and that time be set aside for active interpretation (that is, small groups immediately pondering the implications of presentations). The best prior models for this conference were taken to be the Macy Conferences (Fremont-Smith 1961; Leeds-Hurwitz 1994). Although the explicit emphasis of the Macy Conferences was on facilitating interdisciplinary conversations rather than intercultural dialogues, and they leaned heavily toward the exact sciences, several of the organizers' key decisions proved valuable. From that model we knew to keep the event small, to choose a location away from distractions, so that all participants would be present for all major components, as well as to have a clear focus, and formal syntheses of what had been learned at specific points. In discussing the Macy (and similar) conferences, Fremont-Smith (1961) emphasized the need to provide a context in which informal conversations occurring outside normal scientific meetings would be "brought into the conference room" by maintaining "informality of mood" as well as the possibility of interruptions (20), in his terms, a matter of "conversation" versus "speech" (another way to express Mead's many-to-many design in lieu of the more typical one-to-many structure). Fremont-Smith also emphasized the importance of establishing a context where participants could ask a lot of questions, as well as the reduced defensiveness linked to questioning conclusions during a casual rather than formal context, and the resulting development of a community of practice (although not in quite those words, of course; see Wenger, McDermott, & Snyder 2002 for more about CoP).

In keeping with the topic of intercultural dialogue, we not only provided a conference where people discussed their work on that topic, but provided as well multiple opportunities for one-on-one and small group dialogues. As Freeman (2008) points out, meetings are "dialogic, not monologic" (17) because "We construct common objects of interest through discussion: we learn *with* others as much as from others" (18). Conference participants thus talked to each other while simultaneously talking about their research, practicing intercultural dialogues while discussing them.[4]

> This was one of the most enjoyable conferences I've attended. The small size and the length (and the format of the discussions, as well as the social activities) allowed me to meet and interact with people in meaningful ways. I also appreciated the discussion questions in the program, which helped us to stay focused in our small groups.[5]

I chaired the Organizing Committee; Nazan Haydari served as Local Arrangements Chair; the conference itself was the culmination of a conversation between us started in Dresden in 2006. All other organizers and participants are listed in Appendix 1 because the event would not have been the same without these specific people. The group was international in origin and eclectic in interests: of the papers that successfully passed through academic peer review (the acceptance rate was 55%), eighteen were submitted by US scholars, nine from international scholars residing in the US, six from Turkish scholars, and nine from other countries. A total of sixty-six people participated, including those available for the photo below taken by one of the participants, Ruma Sen. The conference would have benefitted from even greater international participation, but this was not a bad start.

The heart of our conference design was a sequence of seven small group discussions on topics of interest to participants (derived from a reading of all accepted papers). Participants were divided into six small groups, and gathered at round tables; the organizers served as facilitators for these exchanges. This meant clusters of up to ten people per table. Rather than present a research report once, participants were asked to use their papers as a resource for multiple overlapping conversations. Most small group interactions were preceded by a plenary presentation related to the topic at hand, and followed by a discussion of the whole permitting public presentation and then at least some synthesis of ideas across clusters. Speakers outside the core group of presenters were invited to make plenary presentations in order to begin each conversation, with various individuals presenting conclusions to the whole. By the end of the event, virtually everyone had found an opportunity to speak to the entire group.

FIGURE 1 Conference Participants

> I actually met and interacted with *everyone* . . . But I can't say enough about how much I appreciated the innovative format of the conference—*just* what I was looking for, just what I needed. We need more of this.

After presentations on the *key concepts* of communication, culture, and context by Donal Carbaugh, representing the organizing committee, and the international significance of the concept of intercultural dialogue by Katérina Stenou, representing UNESCO, the first small group discussions concerned what *vocabulary* participants considered necessary for analyzing intercultural dialogue, and whether they shared definitions of those terms. The afternoon moved on to the question of what *tools* (methods, theories, approaches) participants found most useful in examining intercultural dialogue. The second day examined *identity construction* and then *popular culture and media analysis*, topics common to a number of the papers submitted. The third day began with Christine Develotte of the French Institut National de Recherche Pédagagique describing her use of online technology to facilitate international dialogues between students, leading into small group consideration of how to *teach* the concepts necessary to intercultural dialogue. That afternoon Lisa Rudnick, of the United Nations, presented a challenge: she very much wanted to have certain types of cultural data available in the applied context, but found it lacking, and wanted to know why this was the case; the small groups following focused on issues of *applied research* related to intercultural dialogue. The last day was devoted to consideration of *next steps*. For each topic, participants were seated at different tables, so nearly everyone got to work through ideas with nearly everyone else. (Appendix 2 provides a detailed outline of events.)

> The format was fantastic. The structure, which moved us through discussion to a specific, goal-oriented conclusion (e.g., what do you want, what do you need, in order to do what you identified as next steps?). Cross-section of participants. Opportunity to spend time with our Turkish colleagues, and different "generations" of scholars together. Istanbul!

The interactive and dialogic nature of the conference allowed individuals to share experiences and ideas in a way not typically facilitated by traditional conference presentation format. Such exchanges revealed issues rarely included in the academic literature. For example, during the small group discussions of identity, several participants brought up the difficulty of integrating certain political issues or identities into Intercultural Communication courses. Similarly, during exchanges on methodology, participants raised concerns regarding researcher ethics and responsibilities, the relationship of the researcher to the population studied, and the potentially political nature of conducting research within Intercultural Communication. Such debate allowed space for the participants to criticize their own methodological choices and hear the advantages and disadvantages of other possibilities.

The small group discussions (demanding and fruitful). The itinerary through the days of the conference—development of content. The hospitality of the people—being a guest means something special in Turkey.

In addition to the various formal and informal exchanges during the conference, a number of special events and field trips took advantage of our location in Istanbul. The goal was to permit further opportunities for one-on-one and small group conversations, as a way to develop a cohort interested in related topics to discuss current research on intercultural dialogue, and to set a future research agenda. The local host, Maltepe University, offered their superb 5-star hotel and conference facility for our use. The distance from downtown (about an hour) had the desirable side effect of ensuring that participants attended all the formal sessions before dispersing for sightseeing or field trips in the afternoon or evening as scheduled in the program, and sightseeing occurred in tandem with other participants, supplemented by a local academic as guide and translator. In addition, local expertise was used to create the support materials: the conference logo,[6] website, and posters used to advertise the event as well as the programs, notebooks, mugs, and tote bags given out to participants (all designed by Ozer Karakus and Ebru Ozbakir).

Criteria taken into consideration in the selection of the events and activities to be included in the program were:

1. Including a range of Maltepe University activities, such as documentaries and research projects, related to the theme of the conference;
2. Encouraging interaction between the locals and the participants;
3. Reflecting the cultural and historical activities of the city; and
4. Creating adequate opportunities for sightseeing.

"The Bridge" visual exhibition (organized by Hatice Öz and included original art designed by local artists for this event)[7], video documentaries produced at Maltepe University (produced for other purposes, but supplemented by presentations from the filmmakers describing their goals and techniques), and the Polonezköy field trip organized by the research team conducting an oral history project in the area (preceded by a description of their project and results), all gave us the opportunity to share university-level local activities with the participants as well as reflecting the cultural diversity of Istanbul.[8]

FIGURE 2 Conference Logo

> I really liked the intensive discussions. I loved the smaller size and the ability to eat together and work together at one location and build meaningful relationships.

Not permitting formal presentation of papers via a traditional panel format had the advantage of ensuring that participants actually spent the entire conference talking to one another about their ideas, in order to be sure that everyone else learned about their projects, and their major conclusions. The disadvantage was that participants had no opportunity to present their work once, coherently, to everyone simultaneously. Holding group dialogues on all topics without providing formal evaluation of the ideas by respondents meant this event was unusually uniform in terms of status and rank. This was labeled "horizontal" by the group, while traditional conventions are "vertical" in that rank and status matter much more, with senior faculty serving as panel chairs and respondents, and plenary speakers, for example. The disadvantage was that a few participants said at the end they would have liked to feel there was some clear sense of which ideas were the "best."

This was an especially productive conference in terms of further activities generated. On the last day during planning for future action, I requested of participants that they take responsibility for outcomes they considered worth pursuing, rather than assign conference organizers indefinite responsibility. Perhaps making this explicit explains why so many of the participants accepted leadership roles for further activities. Specifically:

- ► Chitra Akkoor organized a panel at NCA's November 2009 convention held in Chicago, to share with a broader audience what had occurred at our conference, and provide an opportunity for participants to connect again.[9]

- ► I constructed a wiki (now deprecated) as an easy way for participants to share information and follow up on the conference conversations; many photos were posted there, as well as information of general interest about related publication opportunities and conferences.

- ► Evelyn Ho organized a pre-conference for the International Communication Association's convention held in Singapore during June 2010, to follow up the question of key terms in intercultural dialogue.

- ► With substantial advice from the NCA and ICA officers at the conference (Patrice Buzzanell representing ICA; Betsy Bach, Dawn Braithwaite, and Lynn Turner representing NCA), I prepared a proposal for the Council of Communication Associations, and in spring 2010 the Center for Intercultural Dialogue was established as a communication clearinghouse, a vehicle to help international scholars connect in the short term, and a potential source of small grants to continue international collaborative research in the long term (the Center's website is available at centerforinterculturaldialogue.org).

- ► Participants met others with related research interests and designed collaborative projects; a variety of conference presentations and publications resulted.

▶ Prue Holmes edited a special issue of the *Journal of International and Intercultural Communication* including a number of papers originally prepared for the conference.

▶ And, of course, this book is itself a major result of the conference.

I appreciated the format of the conference. I have only attended about 10 conferences but for the first time this conference felt like the way a conference should be. The small group discussions were both fruitful and useful. The conversations were very collaborative, supportive, challenging, and critical. Given the diversity of participants I believe that the conference itself embodied the theme of intercultural dialogue. I also not only met people that I will keep in contact with, but I feel that I have made new friends. The facilities and organization of the conference were wonderful. Thank you!!!

One of the surprises of the conference was the extent to which graduate students (both master's and doctoral level) expressed considerable interest in participating. In the end, ten of the thirty-six attending participants with accepted papers were graduate students. There were two positive results: first, in this format, these students had the opportunity to meet senior faculty from several countries with whom they would not normally get to spend time at international conventions; and second, they formed a strong cohort to continue meeting and working together in the future.

Given the topic of intercultural dialogue, it proved relatively easy to include representatives of the UN and UNESCO. This demonstrated the significance of the topic for real-world issues, and moved comments in the direction of the need for further applied research. A variety of activities related to applied research occurred after the conference, and owe at least part of the logic of their existence to conversations begun there.

The whole experience is very inspiriting for my research. Great job—I think it's the best conference I've ever been to.

This conference drew considerable interest from graduate students and faculty in Turkey, especially those affiliated with Maltepe University, our host, but also from several other universities. The organizing committee agreed to include them in a variety of capacities, and waived the conference registration fee for local scholars willing to serve as hosts, tour guides, translators, or work at the registration desk. This proved enormously successful, as the US and other international guests were delighted with the opportunity to interact directly and often with Turkish scholars. And it was clear that the Turkish scholars made connections for the future and considered their time well spent.

4. Conclusion

Maltepe University proved an ideal location for this conference, and 2009 was the perfect time. That Turkey had requested membership in the European Union, that Istanbul had been selected as the European Capital of Culture for 2010, and this university's own interest in establishing an international presence all help to explain both the willingness of the institution to provide generous support, and the significant interest of international scholars in attending an event in Istanbul in the summer of 2009. Holding the conference in Istanbul was a substantial draw for attendees: while few of those based outside Turkey knew Maltepe University, they came because of the topic and to see the city of Istanbul.

> Format—the discussion groups allowed us to engage in a sophisticated, complex, and fascinating discussion. Likewise, the method of participant selection allowed for new and more mature voices to be heard. Participants—without exception, I truly enjoyed the participants. The international presence was wonderful.

The uncommon conference design proved quite popular, as documented by the quotes from the evaluations sprinkled throughout this description. The focus on dialogue over formal presentations, the deliberate development of a series of related topics over five days, incorporation of visual media and local scholars, field trips related to the topic of the meeting, and time allocated for sightseeing in groups with local guides, were all successful elements. One explicit goal of the conference was to build a strong cohort of scholars with similar interests who would get to know each other and develop joint research projects, and the conference design worked to facilitate this.

> The "Wendy format of conferencing"—the workshop format with discussion opportunities across a range of ideas, perspectives, and disciplines. Interdisciplinarity and listening to voices other than American scholars.

> You changed my whole concept and understanding of "conference." Roundtable discussions were really effective. People were full of different ideas. I came here with five questions and I am leaving with fifty of them. But, I guess that is the whole idea behind the conference.

And, of course, it was.

References

Capes, M. (Ed.). (1960). *Communication or conflict? Conferences, their nature, dynamics, and planning*. London: Tavistock.

Craig, K. (June 6, 2006). Why "unconferences" are fun conferences. *Business 2.0 Magazine*. Retrieved from http://money.cnn.com/2006/06/05/technology/business2_unconference0606/index.htm

Freeman, R. (2008). Learning by meeting. *Critical Policy Studies, 2*(1), 1–24.

Fremont-Smith, F. (1961). The interdisciplinary conference. *AIBS Bulletin, 11*(2), 17–20, 32.

Ingebretsen, M. (2008). Unconferences catch on with developers. *IEEE software, 25*(6), 108–110.

Leeds-Hurwitz, W. (1994). Crossing disciplinary boundaries: The Macy Foundation Conferences on Cybernetics as a case study in multidisciplinary communication. *Cybernetica: Journal of the International Association for Cybernetics, 3/4*, 349–369.

Mead, M. (1968a). Preface and acknowledgements. In M. Mead & P. Byers, *The small conference: An innovation in communication* (pp. v–vii). Paris: Mouton.

Mead, M. (1968b). The conference process. In M. Mead & P. Byers, *The small conference: An innovation in communication* (pp. 1–54). Paris: Mouton.

Mead, M., & Byers, P. (1968). *The small conference: An innovation in communication*. Paris: Mouton.

Powell, K. (2005). Small conferences pay their way. *Nature, 438*(7066), 264–265.

Ravn, I., & Elsborg, S. (2007). Creating learning at conferences through participant involvement. Presented at the Academy of Management annual meeting, Philadelphia, PA. Retrieved from http://www.universitaetbielefeld.de/(de)/exzellenz/lehre/docs/Ravn_og_Elsborg_-_Creating_Learning_at_Conferences.pdf

Ravn, I., & Elsborg, S. (2011). Facilitating learning at conferences. *International Journal of Learning and Change, 5*(1), 84–98.

Reid, J. J. (1992). The annual meeting as text or exhibition. *American Antiquity, 57*(3), 391–392.

Simpkins, A. B. (2009). Designing an innovative conference. *Bridges* [Federal Reserve Bank of St. Louis]. Retrieved from http://www.stlouisfed.org/publications/br/articles/?id=1031

Wenger, E., McDermott, R., & Snyder, W. M. (2002). *Cultivating communities of practice: A guide to managing knowledge*. Boston: Harvard University Press.

Wiessner, C. A., Hatcher, T., Chapman, D., & Storberg-Walker, J. (2008). Creating new learning at professional conferences: An innovative approach to conference learning, knowledge construction and programme evaluation. *Human Resource Development International, 11*(4), 368–383.

Wolstenholme, G. E. W. (1964). Obese degeneration of scientific congresses. *Science, 145*(3638), 1137–1139.

Zelinsky, W. (1994). Conventionland USA: The geography of a latterday phenomenon. *Annals of the Association of American Geographers, 84*(1), 68–86.

APPENDIX 1

List of Participants

Organizing committee members

Donal Carbaugh (US: University of Massachusetts)
Kristine Fitch (US: University of Iowa)
Nazan Haydari (Turkey: Maltepe University)
Tamar Katriel (Israel: University of Haifa)
Wendy Leeds-Hurwitz (US: University of Wisconsin-Parkside)
Yves Winkin (France: Ecole Normale Supérieure Lettres et Sciences Humaines; now Ecole Normale Supérieure de Lyon)
Saskia Witteborn (China: Chinese University of Hong Kong)

Participants with accepted papers

Chitra V. Akkoor (US: University of Iowa)
Susan Davidson Allen (US: University of Maryland)
Jolanta Aritz (US: University of Southern California)
Susan Berry Baca (Denmark: Aalborg University)
Jennifer Billings (US: Monterey Institute of International Studies)
Charles Braithwaite (US: University of Nebraska)
William J. Brown (US: Regent University)
Lindsay Regan Calhoun (US: Marshall University)
Hsin-I Cheng (US: Santa Clara University)
Jolanta A. Drzwiecka (US: Washington State University)
Selva Ersoz (Turkey: Maltepe University)
Elena Esquibel (US: Southern Illinois University)
Aybuke Filiz (US: Portland State University)
Cecile Garmon (US: Western Kentucky University)

Serra Tevhide Gorpe (Turkey: Istanbul University)
Tabitha Hart (US: University of Washington)
Evelyn Y. Ho (US: University of San Francisco)
Prue Holmes (New Zealand: University of Waikato)
Sermin Ildirar (Turkey: Istanbul University)
Stephen Alan King (US: Delta State University)
Elena Khatskevich (US: University of Massachusetts)
Erla Kristjansdottir (Iceland: Reykjavik University)
Bernadette Longo (US: University of Minnesota)
Janeet MacLennan (Puerto Rico: University of Puerto Rico)
Maria Flora Mangano (Italy, independent scholar)
Eric Morgan (US: New Mexico State University)
Eddah Mutua-Kombo (US: University of Minnesota)
Neslihan Önder (Turkey: Uludag University)
Secil Pacaci Elitok (Turkey: Maltepe University)
Gudrun E. Reimerth (Austria: University of Applied Sciences)
Todd Lyle Sandel (US: University of Oklahoma)
Aynur Sarisakaloğlu (Austria: University of Salzburg)
Lisa Schreiber (US: Millersville University)
Ruma Sen (US: Ramapo University)
Melissa Elizabeth Steyn (South Africa: University of Cape Town)
Saskia Witteborn (Hong Kong: Chinese University of Hong Kong)

Invited Guests

Betsy Bach (then NCA President)
Dawn O. Braithwaite (then NCA First Vice President)
Lynn Turner (then NCA Second Vice President)
Patrice Buzzanell (then ICA Immediate Past President)

Invited Speakers

Bahattin Akşit (then Director, Maltepe University Research and Implementation Center for Humanities and Social Sciences, Istanbul, Turkey)
Hakan Aytekin (Documentary filmmaker, Maltepe University, Istanbul, Turkey)
Dan Banda (Documentary filmmaker, then University of Wisconsin-Parkside, US)
Peyami Çelikcan (then Dean of Communication Faculty, Maltepe University, Istanbul, Turkey)
Christine Develotte (Institut National de Recherche Pédagogique [now Institut Français de l'Éducation], Lyon, France)

Matthew Gumpert (Director, Istanbul Studies Center, Kadir Has University, Istanbul, Turkey)

Şahin Karasar (Maltepe University, Istanbul, Turkey)

Lisa Rudnick (Security Needs Assessment Protocol, United Nations Institute for Disarmament Research, Geneva, Switzerland)

Katérina Stenou (then Director, Division of Cultural Policies and Intercultural Dialogue, UNESCO, Paris, France)

Additional Turkish faculty and graduate students who participated

Tülay Atay-Avşar (Mustafa Kemal University, Hatay, Turkey)

Gülçin Çakıcı (Maltepe University, İstanbul, Turkey)

Seda Erel (Maltepe University, İstanbul, Turkey)

Gülçin Coşkun (Maltepe University, İstanbul, Turkey)

Özlem Oğuzhan (Maltepe University, İstanbul, Turkey)

Rona Kırmızı (Maltepe University, İstanbul, Turkey)

Müberra Yüksel (Kadir Has University, Istanbul, Turkey)

Sevgi Kalkan (Maltepe University, Istanbul, Turkey)

Serkan Öztürk (Maltepe University, Istanbul, Turkey)

Mustafa Kara (Maltepe University, Istanbul, Turkey)

Gökcen Cıvaş (Maltepe University, Istanbul, Turkey)

Özge Baydaş (Maltepe University, Istanbul, Turkey)

Conference Program

Wednesday, July 22

2:00 to 5:00 pm	Conference Registration Entry
4:00 to 5:00 pm	**"Bridge": Conference Exhibition Opening Reception** Exhibition Hall, Communication Building
5:00 to 7:00 pm	**Learning Cultures Through Documentaries** Sinemar 2, Communication Building **The Colors of Anatolia: Birth, Wedding and Death** *Presenters:* Peyami Çelikcan; Şahin Karasar
7:00 to 7:30 pm	**Reflections on Communication, Culture, and Context** Sinemar 2, Communication Building **Reflections on Communication, Culture, and Context** *Presenter:* Donal Carbaugh, University of Massachusetts Amherst
7:30 to 11:00 pm	Opening Dinner Reception Teras Restaurant

Thursday, July 23

7:00 to 8:30 am   Breakfast

8:30-9:00 am   **Intercultural Dialogue on the World Stage**
Katérina Stenou, Director, Division for Cultural Policies and
  Intercultural Dialogue, UNESCO
Context and Definitions, Istanbul Hall

9:00 to 9:45 am   Small Group Discussions

9:45 to 10:30 am   Group Reports

10:30 to 11:00 am   Morning Break

11:00 to 12:00 pm   **Taking Stock of Tools used by Participants**, Istanbul Hall
Small Group Discussions

12:00 to 1:00 pm   Report of Small Groups

1:00 to 2:00 pm   Lunch

2:00 to 4:00 pm   **Showing Cultural Identity on Film**
Sinemar 2, Communication Building
Presenter: Dan Banda, University of Wisconsin-Parkside

after 4:00 p.m.   **Parallel Activities**
Option 1: Cultural field trip to Polonezköy
Option 2: Discussion on Documentaries
A Letter for Tomorrow, Hakan Aytekin, Director
Dan Banda, Director
Option 3: Sightseeing

7:00 to 9:00 pm   Dinner

Friday, July 24

7:00 to 8:30 am   Breakfast

8:30 to 9:30 am   **Identity Construction,** İstanbul Hall
Small Group Discussions

9:30 to 10:30 am   Report of Small Groups

10:30 to 11:00 am   Morning Break

11:00 to 12:00 pm   **Popular Culture and Media Analysis,** İstanbul Hall
                        Small Group Discussions

12:00 to 1:00 pm   Report of Small Groups

1:00 to 2:00 pm   Lunch

2:00 to 10:00 pm   Sightseeing in Istanbul

Saturday, July 25

7:00 to 8:30 am   Breakfast

8:30 to 9:00 am   **"Lyon seems pretty cool": Teaching culture online,** İstanbul Hall
                        Presenter: Christine Develotte, Institut National de Recherche
                        Pédagogique

9:00 to 10:00 am   **Teaching Intercultural Communication**
                        Small Group Discussions, İstanbul Hall

10:00 to 11:00 am   Report of Small Groups

11:00 to 11:30 am   Morning Break

11:30 to 12:30 pm   **Applying Cultural Research,** İstanbul Hall
                        Presenter: Lisa Rudnick, Security Needs Assessment Protocol, United
                        Nations Institute for Disarmament Research, Geneva, Switzerland

12:30 to 1:30 pm   **Applied Intercultural Dialogue,** İstanbul Hall
                        Small Group Discussions

1:30 to 2:30 pm   Lunch

2:30 to 4:00 pm   Reports of Small Groups

Cultural Field Trip to Kuzguncuk Area
The field trip will include an optional dinner (not included in the conference registration fee).

Sunday, July 26

7:30 to 9:00 am	Breakfast
9:00 to 10:00 am	**Setting an Agenda for the Future,** İstanbul Hall Small Group Discussions
10:00 to 10:30 am	Morning Break
10:30 to 12:00 pm	**Setting an Agenda for the Future,** İstanbul Hall Report of Small Groups
12:00 to 1:00 pm	Lunch
1:00 to 2:30 pm	**Making it Happen: Discussion of the Whole,** İstanbul Hall *Presenters:* Betsy Bach, President, NCA Dawn O. Braithwaite, First Vice President, NCA Lynn Turner, Second Vice President, NCA Patrice M. Buzzanell, Immediate Past President, ICA Matthew Gumpert, Center for Istanbul Studies, Kadir Has University Belma Akşit & Bahattin Akşit, Maltepe University Research and Implementation Center for Humanities and Social Sciences (MÜTAM)
2:30 to 4:00 pm	**Impact Statements,** İstanbul Hall
6:30 to 11:00 pm	Closing event: Dinner and a Bosporus River Cruise

Endnotes

1. Zelinsky (1994) provides a detailed description of typical activities in what he labels "conventionland."

2. Craig (2006) and Ingebretsen (2008) discuss specific examples of unconferences; Kaliya Hamlin's blog (http://www.unconference.net) provides basic history and concrete details of unconferences in general, as well as many specific techniques, including fishbowls and world cafes. In addition to works discussed elsewhere in this chapter, a few other relevant discussions of conference structure can be found in Capes (1960); Mead and Byers (1968); Powell (2005); Wiessner et al. (2008); and Wolstenholme (1964); with Freeman (2008) being the most detailed and thoughtful current consideration of how learning occurs during professional meetings such as conferences. Despite these sources, on the whole, the literature on this topic is surprisingly slim.

3. NCA provided a grant of $10,000 for this conference, encompassing an online peer review process, development of a dedicated website, and design of supporting materials such as posters and programs, as well as travel grants for ten of the participants. Maltepe University provided local support in the form of free space with all necessary equipment and staff, and substantially underwriting hotel and restaurant costs, which permitted an unusually low conference registration fee covering far more than typical (all materials, two field trips, and all meals on-site, including a formal welcome banquet with entertainment). The support of both was essential to the success of the conference, as was the large number of Turkish scholars who served on the local arrangements committee, helping organize various elements of the event.

4. This sort of circular link between the topic and the design, while still uncommon, is not unique. Simpkins describes another example: "The structure of the 2009 Exploring Innovation conference was designed to be, in itself, an example of innovation" (2009, n.p.).

5. All quotes are drawn from the conference evaluations completed anonymously by participants at the end of the event.

6. With the agreement of all concerned parties, the logo was then converted to the logo of the Center for Intercultural Dialogue (http://centerforinterculturaldialogue.org).

7. "The Bridge" Exhibition (organized by Hatice Öz) was an attempt to create a space for intercultural exchange and dialogue through the depiction of local cultural varieties in Istanbul. The exhibition consisted of thirty-nine visual designs on the

thirty-nine districts of Istanbul, with designers participating in the representation of different stories on various cultural spaces. Works by the following designers were presented: Melike Akgül, Ceyhun Akgün, Salih Akkemik, Ayşe Nil Aksoy, Orhan Ardahanlı, Yunus Ay, Hakan Aytekin, Arif Bağcivan, Nazlı Benlioğlu, Didem Çatal, Sonat Çatal, Kenan Direk, Armağan Gökçearslan, Cem Gül, İdil Güral, Ferruh Haşiloğlu, Bahar Kaplan, Özer Karakuş, Arda Kaya, Rauf Kösemen, Nesgis Kul, Hatice Öz, Ebru Özbakır, Mehmet Özen, Merve Poray, Özge Baydaş Sayılgan, Tuğberk Şallı, Eda Bürge Tekin, Onur Toprak, Murat Tunç, Özden Pektaş Turgut, Banu İnanç Uyan, Osman Ürper, Oktay Yalın, Emel Yurtkulu, Adem Yücel.

8. Polonezköy forms a surprisingly intact Polish community geographically located in Turkey. The second field trip, to Kuzguncuk, included a visit to a Greek Orthodox church.

9. Although the deadline for submission of panel proposals had long passed by the time this conference occurred, the programming chair for the 2009 NCA convention, Dawn Braithwaite, was present at Maltepe, and agreed to schedule a breakfast meeting if a formal proposal could be submitted almost immediately; Chitra rose to the occasion, and the breakfast meeting made the schedule. About twenty people attended, including not only participants from Istanbul but others who were simply curious about the topic and wanted to learn what had occurred at the earlier event.

PART II

Dialogue for Peacebuilding and Reconciliation

2

Community Driven Peacebuilding Approaches: The Case of Post-Genocide Rwanda

Eddah Mbula Mutua

Key Words

- ► Post-genocide Rwanda
- ► Peacebuilding
- ► Peaceful co-existence
- ► Community driven approaches

1. Introduction

The notion of post-conflict peacebuilding has grown increasingly contentious and problematic in recent years. Various scholars have raised concerns about the appropriate levels (global, national, regional, or local) at which post-conflict resolution and reconstruction plans should be conceived and determined (Betts 2005; Donais 2009; Nhema & Zeleza 2008). This chapter contributes to this debate by discussing the limitations of dominant peacebuilding discourses and agendas and calling attention to community driven approaches. It contends that community driven approaches engender collective action toward reconstruction, reconciliation, and co-existence. The approaches discussed focus on ways that

Rwandans construe their own experiences of the genocide and respond by locating peace-building efforts at the center of their everyday life. This view to peacebuilding echoes Erin Baines' (2010) invitation to scholars to pay attention to "more informal, socio-cultural processes outside the purview of the state, particularly for how they promote social construction at the micro-level" (409). These informal contributions are critical to social change as they are grounded in local knowledge and experiences and are cognizant of the complex local dynamics that are most relevant to people's lives.

This chapter is structured in several sections. The first part sets the context that provides a justification for contextual factors deemed necessary to theorize community driven approaches in post-genocide Rwanda. This is followed by theoretical discussion about trends in dominant peacebuilding approaches and the need for ethical considerations. A counter narrative to dominant peacebuilding approaches that draws from post-colonial theory is provided. Select community driven peace initiatives to showcase "peacebuilding in practice" in Rwanda are discussed. Last but not least, the possibilities for community driven approaches in promoting peace, national reconstruction, and reconciliation efforts in post-genocide Rwanda are highlighted.

2. Rwandan Context

The troubled history of Rwanda renders itself as a critical factor in creating conditions for citizens' participation in community activities to attain sustainable peace. There is no one agreed narrative about the source of violence in Rwanda. Corey and Joireman (2004) observe that competing interpretations of Rwanda's historical events—historical, anthropological, and political perspectives—are dissimilar for Hutu and Tutsi and have been used to justify violence. Whatever ideological perspective prevailed in justifying the 1994 genocide, another reality is needed to converge Rwandan peoples' collective memories to reconciliation and peace[1]. The mass participation in the genocide, resulting in the death of an estimated 800,000 people in 100 days, left the country in ruins (Dallaire 2003; Mamdani 2001; Prunier 1995) after Rwandans turned against fellow Rwandans; their friends, neighbours, spouses, relatives, students, patients, and colleagues.

The landscape of Rwanda was transformed by the violent killings, sexual violence on Tutsi women and girls, inhumane acts including corpses left unburied, live and dead bodies dumped in latrines, government officials, nurses, nun, and priests turning into murderers and destruction of government, legal, and cultural institutions all transformed Rwanda's landscape. Metaphorically, transformation of Rwandan landscape refers to the destruction of every aspect of life by the genocide—geographical, physical, emotional, and psychological and also the renewal of how Rwandans (need to) interact in the post-genocide setting. For example, in 2003, a political decision by President Kagame to release 40,000 perpetrators of the genocide left no doubt that Rwandans would have to work together to heal, trust each other, and co-exist. Additionally, the law to prohibit ethnic identification would mean re-naming of the Rwandan people[2]. The difficulty of genocide survivors to live in the face of pain and anger, mass graves, destruction of home in the place Rwandans call home, children born out of rape, HIV/AIDS, "Never Again" messages, are some of the reminders of the genocide. Hatzfeld (2007) documentation of testimonials of living in Rwanda after the genocide reveals the difficult past, and Rwandans' sense of how it has changed them forever and everything they do. Memory of the genocide may never fade even as Rwandans reconstruct their lives and institutions in the post-genocide setting. However, one memory that will remain in history books is the madness of the genocide and its inability to "prove innocence because it (genocide) was cruel" (A. Urusaro, personal communication July 20, 2004).

Despite the mass violence, Rwandans have not resigned to social inertia. There are efforts to heal the reality of hatred as victims and perpetrators of the genocide strive for peaceful co-existence. Community members' urgency to legitimize collective action is what has become one way to define and address the needs of a post-genocide setting. It shapes the what, how, and why questions about peaceful co-existence. Baines (2010) observes that such are efforts "at people's disposal to reconcile the day-to-day wrongs committed amongst themselves and to renew moral fabric and rebuild social trust" (411). They are an attempt to give voice and visibility to ordinary citizens to reconstruct their lives at the local level. This pragmatic approach defines local as:

> . . . a set of micro-level relationships between everyday people striving to get on with life, and along with each other, after mass violence. Part of this process of repair involves drawing upon existing socio-cultural resources to acknowledge and then move past the wrongs committed by one another (Baines 2010, 412).

Given the complexity of the Rwandan experience, efforts toward peaceful co-existence by both victims and perpetrators of the genocide may be what is relevant to their context. This chapter argues that critique of dominant post-conflict peacebuilding approaches is what should lead us to consider the relevance of community driven peace approaches in Rwanda.

3. Trends in Dominant Peacebuilding Approaches

The debate over approaches to post-conflict peace, justice, reconciliation, and reconstruction continues to dominate literature on contemporary peacebuilding processes. The questions that purview the debate is about whether or not post-conflict resolution and reconstruction approaches are to be determined globally, nationally, regionally, or locally (Baines 2010; Betts 2005; Donais 2009; Lundy & McGovern 2008; Meyerstein 2007; Nhema & Zeleza 2008). Donais (2009) points to the complex relationship between insiders (local actors) and outsiders (international/regional actors) approaches which have resulted into tensions about how to operationalize local ownership principles in contemporary peacebuilding. This tension is evident in ways that local actors utilize local resources and experiences to initiate and own local processes, and how international and some local actors orchestrate processes "conceived as 'universal' conception of justice" (Lundy & McGovern 2008, 268). For example, the increasing role of Western funded international and local Non-Governmental Organizations (NGOs) in many post-conflict societies tends to over-shadow informal local efforts initiated by citizens to rebuild their communities after mass violence. Nhema and Zeleza (2008) observes that while the role of external actors is indeed laudable, Africa will have to rely increasingly on its own to provide long-term solutions to its own problems within the framework of its sub-regional groupings and the African Union and the United Nations.

Scholars have criticized international systems which superimpose Western democratic values on post-conflict societies and by so doing influence how peacebuilding is conceptualized and practiced (see Roland Paris 2002 and Oliver Richmond 2007 as cited in Donais 2009, 5). The Western view that peacebuilding "is about transforming war-shattered polities into functioning liberal democracies where the liberal democratic framework is seen not only as the gold standard of good governance, but also as the most secure foundation for sustainable peace" (Donais 2009, 5–6). This hegemonic view of post-conflict peacebuilding fails to fully recognize the relevance of local realities to peacebuilding. The Western framework limits the engagement of local communities because (i) a global-local dichotomy is constructed to advance Western political and legal approaches, (Donais 2009); (ii) the 'local' is reproduced through the lens of the universal, to the neglect of the socio-cultural (Baines 2010, 413); and (iii) appreciation of post-colonial hybrid forms of peacebuilding approaches is prevented (Meyerstein 2007).

Problematizing dominant peacebuilding approaches allows actors to dialogue Rwandan ways of knowing in enriching the field of peacebuilding. This is a dialogue with a potential to clarify issues scholars and development practitioners grapple with and make the notion of post-conflict peacebuilding in diverse contexts difficult. In proposing this dialogue, it must be noted that not all conflict contexts are the same. As such, this may explain factors that require certain conflict contexts to adopt context-specific peacebuilding approaches. In post-genocide Rwanda, the context-specific approach to peacebuilding reveals the limitations of and resistance to certain dominant peacebuilding approaches. A good example is the International Criminal Tribunal of Rwanda (ICTR). The tribunal has been criticized for its western legal approach (See Yazdani 2010). In addition, lack of proximity to the place where the violence occurred and majority of people affected illustrates disconnect of ICTR with many Rwandans. With this in mind one can see to a large extent, the relevance of Gacaca traditional justice system which was preferred for its relevance to communities where it operated and recognition of local culture and knowledge system.

In response to the limitations posed by dominant western approaches, scholars are now advocating for increased attention to approaches which are culturally and contextually grounded on the local realities of conflict contexts (Abu-Nimer et al. 2007; Hoover 2011; Lundy & McGovern 2008). This view challenges the liberal peace approach by stressing the importance of tradition and social context in determining the legitimacy and appropriateness of particular visions of political order, justice, or ethics (Donais 2009). For example,

Lahiri (2009) recognizes Gacaca model in Rwanda as endeavoring to be culturally proxi-mate, participatory, and cathartic[3]. Hudson (2009) emphasizes the inclusion of gender in the analysis of peacebuilding models in Rwanda and Cote d'Ivoire as essential elements to con-structing responsible and comprehensive peacebuilding policies and practices. Cole and Norander (2011) propose gendered peacebuilding.

Similarly, scholarship in intercultural dialogue offers relevant insights about how to engage in the practice of intercultural dialogue in conflict situations to promote human dig-nity, equality, mutual respect, sustainability, alliance building, critical self-reflection, and promotion of deeper understanding of difficult social issues (See Ganesh & Holmes 2011; Hoover 2011; Kastel 2010; Nagda 2006; and Orbe 2004). The shifting paradigm that acknowledges context and experiences of victims of violence is what forms the core of com-plex processes and actions out of which local peacebuilding initiatives are developed. In the following section, I offer an expanded discussion about factors that form the core of com-munity driven peacebuilding approaches in Rwanda. It serves as an introduction to African indigenous ways of knowing and empiricism.

4. Core of Community Driven Approaches

Local culture and conflict context in post-conflict peacebuilding explains complex actions partaken by many Rwandans to build peace. Thus the significance of community driven peacebuilding approaches is largely informed by ways that Rwandans interpret and perform local Rwandan ways of knowing and African empiricism. Taylor and Nwosu (2001) posit that the goals of African empiricism are to discover and illustrate how African centered explanations help to enhance the understanding of unique patterns of how Africans think, feel, and act in developing effective strategies for conflict management. In post-genocide Rwanda, the response by both victims and perpetrators of the genocide to rebuild the coun-try entails grounding meaning assigned to collective action in the local knowledge systems. Such response underscores the relevance of Rwandan culture, epistemology, and ontology as significant elements in forming the framework for individual and collective commitment to peacebuilding. Put together, these elements of Rwandan way of life empower Rwandans (as local actors) to produce an alternative narrative to Western political-legal framework of peacebuilding.

Nyamnjoh (2012) points to the importance of considering and engaging with African cultures as the dynamic, nuanced, negotiated, and open-ended realities they are. Rwandans' engagement with their culture in the post-genocide setting reveals its value as a resource for peacebuilding. The impact of the genocide on cultural institutions illustrates how culture is dynamic and not bounded. For example, the loss of men in the genocide and subsequent shift in gender roles has opened opportunities for societal growth. Acquaro and Landesman (2003) acknowledge the rise of matriarchy as offering unprecedented opportunity to trans-form Rwanda. Moreover, the new cultural context created by experience of the genocide provides the basis to generate knowledge that defines post-genocide peacebuilding. It is knowledge created in a context where the future and aspirations of Rwandans are reconstructed and performed.

Rwandan epistemological interpretation of the genocide by perpetrators, victims, and survivors offers scholarly platform to broaden the understanding of post-conflict peacebuilding. Take for instance, ways that the actions of Rwandans in response to their adversity create awareness about (i) experience that "moves to expression" (Madison 2005, 150) and, (ii) politics of representation and knowledge as well as questions pertaining to ethics of speaking for and about others (see Linda Alcroff 1991). In understanding the epistemological view Rwandans seek to privilege, we may want to ask the question: should peace be defined as an end in itself or as a multidimensional concept, in what context, by whom, and for what purpose? The Rwandan effort to engage in peacebuilding approaches located in local culture and experience of the genocide may be the model to offer homegrown insights to post-conflict peace in Africa not entirely dependent on outside actors.

In post-genocide Rwanda and Africa as a whole, there are many concerns that form the competing and conflicting interests in peacebuilding discourse. For example, given the complexity of peacebuilding in Africa, can we ignore the postcolonial element? Can peacebuilding research obliterate postcolonial nuances? Sultana (2007) has observed that the idea of "neocolonial representations is an important concern as writing 'with' rather than writing 'about' is a challenge that scholars have taken up in order to redress concerns about marginalization, essentialisms, and differences in representations (375). Rethinking post-conflict peacebuilding calls attention to the relevance of locating peace within the Rwandan experience (knowledge system, culture, history, and politics). Taking these factors into consideration, subsequently theorizing peacebuilding becomes the priority and desires of a people divided by violence. How do intercultural communication scholars make meaning of Rwandan efforts to redefine peacebuilding as part and parcel of their everyday life?

Increased engagement with the Rwandan experience as locus of analysis is needed to privilege Rwandan ways of knowing. Linda Smith (1999) castigates research practices that are deeply embedded in the multiple layers of imperial and colonial practices and still employed to deny the validity of indigenous peoples' claim to their existence such as the right of self-determination, survival of forms of cultural knowledge among others. In response, Sultana (2007) urges for attentiveness to histories of colonialism, development, globalization, and local context to avoid exploitative research or perpetuation of relations of domination and control.

Historically, African knowledge has been subject to destructive forces notably Western economic and epistemological models that threaten its survival (Mahmood Mamdani as cited in Kigotho 2011). As a result, this colonial legacy has allowed for Western scholars, practitioners, and institutions such as the United Nations to dominate the sphere of knowledge about post-conflict peacebuilding and offer Western models as the "fix" to Africa's conflict situation including post-genocide Rwanda. The practice sets precedence to universalize peacebuilding principles at the expense of local knowledge created by victims and perpetrators of the genocide. There is a need to reverse trends that tend to marginalize indigenous knowledge. Nyamnjoh (2012) has suggested that global conversations and cooperation among scholars are a starting point in a long journey to equalization and recognition of marginalized epistemologies and dimensions of scientific inquiry. Martin and Butler (2001) propose that intercultural communication research be based on an ethic of speaking with and taking into account cultural and paradigmatic norms. The suggestion for inclusiveness prepares those interested in understanding the Rwandarized peace model to enhance the mutuality to acknowledge the local experience. It creates space for possible intercultural dialogue between Rwandans and outside actors.

5. Examples of "Peacebuilding in Practice"

I use "peacebuilding in practice" (term borrowed from Cole & Norander) to illustrate peace efforts initiated by community members in different contexts in Rwanda. I was honored to visit and observe community members participate in these peace initiatives. The emphasis placed on community participation prompted me to theorize ways that Rwandans assign meanings to peace efforts in a post-genocide setting. Descriptions of peace activities provided reveal how meaning is constructed in active form of utilizing local resources manifested in cultural traditions, local ways of knowing, and communities' sense of urgency. These efforts systematically integrate intercultural dialogue and community building as key elements to peacebuilding in post-genocide Rwanda. There are benefits to recognizing these community efforts as significant to the peacebuilding process in Rwanda. Failure to do so, as Baines (2010) warns "all of this slips under the radar when "justice" is studied from universal definitions and standards; or where the "local" is defined solely as space for intervention, not comprehension, not knowledge, not capacity" (430). The activities described below represent the context they are performed in as a space for knowledge and capacity to transform conflict.

5.1. Interuniversity Arts Festival

Interuniversity Arts Festival is an annual three day event at National University of Rwanda (NUR). Participating students from universities in Rwanda, Uganda, Burundi, and Democratic Republic of Congo (DRC) perform peace messages in different artistic forms including music, drama, drumming, storytelling, and dance. The songs performed at the festival reiterated the value of community members in utilizing local culture as a resource for peace in the East African region. The six languages spoken in the region namely Kinyarwanda, French, English, Kiswahili, Lingala, and Kirundi were featured in a song performed by students from DRC which called for peace in Congo, Rwanda, Burundi, and Uganda. Response to the song by the audience mainly comprised of students and community members was indicative of a people's yearning for peace. The chorus line *"Amani""Amani""Amani"* (Peace) was chanted through the auditorium as the performers used call-response style to involve audience members. Similar messages of peace were communicated in two plays performed at the festival depicting the ills of the genocide.

5.2. "Kuchi" (Why)

This one-man act performed in Kinyarwanda (Rwandan native language) recounted the history of Rwanda by use of rhetorical questions, symbolism, props, and call-response. The act began with a rhetorical question: "why are Rwandans in Burundi, Uganda, Kenya, and Congo?" Without a response from the audience, the actor proceeded to use his props—three buckets half-way filled with water. The act of mixing water in three buckets in silence prompted more thought-provoking questions directed at the audience. For example, the actor inquiring from the audience about the difference in the water and subsequent response "no" reveals the symbolic meaning of the act, that is unity between Rwandans. The three buckets of water symbolized the Tutsi, Hutu, and Twa.

5.3. "Ibyonabonye" (What I Saw)

Ibyonabonye, an all-female cast performance enacted how people were killed, women raped, property destroyed, and the consequences that followed the genocide (distrust, anger, fear, loss of family members, friends, etc). The wielding of machetes, tears, and screaming on the stage was a reminder of the terrible events witnessed during the genocide. On the other hand, the deep silence that followed the end of the act communicated a message Rwandans desire for their country: *"Ntibizongera kubaho ukundi"* (Never Again).

5.4. Butare Legal Clinic

This is an initiative where NUR collaborates with the local communities to promote legal education and community based conflict resolution in Butare district. Community members gather at Butare Municipal Hall on designated days to address causes of conflict in the community. NUR third year law students and trained legal assistants listen to conflicts reported about land ownership disputes, child custody, sexual harassment, women's rights, among others. Most of the attendees to the clinic are women seeking to resolve conflicts with family members and neighbors. Most of the conflicts reported have legal implications but also include challenges facing Rwandans in their everyday lives such as HIV/AIDS and poverty. The legal clinic allowed women with no formal education to understand and apply legal knowledge in ways that make law relevant to their lives and local culture. For example, some women reported their preference for the clinic to relevant government authorities because it was not punitive. It allowed women to resolve family matters amicably unless the issue at hand needed the attention of the legal system. The success of the clinic was attributed to culturally sensitive and community centered approaches that enable community members and in particular women to advance their knowledge about legal rights and conflict management skills. These are skills women need as they seek to embrace their redefined roles as peacemakers in the post-genocide setting. Women may be walking in the clinic as victims but they exit the door as peacemakers.

Popularization of community driven approaches to peacebuilding by university students reveals the critical positioning of community members to make peace. This level of critical consciousness allows community members to face their own circumstances and define the agenda for peace. It is captured in their words, actions, and aspirations for Rwanda.

5.5. Women's Movement

The relevance of community driven peacebuilding approaches was crystallized during an interview with Mrs. Theresa Bishagara, President of *Twese Hamwe*, national umbrella body of all registered women's groups also known as self-help groups in Rwanda. The symbolic meaning of *"Twese Hamwe"* (Let's go together) justifies the proliferation of women's groups as an avenue of voice and urgency. The need to promote cooperative values and expand social networks is evident in diversity of groups organized according to multiple purposes such as (i) support for widows, orphans, victims of sexual violence, disabled women, (ii) economic generating activities, (iii) agricultural/livestock, (iv) HIV/AIDS, girls, and women's education, (v) young women's leadership and girls mentorship, and (vi) conflict resolution education through the arts. It is not possible to describe 'peacebuilding in practice' for each of the women's groups visited. Instead, I offer my overall impression of women's groups as catalyst for Rwanda's future.

As a result of collective efforts by women, multiple generations of Rwandan girls, boys, and men are able to participate in multifaceted peace activities. Women have transformed peacebuilding to become the business of "insiders"—the local people—who possess the drive to initiate, implement, and support indigenous peacebuilding efforts that do not necessarily privilege the role played by "outsiders." These efforts reaffirm Galtung's (2004) understanding of positive peace. Overall, women's organizing has opened doors for active participation in domains of law, economic development through income generating activities, political participation, land ownership, food production and security, health education notably HIV/AIDS education, girls and women's education among others.

5.6. Umuganda

Umuganda is a national community event designated for the last Saturday of every month. It brings together families, neighbors, and leaders to participate in activities geared at strengthening community networks, trust, collective identity, and co-existence. All business premises close from 8:00 a.m. to 12:00 noon. Each family must be represented otherwise a fine is imposed on absentee families. Abui (a member of my host family) and I joined residents of four villages in the Remera and Kacukiro area of Kigali to participate in activities designated for the day which involved clearing bushes, repairing dusty roads, and conducting local elections for village leaders. The large turnout at the event included genocide survivors, victims, and offenders. The active participation of community members including women leaders reaffirmed the idea of collective work by Rwandans is engrained in African communalistic cultural values that emphasize self-help, trust, sustained interactions, social ties, group identity, and responsibility. Additionally, the experience of the genocide cultivates values about self and collective sacrifice, discipline, responsibility, and attentiveness to peace, and co-existence. Umuganda serves to bridge troubled history of Rwanda's "ethnic" identity and a metaphor for how Rwandan communities should function.

6. Conclusion and Lessons Learned

The effects of 1994 Rwanda genocide call for multifaceted approaches to reconcile communities torn apart by political ideology and "ethnic" divisions that have existed in Rwanda over many decades. The prospect for peaceful co-existence is the desired outcome of Rwandans' efforts to reconcile and reconstruct their country. Community driven peacebuilding approaches serve as the basis to create another reality about theory and practice of peacebuilding. Asante (2001) observes that "to provide a radical assessment of a given reality is to create, inter alia, another reality" (72). Conditions of the post-genocide setting have welcomed comprehensible interventions by the people to support the capacity to negotiate and renegotiate the reality of the genocide. Community driven peace initiatives have fostered personal and community relationships among Rwandans which heighten awareness of the complex relationships that must be endured in a post-conflict context. These peace activities serve as forums to respond to personal and collective processes required in constructing shared language and collective identity that present the post-genocide narrative of peace. They privilege Rwandan ways of knowing, local culture, the genocide experience, local urgency, and encourage popular participation as key tenets to post-genocide peace.

Overall, lessons learned from Rwanda offer theoretical insights about post-genocide peacebuilding that deepen and broaden understanding of elements that empower communities to respond to their condition. The local conflict context authenticates ways that define the context as a space for generating innovative ideas about how to build post-conflict peace. Similarly the Rwandan context offers insights that evoke critical examination of the benefits that autonomy and interdependence of victims of violence can bring. And most of all, community based peacebuilding approaches rely on local epistemologies from which Rwandans draw on to instigate potentiality for peace. The urgency to participate in community activities with zeal, energy, and commitment shows that Rwandans realize that they are divided and united by conflict. The future for Rwanda's peace lies in the hands of her people.

References

Abu-Nimer, M., Khoury, A., & Welty, E. (2007). *Unity in diversity: Interfaith dialogue in the Middle East*. Washington DC: U.S. Institute of Peace.

Acquaro, K., & Landesman, P. (2003). Out of Madness, A Matriarchy, *Mother Jones. January/ February.* Retrieved from http://www.motherjones.com/politics/2003/01/out-madness-matriarchy

Alcroff, L. (1991). The problem of speaking for others. *Cultural Critique 20*, 5–32. Asante, M. (2001). Transcultural realities and different ways of knowing. In V. Millhouse, M.

Asante, and P. Nwosu (Eds.). *Transcultural realities: interdisciplinary perspectives on cross-cultural relations* (71–81). Thousand Oaks, CA: Sage Publications.

Baines, E. (2010). Spirits and social reconstruction after mass violence: rethinking transitional justice. *African Affairs, 109*(436), 409–430.

Betts, A. (2005). Should approaches to post-conflict justice and reconciliation be determined globally, nationally or locally? *The European Journal of Research, 17*(4), 735–752.

Cole, C., & Norander, S. (2011). From Sierra Leone to Kosovo: exploring possibilities for Gendered peacebuilding. *Women and Language, 34*(1), 29–49.

Corey, A., & Joireman, F. (2004). Retributive justice: the Gacaca courts in Rwanda. *African Affairs, 103*, 73–89.

Dallaire, R. (2003). *Shake hands with the devil: The failure of humanity in Rwanda*. Canada: Random House.

Donais, T. (2009). Empowerment or imposition? Dilemmas of local ownership in post-conflict peacebuilding processes. *Peace & Change, 34*(1), 3–26.

Galtung, J. (2004). *Transcend and transform: an introduction to conflict work*. Boulder, CO: Paradigm Publishers.

Ganesh, S., & Holmes, P. (2011). Introduction: Positioning intercultural dialogue—Theories, pragmatics and an agenda. *Journal of International and Intercultural Communication, 4*(2), 81–86.

Hatzfeld, J. (2007). *Life laid bare: The Survivors in Rwanda speak*. Translated by Linda Coverdale. New York: Other Press.

Hoover. J. (2011). Dialogue: Our past, our present, our future. *Journal of Intercultural Communication Research, 40*(3), 203–218.

Hudson, H. (2009). Peacebuilding through a gender lens and the challenges of implementation in Rwanda and Cote d'Ivoire. *Security Studies, 18*, 287–318.

Kastel, Z. (2010). And I, where do I come?: experiences in Jewish-Muslim dialogue. *Tikkun 25*(3), 58–71.

Kigotho, W. (2011). Africa home to only 2.3 per cent world's researchers. *The East African Standard.* Retrieved from http://www.standardmedia.co.ke/?id=2000040499&cid=4&articleID=2000040499

Lahiri, K. (2009). 'Gacaca' courts a possible model for local justice in international crime? *International Criminal Law Review, 9*, 321–332.

Lemarchand, R. (1970). *Rwanda and Brundi.* New York: Praeger Publishers.

Lundy, P., & McGovern, M. (2008). Whose justice? Rebuilding transitional justice from the bottom up. *Journal of Law and Society, 35*(2), 265–292.

Madison, S. (2005). *Critical ethnography: Method, ethics, and performance.* Thousand Oaks, CA: Sage Publications.

Mamdani, M. (1993). University crisis and reform: A reflection on the African experience. *Review of African Political Economy, 58*, 7–19.

Mamdani, M. (2001). *When victims become killers: colonialism, nativism and the genocide in Rwanda.* Princeton, NJ: Princeton University Press.

Martin, J. & Butler, R. (2001). Toward an ethic of intercultural communication research. In V. Millhouse, M. Asante, and P. Nwosu (Eds.). *Transcultural realities: Interdisciplinary perspectives on cross-cultural relations* (pp. 283–298). Thousand Oaks, CA: Sage Publications.

Mazrui, A. (1986). *The Africans: A triple heritage.* London: British Broadcasting Corporation.

Meyerstein, A. (2007). Between law and culture: Rwanda's Gacaca and postcolonial legality. *Law & Social Inquiry, 32*(2), 467–508.

Nagda, B. (2006). Breaking barriers, crossing borders, building bridges: Communication processes in intergroup dialogues. *Journal of Social Issues, 62*(3), 553–576.

Ngugi wa Thiong'o (1986). *Decolonizing the mind: the politics of language in African literature.* London: James Curry.

Nhema, A. & Zeleza, T. P. (2008). (Eds). *The resolution of African conflicts: The management of conflict resolution & post-conflict reconstruction.* Oxford, UK: James Currey Ltd.

Nyamnjoh, F. (2012). Potted plants in greenhouses: a critical reflection on the resilience of colonial education in Africa. *Journal of Asian and African Studies. 47*(2), 129–154.

Orbe, M. (2004). Co-cultural theory and the spirit of dialogue. *International & Intercultural Communication Annual, 27*, 191–213.

Paris, R. (2002). International peacebuilding and the 'Mission Civilisatrice.' *Review of International Studies, 28*(4), 637–656.

Prunier, G. (1995). *The Rwanda crisis: history of the genocide.* New York: Columbia University Press.

Richmond, O. (2007). Emancipatory forms of human security and liberal peacebuilding. *International Journal, 62*(3), 458–477.

Smith, L. (1999). *Decolonizing methodologies: research and indigenous peoples.* London: Zed Books.

Sultana, F. (2007). Reflexivity, positionality and participatory ethics: Negotiating fieldwork dilemmas in international research. *ACME: An International E-Journal of Critical Geographies, 6*(3), 374–385. Retrieved from http://www.acme-journal.org/Home.html

Taylor, D., & Nwosu, P. (2001). Afrocentric empiricism: a model for communication research in Africa. In V. Millhouse, M. Asante, and P. Nwosu (Eds.). *Transcultural realities: interdisciplinary perspectives on cross-cultural relations* (pp. 299–312). Thousand Oaks, CA: Sage Publications.

Yazdani, S. (2010). Victims Critique the ICTR. The *Human Rights Brief: Center for Human Rights and Humanitarian Law*. Retrieved from http://hrbrief.org/2010/01/victims-critique-the-ictr-2/

Endnotes

1. The source of ethnic conflict in Rwanda is contested. There is no given answer despite the historical analysis provided in the works of many scholars such as Corey and Joireman (2004), Mahmood Mamdani (2001), and Lemarchand (1970) among others. The competing narratives attribute Rwanda conflict to existing divisions at pre-colonial period and German and Belgian colonialism that elevated the status of Tutsi over the Hutu. Similarly, ethnic identity is contested. The political decision to "erase" "ethnic identity" in favor of a national Rwandan identity speaks to the complexity of identity politics in Rwanda.

2. As noted above, the complex conceptions of ethnic identity and ethnic conflicts may seem to still jeopardize post-genocide peace efforts. However, the contention between ethnic identity and national identity does not seem to slow down efforts to reconstruct Rwanda in ways that view peace as a multidimensional concept. For example, Rwanda's economic success in the East African region, the government's national healthcare programs among other successes call attention to what constitutes successful post-conflict peacebuilding. Is it time to interrogate the relevance of ethnic identity and/or national identity in peacebuilding? In what circumstances do these identities work and/or don't work? My experience in East Africa reveals that attachment to ethnic identity is destructive and threatens elusive peace in the region. Perhaps, Rwanda's move to embrace national identity is what is needed to bring stability to conflict prone African countries.

3. Gacaca refers to traditional form of conflict management where community members participated in resolving conflicts involving families, friends, and/or neighbors. In June 2012 the operations of the Gacaca courts came to an end after about ten years of trying to bring justice to victims of the 1994 genocide. In the post-genocide setting, Gacaca courts took a different role to "prosecute" suspected perpetrators of the genocide. They were state-administered system of 10,000 community based judicial forums that bended traditional restorative and retributive mechanisms to speed up the government's processing of genocide suspects (Ariel Meyerstein 2007). Whether or not the Gacaca courts system delivered justice, its existence in the period after the genocide offered an alternative that local people

could claim ownership, access, and voice. The outcome of the courts has not been spared of criticism by insiders (some Rwandans opposed to the Kagame government) and outsiders (such as International Human Rights groups). For example, a BBC News report acknowledges the good work the courts were able to accomplish and at the same time refers to "controversial justice" that was also a feature of the courts. http://www.bbc.co.uk/news/world-africa-18490348?print=true

3

Dialogue across the Divide: Bridging the Separation in Cyprus

Benjamin J. Broome

Key Words

- ► Cyprus
- ► Protracted conflict
- ► Reconciliation
- ► Peacebuilding

1. Introduction

Famous since ancient times as the birthplace of Aphrodite (the goddess of love, beauty, and fertility), the eastern Mediterranean island of Cyprus is divided today by a buffer zone that ethnically separates the Turkish-Cypriot and Greek-Cypriot communities. The buffer zone was established as a cease-fire line in 1974, when a Greek-led coup against the government of the Cyprus Republic was followed by Turkish military intervention, leading to the creation of two ethnic zones on the island. Intended as a temporary dividing line separating the two sides during negotiations to end the conflict, the buffer zone still is in place today. United Nations (UN) peacekeeping forces, which have been on the island since 1964, when inter-communal fighting led to a division of the capitol city Nicosia, patrol the buffer zone and maintain observation posts along its 180-kilometer length. Despite ongoing negotiations led by the United Nations, no agreement has been reached to end the conflict.[1]

This physical division of Cyprus has affected nearly every aspect of the lives of both Turkish Cypriots and Greek Cypriots—limiting economic growth (particularly for the Turkish Cypriots), social development, advancement of the education system, integration into the international community, and protection of irreplaceable environmental resources. In addition, the ongoing division has served as a constant source of tension between the countries of Greece and Turkey, and is a major roadblock to Turkey's prospects for joining the European Union. These characteristics place Cyprus in a special class of conflicts that are termed *protracted* or *intractable*. Such conflicts are extremely complex, usually involving issues of identity, meaning, justice, and power, and frequently resist even the most determined attempts at resolution (see Coleman 2003).

Perhaps the most unfortunate consequence of the division in Cyprus has been the severing of communication between people in the two communities. With people disconnected from the daily experience of living together, negative images of the other side have been able to proliferate and take root in the educational system, media representations, and social consciousness of the general populace. The psychological burden of the division is heavy, with most people carrying a sense of injustice about the past and anxiety about the future. Although it had the potential to become a model society where individuals of different faiths, languages, and cultural identities live together in peace, Cyprus has become instead a regrettable example of an ethnically divided society.

In the late 1980s and early 1990s, a small group of Turkish Cypriots and Greek Cypriots who were concerned about the continued division of their island started a series of inter-communal dialogue groups. Facing numerous obstacles and varying degrees of resistance, the initial core group continued their efforts over the years, resulting in the gradual expansion of dialogue-related activities that eventually involved hundreds of individuals in both communities. Their work not only resulted in increased understanding, numerous friendships, and working relationships among the participants in these dialogue groups, but they have also helped mitigate the stranglehold of extreme nationalism that grips the politics of both communities (Anastasiou 2008). These positive results are tempered, however, by the continued division on the island. In fact, today the situation is at a stalemate, with the possibility that for the foreseeable future Cyprus will remain ethnically divided and without a political solution to the conflict that has plagued it for nearly half a century.

In this case study, I examine some of the specific ways in which the work of dialogue groups in Cyprus have contributed to the possibilities for peace on the island, while exploring also the challenges and limitations of intergroup dialogue in protracted conflict situations. I will utilize a dialogic framework that was developed to depict the contribution of dialogue to building a culture of peace (Broome, 2013). This framework is based on contact theory (Amir 1969; Hewstone & Greenland 2000; Pettigrew 2011), concepts of reconciliation (Abu-Nimer 2001; Bar-Tal 2009; Galtung 2001; Kelman 2008) and conflict transformation (Lederach 1995, 1997), and research on cooperative/constructive approaches to conflict (Deutsch 1973, 2008). It is proposed that dialogue contributes to sustainable peace in divided societies in five interrelated ways: enabling sustained contact, reducing deep-seated hostility, nurturing greater respect for the other, developing a narrative of peace and hope, and establishing a stronger basis for cooperation. I will use the lens of this framework to examine the dialogue processes in Cyprus, with the goals of both presenting a hopeful picture of the role that dialogue can play in intractable conflicts and offering a realistic view of the challenges that dialogue groups face in making a meaningful impact on the larger society.

I approach this analysis both as a communication scholar and as an active participant in many of the dialogue groups, where I acted as facilitator, trainer, and consultant. Initially, I went to Cyprus as a U.S. Fulbright Scholar, taking up a position that had been established through lobbying efforts of the Turkish-Cypriot and Greek-Cypriot pioneers of the dialogue process in Cyprus. They identified a need for formal expertise in dialogue processes and the desirability of an external third-party to facilitate their efforts, and they convinced the Cyprus Fulbright Commission to bring a scholar who could work with them on a resident basis. My Fulbright fellowship was initially slated for a nine-month period, starting in September 1994, but I stayed in Cyprus another two academic terms through additional funding from Fulbright and USAID. Over the past fifteen years I have continued to work closely with many of the dialogue groups, making numerous trips to the island for various projects. Thus, this chapter is written from the position of an active participant/observer in the dialogue process.[2]

2.   Dialogue and Peacebuilding in Cyprus

In Cyprus, a large number of intergroup dialogue initiatives have taken place in the form of problem-solving workshops, conflict resolution training, interactive design sessions, and special seminars and project groups (see Anastasiou 2002; Diamond & Fisher 1995; Fisher 1997; Hadjipavlou 2004; Laouris 2011). Many of the early activities were facilitated by external third parties, but the impetus for workshops came primarily from local actors. Organizational support for scheduling and holding these activities was offered by various diplomatic entities, in particular the Cyprus Fulbright Commission (CFC). In later phases of the work, a number of non-governmental organizations (NGOs) were established, many of them using funding mechanisms of international organizations such as UNDP (United Nations Development Program), European Commission, and PRIO (Peace Research Institute of Oslo). A more detailed description of the many types of peacebuilding activities in Cyprus are described in Broome (2005).

In this case study I will base my observations and conclusions on the overall set of dialogue activities that have taken place in Cyprus over the past twenty years, drawing particularly from those dialogue sessions in which I have been directly involved as facilitator, trainer, and/or consultant. To help the reader visualize the work of these groups, I will first describe a series of interactive design sessions that took place over a nine-month period in the mid-1990s with a core group of peacebuilders from the two communities.[3] The thirty participants in this core group (15 Turkish Cypriots and 15 Greek Cypriots) represented a broad cross-section of society, including secondary school teachers, university academics, office workers, civil servants, small business owners, and other civil-society actors. They ranged in age from early-twenties to late-fifties, with the majority between thirty-five and forty-five. There was a balance of males and females. Many of the participants had taken part in conflict resolution workshops held during previous years in Cyprus, the US, or various European countries, so some had met each other previously, and most of them had been introduced to concepts of dialogue. The participants used English as the primary language of discussion in the bi-communal setting.

The dialogue sessions were initiated by the participants, and they volunteered their time to attend the dialogue sessions and contributed personal resources to bring food, beverages, and other items. The Cyprus Fulbright Commissions assisted with the logistics and provided funds for workshop materials, and the United Nations Peacekeeping Forces in Cyprus (UNFICYP) provided a meeting space in the old Ledra Palace Hotel, a derelict building caught in the time-wrap of the buffer zone, at that time (and still today) serving as housing for the UNFICYP troops.

Over the nine-month period, the core group met for weekly two- to three-hour dialogue sessions, and in addition held a weekend retreat. The primary focus of discussion centered on the question of how to best advance peacebuilding efforts in Cyprus. The dialogue sessions progressed through three primary phases. In the first phase, the group identified and discussed the perceived barriers to peacebuilding efforts in Cyprus. Their exchange focused on historical, political, cultural, and group-level issues. Because of problems obtaining permissions for the Turkish Cypriots to cross into the buffer zone, several of these initial sessions were held in separate communal settings, with a bi-communal meeting to exchange and discuss the outcomes of their separate discussions. Although holding separate meetings was not initially the intended or desired format, it provided an opportunity for each communal group to work through some of the internally divisive issues without feeling the need to present a "united front" to the other community. This allowed greater variety of opinions to emerge within each group during the mono-communal meetings, and during the bi-communal meetings it helped the other side to understand the diversity of views that exist within each community.

Their intense and thorough discussion of obstacles to peacebuilding set the stage for the second phase of their dialogue, which targeted the creation of a collective vision statement that could guide peacebuilding efforts in Cyprus. In the beginning of this phase, the group again had to meet in separate communal meetings due to permission issues, so each group used this time to propose a set of statements for possible inclusion in the bi-communal vision statement. Fortunately, permissions were soon obtained to meet regularly, and together the bi-communal group selected a set of goal statements that each group felt comfortable including in the overall vision statement. Through a series of structured discussions, they created a graphical portrayal (in the form of a flowchart) of their consensus about the connections among these goals. The discussions held during these dialogue sessions were intense, often emotional, and sometimes led to periods of stalemate, but the participants overcame these difficulties to create a vision for the future that served as a guide for their efforts over the next decade (see Broome 2004 for a detailed discussion of this vision statement and the process of dialogue that led to its creation).

Based on their jointly-created and mutually-embraced vision statement, the group continued their bi-communal meetings into the third phase, in which they proposed and discussed specific ideas for advancing peace between the two communities. They initially generated nearly 250 ideas for activities that could promote reconciliation between the two communities, and from this rather large set of options they created an agenda of fifteen projects they wanted to initiate within the following year. An active recruiting effort was undertaken to find volunteers to staff these projects, and twelve of them were carried forward. These projects included the formation of several additional dialogue groups, each focused on a particular sector of Cypriot society: young business leaders, youth leaders, educators, women's groups, and university students.

In the decade after the core group completed this nine-month series of dialogue sessions, culminating in their collective vision statement and action agenda, dozens of additional bi-communal activities were developed, resulting in several thousand Greek Cypriots and Turkish Cypriots meeting each other in various bi-communal group activities. While some of these groups followed a format similar to the interactive design sessions described above, others held short-term discussions to better understand topics that were important to the future of Cyprus (e.g., the nature and implications of federation as a governing structure), while other groups took on special goal-oriented tasks (e.g., investigating how history books need to be changed to present a less biased view of Cyprus history). Still others came together to engage in particular community service (e.g., cleaning up a graveyard or removing the litter from a beach), while some formed non-governmental organizations (e.g., Cypriot Youth for Peace) to promote reconciliation among specific populations. In the remainder of this section I will explore some of the specific ways I believe these intergroup dialogue initiatives have contributed to the possibilities for peaceful co-existence in Cyprus.

2.1.   Enabling Sustained Contact

In situations where there is little or no contact between conflicting groups, it is easy for bias and prejudice to be reinforced and over time to become institutionalized, further solidifying the boundaries between the parties in the conflict (Hewstone & Greenland 2000). In protracted conflicts, contact between opposing parties is usually limited, and when it does take place, it does not always produce positive results. However, Allport's (1954) original hypothesis, extended by Amir (1969), Cook (1978), Hewstone and Greenland (2000), Pettigrew (2011), and others, suggests that under conditions of equal status, sustained interactions, cooperative interdependence, and social norms favoring equality, intergroup contact can be effective in reducing prejudice. Dialogue groups meeting these requirements have informed policies in multiethnic societies such as Israel (Amir 1969) and Northern Ireland (Knox & Hughes 1996).

In Cyprus, dialogue groups brought individuals together from two communities that had been separated for decades, allowing participants the opportunity to encounter each other as fellow human beings. Participants learned things about the other side that called into question their existing stereotypes and attitudes; they formed strong affective ties with individuals from the other side, which led to inter-group friendships; and they developed a more differentiated view of the other side, realizing that the other community is not homogenous (Pettigrew 2008). As Salomon (2009) suggests, contact changes relational dynamics by placing participants in a position where they can reexamine the ways in which they perceive one another and relate to one another.

In order for dialogue to lead to cooperation, interaction must be sustained over time (Cromwell & Vogele 2009). Multiple instances of positive interactions make it possible for participants to recall their past exchanges when times were more difficult, and they also help participants recognize each other as potential allies or partners in cooperative ventures. Many of the dialogue groups in Cyprus met regularly over a period of months and, in some cases, years, demonstrating a strong commitment to continue even in the face of negative external developments. In this way, they became part of a positive dynamic, creating through regular contact forces that encouraged additional contact. By developing within their own group a positive present, dialogue helped them look toward a shared future.

2.2.   Reducing Deep-Seated Hostility

Intractable conflicts often result in a deep-rooted hostility that is not easy to overcome, even with the best of intentions. The grievances that residents of conflict zones accumulate, especially when violence or division continues over a number of years, leave deep scars of anger, grief, a sense of victimhood and a will for revenge (Bar-Tal 2009). In order to build bridges, a divided society must find a way to break loose from the confining emotions of fear, anger, and hatred that shackle those who have experienced violent conflict.

The 1974 war in Cyprus, which was preceded by a decade of ethnic hostilities, left deep scars in both Turkish-Cypriot and Greek-Cypriot communities. The traumatic events experienced by people caught up in these hostilities cannot be forgotten by those involved, and it's unlikely that all traces of resentment can be erased from the hearts and minds of those who personally experienced great losses. The opportunity to engage in meaningful dialogue, however, helped reduce this hostility in consequential ways in Cyprus. The dialogue groups offered individuals and groups the possibility to move beyond the past while still acknowledging the events that frame the conflict. The pain from past events was at least partially healed when Greek Cypriots and Turkish Cypriots had a chance to interact with one other as fellow human beings, which gave them an opportunity to share with each other the harm they suffered and the pain they experienced because of actions by the other side. Through frank and honest exchange, individuals moved to a point where they could recognize and acknowledge the responsibility of their own side in the conflict. By engaging in such dialogue, they created an awareness of their shared humanity, taking a major step toward healing and reconciliation (Lederach 1997) and setting the stage for building a shared future on the island.

2.3. Nurturing Respect for the Other

The human psychological tendency to dichotomize makes it easy to classify others as either "allies" or "enemies," which often results in former neighbours harming each other simply because they belong to different national/ethnic groups (Mack 1990). In deeply divided societies, limited freedom of movement creates an environment that reinforces mistrust and suspicion, and pushes each side toward partisan and skewed grievances. Preoccupied with asserting their own rights, people become blind to the need for attending to and mending interethnic relations. Those classified as enemies are demonized, and the causes of one's own suffering and experiences of injustice are attributed exclusively to the other.

The intergroup dialogue sessions in Cyprus provided participants with the opportunity to understand each other's culture and everyday concerns, and learn about the other's history and personal experiences. They exchanged personal stories and engaged in mutual analysis of the conflict and its effects, thus legitimizing and humanizing their former adversaries. By listening to each other describe their experiences and views, and by allowing for the authenticity of what they heard, *respect* slowly emerged. Even thought they might not have agreed with what they heard, by hearing and acknowledging the other's perspective without overreacting or disparaging it, they were able to interpret the words and intentions of the other side with "attributional generosity" (Janoff-Bulman & Werther 2008, 159). As respect increased, along with the corresponding trust that often accompanies it, participants slowly and carefully revealed their own hurt and pain, confident that their sharing would find a positive reception from the other. The work in Cyprus served as a good example of Kriesberg's (2004) suggestion that a *regard* for the other usually takes hold in dialogue groups, eventually helping members to accept the possibility that different ways of life can exist side-by-side. As Bar-Tal (2009) notes, through such dialogue the rival can become a legitimate partner in peace and deserving of humane treatment.

2.4. Developing a Narrative of Hope and Peace

In protracted conflicts, the psychological burden imposed by images of the past weighs heavily on the minds of those involved, creating a pathology that permeates society. Memories of violent confrontations tend to dominate the minds of people in the affected society. It is not possible to simply lay aside mental images of lost family members, destroyed homes, shattered livelihoods, the experience of living in refugee camps, acts of violence such as rapes and murders, and other horrors of war. Even those of the younger generation who did not directly experience such incidents are confronted with them on a daily basis through stories from their parents, lessons in school, and constant renditions in the newspapers, radio programs, and television specials.

Like most conflicts that are characterized by physical and psychological violence, Greek Cypriots and Turkish Cypriots are heavily burdened by collective memories of past violence, resulting in individual and societal feelings of fear, anger, and hatred. This produces a climate of negativity, a sense of pessimism about the future, and low expectations about the possibility for resolving the conflict. In such a climate, it is difficult to promote the changes that are necessary to improve relations and establish the infrastructure for peace. To get past the negativity, it is necessary to develop "an emotional orientation of hope" (Bar-Tal 2009, 369).

For those in Cyprus who participated in the dialogue groups, the weight of the psychological burden lessened through their involvement in discussions that examined the dynamics of the conflict, followed by building a collective vision of the future. By harnessing dialogue appropriately, participants found a way to reduce the mental and emotional burdens of the past, while turning their attention toward possibilities for living in peace. The physical barriers did not go away, and their sense of loss and incompleteness were not eliminated, but through dialogue participants were able to cultivate more positive attitudes toward the other side and more optimistic attitudes toward the possibility of peace. Dialogue helped them create what Staub (1996) calls a "positive vision based on humanistic and inclusive ideals without an inherent destructive potential" (147). They gained an awareness of their interconnectedness, common humanity, and shared interests. Although the dialogue sessions themselves were limited to a relatively small percentage of the overall society, and it is not clear to what extent the work of these groups became part of the public consciousness, they interjected into the larger public discussions the option that there may be alternative paths out of the conflict. Developing a narrative framework that places peace at its center is a key element in transforming conflict, helping society visualize a different (and more positive) future.

2.5. Establishing a Basis for Cooperation

In protracted conflicts, cooperation almost always ceases as trust breaks down and group relations deteriorate. This unfortunate consequence means that individuals on opposite sides of a conflict no longer have a way to experience the give-and-take that is part of the process of working and living together. Individuals no longer receive practice in compromising while working out the details of daily problem-solving, making it even more difficult to consider compromise on larger issues that divide the parties. Not only is the experience of cooperation missing, but many issues are left unattended when parties cannot work together, leading to losses for both sides.

As Cromwell and Vogele (2009), Kelman (1999), Osgood (1966), Deutsch (2008), and others suggest, cooperation is the foundation for a peaceful community. By working together on cooperative activities, individuals develop habits that will serve them well in building a common future, and they create commitments that help them move past roadblocks and conscious attempts to sabotage their efforts. Undertaking small but meaningful initiatives can lower tensions and help participants move away from competitive actions. In the view of Morton Deutsch (1973), cooperative relations have characteristics such as effective communication, respect, fair treatment, enhancement of one another's knowledge and skill, and recognition of the legitimacy of each other's interests. Such actions, which must be based on mutual trust, do not come easily, but instead must be cultivated gradually. As Deutsch (2008) notes, it takes repeated experience of successful and mutually beneficial cooperation, in a variety of settings, to build trust between former warring parties.

In Cyprus, the dialogue sessions spawned numerous cooperative projects. Through their experience in intergroup dialogues over a number of years, participants gained important contacts with the other community, and they become much more sensitive to their concerns. In addition, they also become aware of some of the issues that might cause misunderstanding and conflict, while learning some of the skills for dealing with differences. Through the intergroup dialogue initiatives group members learned to talk about divisive issues in ways that avoid unintentional provocation, placing them in a better position for success in cooperative initiatives. While the political situation prevented any large-scale cooperation in the business sector, other cooperative ventures across community lines were accomplished through determined initiative by individuals who understood their importance, who were aware of the potential difficulties, and who were committed to their success. From sustained participation in dialogue sessions, participants built strong communication links for cooperation and identified suitable tasks that could hold potential for success. Without a political solution to the conflict, the types of cooperative projects are limited in Cyprus, but when an official framework is in place that allows for closer working relationships, those Turkish Cypriots and Greek Cypriots who participated in the dialogue sessions will be in a good position to move forward with cooperative projects that lie at the heart of building a functioning society.

Even though the dialogue groups have made important contributions to the possibilities for peace, the political deadlock unfortunately remains, and it is difficult sometimes to maintain hope for significant progress on a settlement in the near future. Of course, dialogue in and of itself cannot provide a political solution to the conflict in Cyprus. In spite of the very real and meaningful progress obtained through dialogue, there are many limitations to its impact, which will be explored in the final section.

3. Challenges to Dialogue

Building peace in protracted conflicts is a lengthy and difficult road, requiring an evolution in societal views and orientations. Dialogue can promote a new set of guiding beliefs and ideals, but there are many challenges that confront those involved in intergroup dialogue initiatives. Even when the initiatives are successful, there may be limitations to the impact dialogue can have on the larger social fabric. The dialogue activities in Cyprus provide several useful lessons about these challenges, including both obstacles and limitations.

First, it is important to keep in mind that it is not always possible or appropriate to bring people together, even though the participants themselves may be willing to meet with each other. Among other impediments to dialogue, there is often strong resistance from authorities and/or the general population. Especially when those at the top of the power hierarchy find dialogue a threat to their views and positions, they will often place roadblocks in the way of groups meeting together. In Cyprus, during the early stages of the dialogue activities, the existence of a buffer zone separating the two communities meant that special procedures had to be followed to obtain permissions before any meetings could be held. Permissions were difficult to obtain and often denied, leading to endless frustration and inconvenience for everyone. For over six years, from January 1997 until April 2003, there were no permissions given for dialogue groups to meet in the buffer zone. Participants found ways to continue contact during this period—through electronic exchange, workshops organized outside Cyprus, and meetings at a mixed village that was located on the British Sovereign Base area—but it required a great deal of patience and persistence on the part of the participants and organizers to keep the dialogues moving forward. Without regular meetings, sustained discussions that are so important in maintaining progress could not take place. Sometimes it is not possible to overcome these obstacles and dialogue may not be feasible.

Second, simply bringing participants together in the same physical space, even if they have the willingness to interact with the other side, is insufficient for dialogue to actually happen. Particular attention must be given to the design of the dialogue. Special care must be taken to select a suitable forum as well as devise appropriate methods and structures for dialogue, ones that ensure all voices can enter the discussion in a meaningful way. In most of the dialogue groups in Cyprus, careful efforts were made to design sessions appropriately, but when the dialogue sessions were less thoughtfully designed, the groups were rarely productive and usually stopped meeting after one or two sessions. Facilitation of dialogue is a very complex process, even in the best of circumstances, but the chances of success are much greater when experienced facilitators employ proven methodologies and techniques for creating a safe climate and encouraging meaningful interaction. Unfortunately, the training required for proper facilitation of dialogue is not always available, and many dialogue groups will experience problems without it.

Third, societal, regional, and even international events can significantly alter the course of dialogue. Dialogue groups are not isolated from the changing context of the conflict, and the dynamics of the conflict will act as constraints and impose limitations on what can be accomplished. Overall, it is much easier for individuals and groups engaged in dialogue to succumb to the misgivings, loss of hope, and renewed hostility brought on by stalemate or regression in progress than it is to safeguard and protect the trust, cooperation, and respect they have developed in the group. The groups in Cyprus have been the victim of numerous domestic and international developments over the years. In general, the two sides in Cyprus have seldom had leaders who simultaneously supported a solution, leading to a lack of synchrony between the two sides at the political level. This discrepancy was reflected in the dialogue groups: at times one side or the other was excited and hopeful about the possibilities for a settlement, and at other times they were deflated because their efforts and hope were not shared by the other side. Many other events, too numerous to describe here, have affected the dialogue activities, and in every case they affected the willingness of people to participate, making it much more difficult for people to take the risks that are inherent in dialogue initiatives.

Fourth, we must realize that the attitudinal, emotional, and behavioral changes that occur in the dialogue groups do not automatically transfer to those outside the small circle of participants, and there is no clear path for ensuring that this happens. Although more than 2,000 people have participated in some form of dialogue group in Cyprus, only a small percentage of these took part in groups that met consistently over a long period. While the overall number of participants in dialogue activities is not insignificant, especially in the context of an overall population of less than one million, in the larger society the dialogue activities have not been embraced. Although it is not necessary for everyone in the general population to participate in a dialogue group, it is unlikely that the type of transformation sought through dialogue will occur until there is large-scale support for the goals of dialogue.

Fifth, we should be aware that dialogue groups may be unwittingly "used" by officials and others for their own purposes. Hopefully this is not often the case, but it is a danger that should be given attention by anyone promoting dialogue in the face of intractable conflict. In Cyprus, the existence of dialogue groups was more compatible with the Greek-Cypriot interests, whose political rhetoric emphasized re-uniting the communities (bringing back a period when the Greek Cypriots were dominant in the society), than with the Turkish Cypriot interests, whose rhetoric emphasized division (presumably to protect their community from political and economic domination by the Greek Cypriots). Thus, the Greek Cypriot officials did little to officially stand in the way of the dialogue groups; rather, they would sometimes point to the dialogue groups as evidence of how Turkish Cypriots and Greek Cypriots could live together peaceably if there were no Turkish military presence on the island. In the early stages of the dialogue initiatives, the Turkish Cypriots actively discouraged participation in dialogue groups in part because they feared these groups would be used by the Greek-Cypriot side to further their unification argument. The Turkish-Cypriot rationale for maintaining the separation, which argued that it was not possible for the two communities to live together, was perceived by the Turkish-Cypriots leadership as undercut by the dialogue groups. Although dialogue groups could become tools of those opposed to a solution, the potential benefits of dialogue usually outweigh the costs associated with the possibility of being used by those in power. Nevertheless, it is prudent for organizers to be aware of the potential for playing into the hands of those with ulterior motives, and steps should be taken to minimize the negative impact.

Sixth, it is imperative to consider the appropriateness of dialogic approaches and methodologies for the cultural settings in which they are being applied. Generally, dialogue is consensual in its assumptions and implementation, and most approaches to dialogue are based on active, open talk. Such practices are not always compatible with accepted cultural norms, or one of the cultural groups might be more comfortable than the other group with highly-verbal interaction. In Cyprus, there was an overall embrace by both communities of western forms of dialogue, but the approaches that were implemented may have been a better fit for the Greek Cypriots, who are more expressive, emotional, and action-oriented than the Turkish Cypriots, who tend to be more reserved and careful in their deliberations. Such differences in style require more careful facilitation and greater attention to design of dialogue meetings. Ways must be found to make sure that all members have sufficient opportunity to participate and that one style of interaction is not privileged.

Additionally, we must keep in mind that language issues can affect dialogue groups, especially those that bring together participants across ethnic and cultural lines. In Cyprus, neither community speaks the language of the other, so most of the groups used English as the language of discussion. Because Cyprus is a former British colony, and many are educated in the UK or US, a common language could be used; nevertheless it limited participation to those with sufficient proficiency in English, and it posed problems in expression for participants who were less comfortable in English. Interpreters can be used, but subtleties of translation can lead to misunderstanding, affect spontaneity of expression, and interrupt the flow of conversation. In general, language differences often present difficulties, and dialogue may be limited when participants do not share a common language.

Seventh, we must ask how the dialogic process itself can become incorporated in everyday practices of society. If dialogue is primarily limited to specially-arranged events, the dialogue groups will remain as fringe activities with limited impact on the overall conflict. The groups in Cyprus made many attempts to integrate dialogue into the fabric of society: efforts were made to bring a more balanced view of the other into the curriculum of the education system; a number of multi-ethnic NGOs were established; community-based dialogue groups were formed; cultural mechanisms such as literature, films, and theatre were offered in the hope of promoting greater dialogue in everyday conversations; programs were developed for the mass media in the hopes of making it is less adversarial; and when there was opportunity for input into the political negotiations, participants pushed for establishing official units and mechanisms responsible for promoting dialogue at all levels of society. Although some of these efforts had limited success, they were intended to help institutionally anchor dialogue, with the goal of shaping and solidifying its place in society.

By creating tangible ways to incorporate dialogue in various societal structures, the hope is that dialogue will happen naturally in response to conflict, and that dialogue will be used as the means to design an appropriate infrastructure for peace. These objectives are particularly challenging, however, and dialogic activities are often resisted by those whose advocacy would be most critical in their adoption. In the case of Cyprus, the overall society in both communities remains adversarial and far from ready to accept dialogue as the primary means of dealing with the conflict, in spite of many valiant efforts on the part of the peacebuilding community.

In bringing to a close this brief examination of dialogue processes in Cyprus, we must recognize that there are many unknowns about dialogue—we can't always know if it is appropriate or how it will unfold when it takes place. Fortunately, meaningful steps forward are often visible, and these small indications of progress provide hope for transforming societies such as Cyprus, creating eventually a culture in which dialogue is viewed as the means for dealing with differences and settling the disputes that arise from them. Although Cyprus is a long way from achieving such a result, the potential for dialogue to keep alive the possibility of peaceful co-existence on this beautiful Mediterranean island is reason enough to continue the quest. For the individuals who have made great personal and professional sacrifices toward promoting dialogue, the *process* of building peace provides the impetus to continue working, even in difficult circumstances, toward what some would view as idealistic ends.

References

Abu-Nimer, M. (Ed.). (2001). *Reconciliation, justice, and coexistence: Theory and practice*. Lanham, MD: Lexington Books.

Allport, G. (1954). *The nature of prejudice*. Boston: Beacon Press.

Amir, Y. (1969). Contact hypothesis in ethnic relations. *Psychological Bulletin, 71*(5), 319–342.

Anastasiou, H. (2002). Communication across conflict lines: The case of ethnically divided Cyprus. *Journal of Peace Research, 39*(5), 581–596.

Anastasiou, H. (2008). *The broken olive branch: Nationalism, ethnic conflict and the quest for peace in Cyprus* (Vol. I: The Impasse of Ethnonationalism). Syracuse, NY: Syracuse University Press.

Bar-Tal, D. (2009). Reconciliation as a foundation of culture of peace. In J. Rivera (Ed.), *Handbook on building cultures of peace* (pp. 363–377). New York: Springer.

Broome, B. J. (1997). Designing a collective approach to peace: Interactive design and problem-solving workshops with Greek Cypriot and Turkish Cypriot communities in Cyprus. *International Negotiation, 2*(3), 381–407.

Broome, B. J. (2003). Responding to the challenges of third-party facilitation: Reflections of a scholar-practitioner in the Cyprus conflict. *Journal of Intergroup Relations, 26*(4), 24–43.

Broome, B. J. (2004). Reaching across the dividing line: Building a collective vision for peace in Cyprus. *International Journal of Peace Research, 41*(2), 191–209.

Broome, B. J. (2005). *Building bridges across the green line: A guide to intercultural communication in Cyprus*. Nicosia: United Nations Development Program.

Broome, B. J. (2013). Building cultures of peace: The role of intergroup dialogue. In J. G. Oetzel & S. Ting-Toomey (Eds.), *Sage handbook of conflict communication: Integrating theory, research, and practice* (2nd ed.), (pp. 737–762). Los Angeles: Sage.

Coleman, P. T. (2003). Characteristics of protracted, intractable conflict: Toward the development of a metaframework. *Peace and Conflict: Journal of Peace Psychology, 9*(1), 1–37.

Cook, S. W. (1978). Interpersonal and attitudinal outcomes in cooperating interracial groups. *Journal of Research and Development in Education, 12*, 97–113.

Cromwell, M., & Vogele, W. B. (2009). Nonviolent action, trust, and building a culture of peace. In J. Rivera (Ed.), *Handbook on building cultures of peace* (pp. 231–244). New York: Springer.

Deutsch, M. (1973). *The resolution of conflict: Constructive and destructive process*. New Haven, CT: Yale University Press.

Deutsch, M. (2008). Reconciliation after destructive intergroup conflict. In A. Nadler, T. E. Malloy, & J. D. Fisher (Eds.), *The social psychology of intergroup reconciliation* (pp. 471–485). Oxford: Oxford University Press.

Diamond, L., & Fisher, R. J. (1995). Integrating conflict resolution training and consultation: A Cyprus example. *Negotiation Journal, 11*(3), 287–301.

Fisher, R. J. (1997). *Interactive conflict resolution*. Syracuse: Syracuse University Press.

Galtung, J. (2001). After violence: Reconstruction, reconciliation, resolution: Coping with visible and invisible effects of war and violence. In M. Abu-Nimer (Ed.), *Reconciliation, justice, and coexistence: Theory and practice* (pp. 3–24). Lanham, MD: Lexington Books.

Hadjipavlou, M. (2004). The contribution of bicommunal contacts in building a civil society in Cyprus. In A. Eagly, R. Baron, & L. Hamilton (Eds.), *The social psychology of group identity and social conflict* (pp. 193–213). Washington D.C.: American Psychological Association.

Hadjipavlou, M. (2007). The Cyprus conflict: Root causes and implications for peacebuilding. *Journal Of Peace Research, 44*(3), 349–365.

Heraclides, A. (2011). The Cyprus gordian knot: An intractable ethnic conflict. *Nationalism & Ethnic Politics, 17*(2), 117–139.

Hewstone, M., & Greenland, K. (2000). Intergroup conflict. *International Journal of Psychology, 35*(2), 136–144.

Janoff-Bulman, R., & Werther, A. (2008). The social psychology of respect: Implications for delegitimization and reconciliation. In A. Nadler, T. E. Malloy, & J. D. Fisher (Eds.), *The social psychology of intergroup reconciliation* (pp. 145–165). Oxford: Oxford University Press.

Kaymak, E., Lordos, A., & Tocci, N. (2008). *Building confidence in peace: Public opinion and the Cyprus peace process*. Brussels: Centre for European Policy Studies.

Kelman, H. C. (1999). Transforming the relationship between former enemies. In R. L. Rothstein (Ed.), *After the peace: Resistance and reconciliation* (pp. 193–205). Boulder: Lynne Rienner Publishers.

Kelman, H. C. (2008). Reconciliation from a social-psychological perspective. In A. Nadler, T. E. Malloy, & J. D. Fisher (Eds.), *The social psychology of intergroup reconciliation* (pp. 15–32). Oxford: Oxford University Press.

Ker-Lindsay, J. (2011). *The Cyprus problem: What everyone needs to know*. Oxford: Oxford University Press.

Knox, C., & Hughes, J. (1996). Crossing the divide: Community relations in Northern Ireland. *Journal of Peace Research, 22*(1), 83–98.

Kriesberg, L. (2004). Comparing reconciliation actions within and between countries. In Y. Bar-Siman-Tov (Ed.), *From conflict resolution to reconciliation* (pp. 81–110). Oxford: Oxford University Press.

Laouris, Y. (2011). *Masks of demons: A journey in the discovering and breaking of stereotypes in a society in conflict*. Charleston: CreateSpace.

Lederach, J. P. (1995). *Preparing for peace: Conflict transformation across cultures*. New York: Syracuse University Press.

Lederach, J. P. (1997). *Building peace: Sustainable reconciliation in divided societies*. Washington, D. C.: United States Institute of Peace.

Mack, J. (1990). The enemy system. In V. D. Volkan, J. V. Montville, & D. A. Julius (Eds.), *The psychodynamics of international relationships vol. I: Concepts and theories* (pp. 83–95). Lexington MA: Lexington Books.

Osgood, C. E. (1966). *Perspectives in foreign policy*. Palo Alto, CA: Pacific Books.

Papadakis, Y. (2006). *Echoes from the dead zone: Across the Cyprus divide*. London: I.B. Tauris & Co.

Pettigrew, T. F. (2008). Future directions for intergroup contact theory and research. *International Journal of Intercultural Relations, 32*, 187–199.

Pettigrew, T. F. (2011). *When groups meet: The dynamics of intergroup conflict.* New York: Psychology Press.

Salomon, G. (2009). Peace education: Its nature, nurture and the challenges it faces. In J. Rivera (Ed.), *Handbook on building cultures of peace* (pp. 107–121). New York: Springer.

Staub, E. (1996). The psychological and cultural roots of group violence and the creation of caring societies and peaceful group relations. In T. Gregor (Ed.), *A natural history of peace* (pp. 129–155). Nashville, TN: Vanderbilt University Press.

Volkan, V. D. (1979). *Cyprus—war and adaptation. A psychoanalytic history of two ethnic groups in conflict.* Charlottesville: University Press of Virginia.

Endnotes

1. For more details on the Cyprus conflict, see: Anastasiou 2008; Hadjipavlou 2007; Heraclides 2011; Kaymak, Lordos, & Tocci 2008; Ker-Lindsay 2011; Papadakis 2006; Volkan 1979. See also reports produced by the International Crisis Group, available at http://www.crisisgroup.org/en/regions/europe/turkey-cyprus/cyprus.aspx, and the PRIO Cyprus Centre, available at http://www.prio.no/Cyprus.

2. I have described my involvement in greater detail in earlier publications (see Broome 2003, 2005).

3. This nine-month period was the initial stage of my Fulbright fellowship, during which I facilitated the dialogue sessions described in this case study (see Broome 1997).

PART III

Building Dialogue in/for Education

4

Multiculturalism, Contact Zones, and the Political Core of Intercultural Education

Susana Gonçalves

Key Words

- ► Intercultural education
- ► Intercultural pedagogy
- ► Contact zone
- ► Political action
- ► Global citizenship

1. Introduction

From mid-semester onward students frequently tell me that suddenly everything going on in society seems related to what we've been discussing in our class, *Intercultural Education*. To me this is a sign of deep learning—they now engage differently with previously familiar phenomena. Below are some issues brought up in our discussions:

- ► the complex relationship between immigration and the historical, economic, and political context of the society;

▶   the vestiges of colonial mentality in contemporary Portuguese society;

▶   the symbolic power of words in labeling people—for example, using "that black" instead of "that person," "a Gypsy" instead of "someone," or headlines denouncing crimes by "an eastern European immigrant," thus associating immigration with criminality;

▶   the symbolic relationship between cultural dynamics and cultural hybridization— the Portuguese generally perceive themselves and their culture as cohesive and homogenous, even though our national heritage contains traces of innumerable cultures;

▶   universality of celebrating births, honoring the dead, educating children, and cultivating identities, despite their varying expressions in different cultural settings;

▶   the subtle yet persistent stereotypes, myths, and preconceptions of the Other, even in societies like Portugal, that is claimed to be open and hospitable;

▶   and lastly, perception of certain cultures or people as "good" or "bad," depending on circumstances or historical context.

This last reflection arrives almost as an epiphany—it is fundamental to understand the importance and political aspect of intercultural education in global and multicultural societies. The students reflect on their experiences in the class with expressions like "I had never noticed this before," "I never thought about it this way," or with words of empathy or indignation like "now I understand how this person feels in this situation." These are the fruits of individual experiences engaged in critical interrogation and revising personal worldviews. Intercultural sensibility and competence can be achieved through simple resources and techniques under the guidance of the teacher. These instruments of change form the main focus of this chapter.

2.   Concepts

Contemporary holistic approaches which fully engage students in the learning process are now the hallmarks of good teaching and learning. Action is an effective binder of ideas and emotions—learning by doing—and as cognitive research has shown (Damasio 2000; Goleman 1996), thinking and feeling are naturally integrated into teaching.

Teachers, therefore, undertake the important role of exerting influence over the minds, values, and attitudes of their students. In selecting teaching materials, teachers do not only reflect on their conceptual and methodological approach, but also make a value judgment about what is important. Their methods and educational strategy define a range of political and social attitudes toward authority, conformism, tolerance, and resilience that will remain through the lives and actions of the students, as citizens.

"Head, heart and hands" is a well-known formula in active teaching methods (advocated by Johann Pestalozzi) in adult education (Knowles 1975) and in popular and informal education programs (such as Paulo Freire 1975). Dialogue is closely related to this method; dialogue on campus leads to dialogue in wider society, enabling students to become active and committed promoters of social change. Besides training professionals, universities should carry the role of educating responsible citizens (cf. Bergan & van't Land 2010), where active methods are essential. Student-centered teaching is the most appropriate model for promoting active citizenship in students. Active learning enhances the skills of sustainability (Dawe, Jucker, & Stephen 2005), as well as the ability to learn from diversity (Moreno et al. 2006) and observe the social reality with a critical and interventionist eye (Justice et al. 2007).

Intercultural education and its political dimension go hand in hand with active learning and responsible citizenship. In my teaching, I aim for the creation of transcultural, cosmopolitan, and globally sustainable identities among students. Global citizenship can be defined as the knowledge and skills necessary for social and environmental justice (Andrzejewski 1996 in Andrzejewski & Alessio 1999). UNESCO gives us the ideal starting point for a model of sustainable education, global and intercultural: education is "a vital part of all efforts to imagine and create new relations among people and to foster greater respect for the needs of the environment" (1997, paragraph 38). Sustainable Education is an international education, intercultural and interactive (UNESCO 1997, 2010), consisting of relevant curricula, content, and effective student-centered methods.

In defining teaching strategies and methods, I borrow concepts from cultural studies, sociology, and critical theory, such as contact zone, transculturation, ethnoscape, otherness, cosmopolitanism, and social sustainability. "Contact zone" was coined by Pratt (1991) to mean "social spaces where cultures meet, clash, and grapple with each other, often in contexts of highly asymmetrical relations of power, such as colonialism, slavery, or their aftermaths as they are lived out in many parts of the world today" (33). We may broaden the concept to include not only tangible social spaces where cultural encounters occur, but also symbolic spaces that work as media for social encounters and intercultural learning (e.g., books, photography, films). Cultural boundaries are most frequently crossed in contact zones. Compelled to pay attention to diversity, the subject, even if resistant, will learn something of the Other's lifestyle, beliefs, and behavior, eventually being able to see beyond the superficial differences and realize the similarities between cultures.

Students can only properly develop their own sensibilities and intercultural competence when given opportunity to enter multiple contact zones. Contact zones are neither comfort zones, nor war camps. There is risk, uncertainty, and power struggles, but also opportunity, transculturation, and possible collaboration across cultures and social classes. In the process hidden voices might be heard and cultural fusion/symbiosis or transformation might occur.

Transculturation can be useful in intercultural education to help students understand what it means to be a member of a minority, an oppressed group, or simply an outsider. This process relates to hybridity (Bhabha 1990, 1996), which describes the "narrative" constructions arising from the "hybrid" interaction of contending cultural forces and cultural traditions. It can also be discussed in comparison to the concept of ethnoscape introduced by

Appadurai (2006) to describe the transnational, intercultural, and global activities of global transitioning people.

Like pollinating bees, these moving groups naturally bring learning and cultural trans-fusion across frontiers. Travelers, immigrants, and mobile professionals are modern nomads who promote the revitalization of cultures. This transformative movement occurs within the ethnoscapes, "the landscapes of group identity" and contact zones.

Cultural dynamism (and even cultural survival) is at great disadvantage without these intercultural encounters. However, this is not obvious to everyone. In fact, it should be noted here that the notion of Otherness, related to racism as differentiation and leading to exclu-sion (Balibar 2005) emerges after cultural encounters. The ability to see the Other as equal and see ourselves as different places us in democratic parity. Like other aspects of demo-cratic citizenship, social and cultural parity should be the subject of intentional teaching. It is a matter of intercultural education.

Politically, social diversity gives new meaning to the belief that citizenship is more an awareness of the rights of others and practice of our duties to society than the vindication of our rights and the requirement of the duties of another. As Appiah (2006) claims, the adaptive and the ethical answer to diversity and globalization is cosmopolitanism. Cosmo-politanism is the ability to see ourselves as humans (thus like any other human creature) as well as cultural beings (thus differing from those belonging to other groups). The aim of cosmopolitanism is not to convert or to produce hybrid groups through blind adherence to the beliefs and patterns of behavior of other cultures but to make us understand and respect others. This is the key to peaceful living together.

All the aforementioned aspects are vital to intercultural programs, which go beyond culture and intercultural encounters and engage also with political and philosophical agen-das for societies which value cohesion, democratic diversity, and sustainable development. Active citizenship implies more than simply manifesting a critical mind and protest when democracy fails. Citizenship, seen as the awareness of the Others' rights and of our own duties, requires that competency for living together mentioned in the well-known UNESCO Delors report (1996). This skill is what broadens our worldviews and our naturally narrow cultural frameworks. Envisaged as both an educational policy and a political manifesto, intercultural education should always be directed toward this vision.

3. Context

My methods and intercultural teaching activities, as related to Intercultural Education, are offered at the College of Education of the Polytechnic of Coimbra in Portugal. This is a compulsory module for the third year students of Social Pedagogy and second year Teacher Training undergraduates, and also an elective for a range of master students in Education programs. Each class consists of fifteen to forty-five students, who are expected to attend thirty to forty-five contact hours (depending on their program) over the course of fifteen weeks.

The aim of the module is to promote intercultural competence and ability to apply a variety of techniques and strategies to minimize stereotyping, prejudice, miscommunication, and cultural conflict in professional settings. The module also aims to familiarize students with theories and concepts that deepen their understanding of multiculturalism, social cohesion, and intercultural dialogue. The syllabus includes the topics such as multiculturalism in contemporary societies; intercultural dialogue and competence; identity, cultural belonging, and intergroup relations; and promoting intercultural education. Practical methods and training techniques of intercultural education (e.g., case studies, simulation, group dynamics, cultural sensitizers) are integrated into the module. Throughout the semester, students participate in various activities, including lectures and group discussions, independent research, talks and debates with guest speakers, and project-based learning assignments. Assessment primarily consists of practical work such as the design and implementation of an intercultural project (discussed in detail below).

It is important to stress that there are usually few minority students in this module. For many, this is the first contact with the issues of multiculturalism and intercultural relations. Many struggle with stereotypes, misconceptions, and lack of information about minorities in Portuguese society (namely, Roma or black people), so this module is an opportunity for them to gain new knowledge, debate the related issues with their peers, teachers, and guest speakers, and start thinking of themselves as cultural beings whose identity is not just a matter of personality but also of cultural belonging.

4. Methods

My teaching strategies, developed over several years, favor activities that uphold knowledge and sensitivity, individual reflexivity, and social intervention, leading to socially active citizenship. This approach is based on critical questioning, dilemmas, critical incidents, group dynamics, analysis of texts from/about other cultures, portfolio work, and projects. The following five approaches represent the strategies and resources I find most useful in developing students' intercultural understanding and awareness of global citizenship.

4.1. Surprising Cases (Drawing on Music, Image, and Film)

Learning requires attention. An effective way to get students' attention is to confront them with intriguing cases that defy logic and expectations. If these scenarios generate ideas and emotions, then learning will be strengthened.

I want my students to not only understand the concept of intercultural sensitivity but also to develop their sensitivity to the Other. To be able to appreciate, understand, and properly communicate with the Other, we must cross cultural boundaries with an awareness of biased worldviews. In the classroom, I illustrate these ideas with a concrete example: the Roma minority in Portugal, a group plagued by negative stereotypes which maintain their ostracism. Many of these stereotypes originate not from cultural issues but from this group's low educational level and socio-economic status. What I try to make clear to students is that our knowledge of this culture is insufficient to make a fair judgment. Some common ideas about the Roma:

► Their culture is impervious to the influence of other cultures,
► They don't mix with other groups,
► They reject our culture,
► They are very cohesive as a group,
► They have their own language, religion, and customs.

These notions are easily disassembled through a simple guessing exercise based on images and snippets of music. Used as pedagogic resources, images and sound complement verbal information, illustrate abstract ideas, and stimulate imagination and critical thinking. Audio-visual resources help students remember the syllabus' key points. They are even more powerful if associated with people and society, stimulating creative, as well as reactive, ideas and feelings (for a list of ideas on the pedagogical use of various multimedia resources see Gonçalves 2011b).

I use Road of the Gypsies (L'Épopée Tzigane) (2xCD, 1996, Network Medien GmbH) as the main source. This audio CD is a beautiful compilation of music from northern India to Western Europe, representative of the gipsy road. It includes a photo-booklet with information on the musicians and their roots. I begin by showing images of Roma people from various regions of the world (Europe, Asia, and USA). I show only the photos from the photo-booklet, hiding the captions and ask students to identify the people in the photos by country, world region, and ethnic group. Then I play pieces of music from the CD and ask them to guess the geographical origin of the songs. The guesses of the students are usually diverse and mostly incorrect. Only rarely are the images and songs identified with Gypsies. After revealing that all photographs are of gypsy musicians and it was their songs we heard, I let them hear the songs again and look at the accompanying booklet to allow them to appreciate the different languages, ways of dressing, sonorities, and cultural elements. In addition to these exercises I use movies about the Roma people which help deepen students' reflection, e.g., *Time of the Gypsies* (1988, Emir Kusturika, UK, Italy, Yugoslavia), *Latcho Drom* (Tony Gatlif, 1993, France) or *When the Road Bends: Tales of a gypsy caravan* (Jasmine Dellal, 2006, USA).

The use of films in the classroom can serve to help students, at a stage in which their experiences in the world are still limited, understand what is happening in the world around them[1]. For students to recognize and reject racism, social injustice, and oppression, they need to feel empathy for those that are victims of such behaviors (see how they are affected), understand their production mechanisms, and develop a sense of active citizenship that can lead to contributing to the prevention of these phenomena. The strong and intense emotional experiences that often occur while watching a film help students get in touch with their own (often forgotten) feelings and experiences, distinguish their origin and why they are perceived as good or bad, and encourage self-awareness and empathy along with emotional intelligence (Gonçalves 2011b).

This experience can be strengthened with additional activities. For example, we may screen a film on racism which helps students understand characters' natures and motives. We may then ask students to role-play victim and aggressor, or other characters in the narrative. These exercises can lead to involving and emotional debates of the material, as situations gain depth once we are part of them, increasing our chances of understanding diversity.

These activities help students realize how Afghan, Spanish, Egyptian, or Albanian Gypsies appear to be more like the people of their home regions than like one another, despite being of the same ethnicity. Comments at the end reveal their disconcerted feelings ("I feel really so ignorant") and they easily draw conclusions such as:

- ▶ the Gypsies mingle with other people and this leads to appropriations of language, religion, and customs;
- ▶ they are united by ethnic identity, but not other dimensions of identity, such as national or religious identity;
- ▶ the Portuguese Gypsies are Portuguese citizens, just as the Romanian gypsies are Romanian citizens;
- ▶ to understand the other, we need to consider their identities in relation to various dimensions, such as socioeconomic class, culture, nationality, and education.

These conclusions are the cognitive bases for the development of intercultural sensitivity. The example shows how still image (photography, cartoons, etc.), film (fiction and non-fiction films and video), and music can be a powerful teaching and learning resource. Images can be used to discuss and understand almost any social phenomenon, controversy, trend, and driver in society.

4.2. Storytelling

Stories connect minds, creating ideas and mindsets. Stories are important cultural products and reservoirs of culture. As mentioned by UNESCO (2010):

- ▶ Stories safeguard and codify information as well as beliefs, and rules for living.
- ▶ Stories remind us of other times and different places and lift us beyond our limiting pre-occupation with the 'here and now'. (…)
- ▶ (…) Each story has a beginning, a middle, and an end. A specific conflict and patterns of conflict resolution are usually embedded within this structure. These can stimulate the development of possible solutions to our own predicaments.

▶ Stories evoke powerful emotional responses. These emotions help us to clarify the way we feel and can fuel the desire for change.

▶ Stories nearly always generate communication. Not only does listening to a story create a warm bond between us, once the story is finished we often automatically turn to each other to talk and to share our responses. Likewise, a good story invariably evokes the longing to retell it to others.

▶ Stories can help us work through traumatic and stressful experiences so we might regain feelings of mastery and develop new insights.

▶ Stories often reflect the viewpoints of indigenous people and so can bring their lessons on sustainability to others.

Nigerian novelist Chimamanda Adichie provides us with a wonderful example. I introduce my students to her talk "The danger of a single story" (http://www.ted.com/talks/chimamanda_adichie_the_danger_of_a_single_story.html). This is an account of the Nigerian diaspora's travel to the US and the writer's personal journey, but also a reflection on the many layers of the stories of our lives. In her words, "Many stories matter. . . . Stories can break the dignity of a people, but stories can also repair that broken dignity." I then suggest non-mainstream reading lists to my students[2], which they can use to "listen" to voices from other cultural backgrounds.

Through narrative, life scenarios are recreated and stir our emotions; through stories we understand others' feelings and learn about times and circumstances beyond our direct experience of life. I have used stories in these ways:

▶ tell the story in class or show videos of personal testimonies and life narratives;

▶ write it myself and read it aloud, asking students to do the same on a chosen theme (the story of my name, the story of an immigrant, a story about racism . . .);

▶ bring children's books to class and distribute them to students (individuals or pairs) to read and interpret. In groups of three or four, students must then create a new story using elements of each book they read;

▶ show pictures and ask students to guess the history of the life (or time) of the individuals photographed.

There are multiple forms of analysis, interpretation, and creation of stories, but it is essential that they contain ideas and emotions. These emotions are what make them memorable for students, and, as they mention, what will then stimulate their curiosity and compel them to learn more about the Other and the themes in the narrative (e.g., what is life like for the immigrants in my neighbourhood? What is the meaning of a certain ritual, symbol, or behavior?)

Literature reconfigures ideas and emotions into the multiple possibilities of human existence, both realistically and fantastically. Literature is essential to intercultural education.

The inclusion of storytelling in intercultural education and in the repertoire of teaching skills for teachers is thus well justified.

4.3. Classroom Guests

Having a guest speaker in the classroom is an excellent way to provoke debate and discussion, to hear stories of life, and to obtain relevant information to a community intervention or project. The project which I will describe in the next section began with some classic lectures on Portuguese colonialism followed by discussions with other teachers, my colleagues, and guests, who had all been born or lived in the former Portuguese colonies (Angola, Mozambique, Cape Verde, Brazil, Sao Tome and Principe, Guinea-Bissau, and East-Timor). Students found these presentations a memorable experience, for the stories told and stimulating discussion that followed, and for the opportunity to learn the details of colonialism (racism and social segregation, power relations, examples of negotiation and dissent, the meaning of being black or white) and how they directly affected those people.

On another occasion I brought a Russian music teacher and an American English as a Second Language (ESL) teacher to the classroom. They spoke about the Cold War and the stereotypes that each political block created about the Other. On yet another occasion, we hosted a group discussion between students and three foreign professionals (American, Macedonian, and Brazilian) who lived in Portugal for over two decades. They talked of mixed marriages, the stereotypes of the Portuguese people, the difficulties of living in a foreign country, cultural shock, and intercultural learning motivated by travel and emigration.

Further, I bring photojournalists and travel photographers to the college and take advantage of the presence of international foreign guests in academic exchange, seminars, and lectures, so that students can learn from these teachers. These meetings are also opportunities for students to develop their intercultural communication skills in a foreign language (e.g., English, French). I organized several study visits that took students out of school and the city, allowing them to hear other people's stories and learn directly about cultures and management structures for living (for example, the High Commission for Immigration and Intercultural Dialogue, which is an interdepartmental support and advisory structure of the Government in respect of immigration, ethnic minorities, and policies on intercultural dialogue).

Inviting colleagues, experts, or representatives of relevant groups or organizations requires a change in mindset from the teacher as "the sage on the stage" to "the guide on the side" (King 1993). This different approach leads students to understand how the issues debated in class go beyond academic theories and apply to everyday life.

4.4. Socratic Dialogue

Democracy requires citizens to be informed and able to engage in social dialogue. Intercultural education is also a preparation for the life in democracy. Unstructured debate between students, frequent in my classroom, is a good tool to learn these ropes, and so is Socratic dialogue, where students arrive at conclusions by themselves. As an example, I will demonstrate the steps I use to lead in-service teacher trainees to the idea of Intercultural Education as political action.

1. I ask what principles they use in their pedagogical relationship with pupils. They usually respond that they seek to be impartial and competent, treat all children with equality and justice, and manage the classroom democratically.
2. I ask what the concepts of equality, justice, and democracy have in common. Values (ethical values, social values) is their first answer. I ask if equality, justice, and democracy are values in society and citizenship. They answer yes, without hesitation.
3. I ask them to reflect on whether these values and principles are universal, if they remain stable over time, are common to different cultures, and similar in different political regimes. If the answer is no, I ask them why. With my guidance and some key examples they should recognize that the pedagogical practices of teachers create different meanings depending on the theoretical, ideological, and axiological notions they hold. I direct the discussion to the tensions and challenges of managing coexistence in multicultural societies. Issues of social justice, discrimination, and free expression of identity are touched upon through examples (news article, case studies, critical incidents involving immigrants or ethnic minorities). I help them note that their statements reveal their political orientations regarding the political management of diversity.
4. I ask them to define the concept of intercultural education and clarify its multiple dimensions (as educational philosophy, as a set of pedagogical practices, as a methodology, with a particular content). Definitions of intercultural education taken from different authors are given, compared, and discussed. Democratic values underlying intercultural education are highlighted.
5. I ask if intercultural education can be seen as political action. Unanimously they recognize that it can.

Intercultural education is not just a set of principles of educational policy but a way to engage citizens in civil society. When students learn this principle the class becomes more "real," giving them a new drive for community learning.

4.5. Community Projects

Intercultural education is vital in fostering a culture of tolerance, interconnectedness, and joint problem-solving. Community projects are strong educational approaches that require the practical use of knowledge and personal/professional skills like the ability to find the best solutions and practices for the challenges or opportunities posed by multicultural environments.

Cultures@esec (Gonçalves, 2011a) is one of the intervention projects I proposed to my students. Students were required to investigate the cultural heritage and identities of African students (from the former Portuguese colonies—CPLP) in Portugal. The project was developed in the context of Intercultural Education during the first semester of 2008–2009. Five Erasmus students (three Finnish, one Turkish, and one Bulgarian) and thirty-four Portuguese students attended the module, but there were no students from other Portuguese-speaking countries. Early in the semester, students formed seven groups to prepare a presentation on each of the CPLP countries. They were expected to contact fellow students on campus from these countries and interview them, introduce the cultures@esec project, seek their collaboration, and invite them to class.

The project required frequent contact between domestic and international students, and cooperation under equal status, joint decisions, and active learning. Simultaneously, both students and invited participants gave their testimonies in a series of plenary sessions. Guests were Portuguese citizens with personal or professional connections to CPLP countries and CPLP citizens (teachers from Brazil and Cape Verde and a student from Mozambique). They shared their life stories, presented resources (movies, images, handicrafts . . .) and debated a variety of themes (the Portuguese presence in Africa, colonialism and post-colonialism, intergroup relations, racism, and other psychosocial phenomena).

The project required students to produce visual material (leaflets, posters, and artistic texts produced for the exhibitions, space/scenic arrangements). Their technical quality and aesthetic balance was guaranteed by a collaborating professor of Design and his/her third year Art & Design students, who contributed with ideas, technical consultancy, and teamwork.

The project results were presented at the semester's conclusion, alongside a conference by Rui Marques (Ex-High Commissioner for Immigration and Intercultural Dialogue), 'Islands and bridges: The relation with the Other.' Students participated actively in the discussion with the invited speaker and in the presentation of their work, sharing what they leaned. Results showed that sharing knowledge and ideas and working under stimulating learning conditions helped to break cultural barriers and prejudice and contributed to fostering intercultural sensitivity and competence. African students, who previously were the most invisible despite their skin color difference, acquired a positive visibility: outside the classroom, other students sought their company, integrated them in their groups, and tried to learn from them.

The Cultures@esec shows how intercultural projects help develop cross-cultural skills. Cooperation under equal status is one of the main pillars for projects that aim to promote students' respect and appreciation of people from other cultures. Inter-ethnic contact is the ideal situation to promote intercultural harmony and the resolution of conflicts related to ethnic diversity but, as shown by Allport (1954), it only works in the presence of some additional conditions: equality of status of the members of interacting groups, cooperative interdependence, and a reassuring normative context that fosters contact and harmony between groups. All these aspects were present in cultures@esec and that is why it succeeded.

Becoming interculturally competent is the result of various opportunities which together foster a new vision of diversity and the will to learn, profit, and enjoy cultural diversity (Gonçalves 2011a).

5. Intercultural Education as Political Action

Intercultural competence is a natural result of intercultural active learning, based on methods like the ones I have described. The classroom should become a lively laboratory for the experience of intercultural contact and learning. The classroom is a protected environment that can be used to simulate various types of contact zones.

In today's world, contact zones are more dynamic and innovative, in large part due to globalization, that "intensifier of social relations in the world" (Giddens 1990, 64). Globalization requires change in learning spaces and action in social space—the diversity of identities, the classic and emerging lead back to the "polis," an obvious cosmopolitanism, and the inevitability of the intercultural encounter with the Other. In multicultural society the Other is not the alien but ourselves: each of us is different, the Other. How do we learn to live with our differences? How may they benefit us? The methods in this chapter may be part of the answer.

I conclude by delineating the political basis of intercultural education, its intentionality, and its principles. This is an important dimension of intercultural education, with enormous implications for higher education. Teachers, particularly those working in the broad field of social and cultural sciences, should be aware of their role as agents of influence. I usually tell my students that intercultural education is a political action, a statement they find surprising because of the Portuguese belief that education/instruction must be politically neutral (as opposed to the authoritarian dogmatism that characterized state and school before the revolution of 1974) and because they are unable to differentiate politics from partisanship.

Any form of education holds a political dimension. Education should aim to raise individuals to the best expression of their virtues to become good citizens. In the case of intercultural education, the result of unavoidable contemporary multiculturalism, the diversity of identities and the risks, opportunities, and challenges that are provided by this diversity must be taken into account. In contemporary societies formal and non-formal education must be multi-, inter-, or transcultural. Multi-inter-transcultural education is not just a matter of democratic principle; it is also a matter of wise judgment and social intelligence.

In our last class, I ask students to evaluate the module's results in terms of learning, satisfaction, and accrued value to their lives. Most mention methodology as the most notable element (the resources, stimulus, questions, and activities, particularly the ones in class). They elect activities like discussion with guests, cooperation with foreign students, viewing and discussing movies and life stories with their colleagues, or being involved in various group dynamic exercises. These activities helped them explore important aspects of social life and resulted in heightened curiosity about other people's worldviews and an increased appreciation of diversity. Many also mention how they feel more able to communicate with foreigners and members of other cultures. Some say they developed an intense wish to travel and explore the world. Others realize that they became less naïve and more open-minded. All of these statements encourage me to continue using student-centered methods.

Knowledge of other people and their culture is better acquired by experience. The above five approaches offer educators ways to promote cultural experiences and foster students' interaction with cultures and people from various cultural, national, linguistic, and religious backgrounds (Gifford et al. 2007). Learners will be less ethnocentric, more empathetic, and able to understand the intentions, feelings, and states of mind of people across cultural borders. These are crucial competencies for social cohesion in multicultural societies.

References

Allport, G. W. (1954). *The nature of prejudice*. Cambridge, MA: Addison-Wesley.

Andrzejewski, J., & Alessio, J. (1999). Education for global citizenship and social responsibility. *Progressive perspectives 1998–99 Monograph Series,1*(2). Retrieved from http://www.uvm.edu/~dewey/monographs/glomono.html#Education for Global Citizenship and Social

Appadurai, A. (2003). Archive_and_aspiration. In J. Brouwer and A. Mulder (Eds), *Information is alive* (pp. 14–25). Rotterdam: NAI Publishers. Retrieved from http://entreculturas.info/system/docs/10/original/Appadurai_Archive_and_Aspiration.pdf?1276464953

Appadurai, A. (2006). Disjuncture and difference in the global cultural economy. In M. G. Durham and D. M. Kellner (eds*.), Media and cultural studies: Keywords* (pp. 584–604). MA: Blackwell Publishing. Retrieved from http://www.intcul.tohoku.ac.jp/~holden/MediatedSociety/Readings/2003_04/Appadurai.html

Appiah, K. A. (2006). *Cosmopolitanism: Ethics in a world of strangers*. London/New York: Penguin.

Balibar, E. (2005). Difference, otherness, exclusion. *Parallax, 11*(1), 19–34.

Bergan, S. & van't Land, H. (2010). *Speaking across borders: The role of higher education in furthering intercultural dialogue* (Council of Europe Higher Education Series No. 16). Council of Europe and International Association of Universities (IAU).

Bhabha, H. K. (1990). *Nation and narration*. New York: Routledge.

Bhabha, H. K. (1996). *Locations of culture: Discussing post-colonial culture*. London: Routledge.

Damásio, A. (2000). *O sentimento de si*. Mem Martins: Publicações Europa- América (8th ed.).

Dawe, G., Jucker, R., and Stephen, M. (2005). *Sustainable development in higher education: Current practice and future developments: A report for the higher education academy*. York: Higher Education Academy.

Delors, J. (1996) (Ed.) *Learning: The treasure within. Report to UNESCO of the international commission on education for the twenty-first century*. Paris: UNESCO.

Freire, P. (1975). *Pedagogia do oprimido* (2nd ed). Porto: Afrontamento.

Giddens, A. (1990). *The consequences of modernity*. Cambridge: Polity Press.

Gifford, C., Gocsál, A., Balint, R., Gonçalves, S., & Wolodzko, E. (2007). *Intercultural Learning for European Citizenship*. London: CiCe.

Goleman, D. (1995). *Emotional intelligence*. New York, Bantam.

Gonçalves, S. (2011a). Intangible culture, cooperation and intercultural dialogue among university students. *Intercultural Education, 22*(1), 83–95.

Gonçalves, S. (2011b). *Learning objects and multimedia resources in citizenship education and education for diversity*. London: CiCe.

Gonçalves, S. (2011c). Multiculturalism and intercultural education from a Portuguese perspective. In J. A. Spinthourakis, J. Lalor, and W. Berg (Eds). *Cultural Diversity in the Classroom: A European Comparison* (pp. 63–78). Wiesbaden: VS Verlag fur Sozialwissenschaften.

Justice, C., Rice, J., Warry, W., & Laurie, I. (2007). Taking an "inquiry" course makes a difference: A comparative analysis of student learning. *Journal on Excellence in College Teaching, 18*(1), 57–77.

King, A. (1993). From Sage on the stage to guide on the side. *College Teaching 41*(1), 30–35.

Knowles, M. (1975). *Self-directed learning. A Guide for learners and teachers.* Englewood Cliffs: Prentice Hall/Cambridge.

Moreno, J. F., Smith, D. G., Clayton-Pedersen, A. R., Parker, S., & Teraguchi, D. H. (2006). The revolving door for underrepresented minority faculty in higher education: An analysis from the campus diversity initiative. *The James Irving Foundation Campus Diversity Initiative Evaluation Project.* Retrieved from www.irvine.org/assets/pdf/pubs/education/insight_Revolving_Door.pdf.

Pratt, M. L. (1991). Arts of the contact zone. *Profession (Modern Language Association) 9*, 33–40.

UNESCO (1997). *Educating for a sustainable future: A Transdisciplinary vision for concerted action*, Report of the International Conference: Education and Public awareness for Sustainability, Thessalonikki, Greece.Retrieved from http://www.unesco.org/education/tlsf/

UNESCO (2010). Module 21: Storytelling. In *Teaching and learning for sustainable development:A multimedia teacher education programme.* Retrieved from http://www.unesco.org/education/tlsf/

Endnotes

1. A partial list of films recommended or screened in class: "Turtles Can Fly" (Bahman Ghobadi, 2006, France/Iran/Iraq); "The Lives of Others" (Florian Henckel von Donnersmarck, 2006, Germany); "*Buddha* Collapsed Out of Shame" (Hana Makhalmalbaf, 2007, Iran); "The Rising: Ballad of Mangal Pandey" (Ketan Mehta, 2004, India); "Water" (Deepa Mehta, 2005, India); "La Heine" (Mathieu Kassovitz, 1995, France); "Caramel" (Nadine Labaki, 2007, Lebanon); "Charulata" (Satyajit Ray, 1964, India); Waltz with *Bashir"* (Ari Folman, 2008, Israel).

2. A partial list of novel recommendations: *Marlboro Sarajevo* (Miljenko Jergović, Bosnia and Herzegovina); *The old man who read love stories* (Luis Sepulveda, Chile); *The White Tiger* (Aravind Adiga, India); *Gadis Pantai* (Pramoedya Ananta Toer, Indonesia); *Mitzváh* (Alain Elkann, Italy); *Like Water for Chocolate* (Laura Esquível, Mexico); *Russendisko* (Wladimir Kaminer, Russia); *The Bridge on the Drina* (Ivo Andrić, Serbia); *Season of Migration to the North* (Al-Tayyeb Salih, Sudan); *The Thing Around Your Neck* (Chimamanda Adiché, Nigeria).

5

Dialogue, a Space *Between, Across,* and *Beyond* Cultures and Disciplines: A Case Study of Lectures in Transcultural and Transdisciplinary Communication

Maria Flora Mangano

Key Words

- ► dialogue
- ► intercultural
- ► transcultural
- ► transdisciplinarity
- ► philosophy of dialogue

1. Introduction

This chapter intends to deepen the meaning of dialogue, drawing on the theoretical contributions of transdisciplinarity and the philosophy of dialogue and applying them to my own teaching experiences. Following my initial study of the possible reciprocity between dialogue among cultures and dialogue among disciplines (Mangano 2010a, 2010b), I then began to explore dialogue as a space where the relationship may occur. My interest in developing this investigation was confirmed in conversations with colleagues who study dialogue from different points of view: sociological, philosophical, and theological, in addition to intercultural dialogue, the perspective I am concerned with in this chapter. Most confirmed that this approach to dialogue has been little investigated.

This case study is based on transcultural and transdisciplinary lectures that I conducted in two academic contexts: courses of dialogue between cultures for undergraduates of an Italian philosophical-theological faculty; and intensive schools of communication of scientific research for young researchers. I consider these activities as a case study of the same method: a transcultural and transdisciplinary approach to the other based on dialogue.

1.1.   The proposal for this research

As I present in the following sections, both transdisciplinarity (Nicolescu, 1987) and philosophy of dialogue (Buber, 1937) suggest a space for a relationship between parts: disciplines, according to the first approach, and individuals, in the second perspective. The proposal for this research is that dialogue also starts in this space, just as relationship does, and together with relationship. Therefore dialogue and relationship are strictly connected: dialogue needs relationship to be realised, and, at the same time, dialogue creates relationship. Dialogue may become a space "of" relationship, more than "for" it. In particular for this case study, dialogue may be a space of relationship between, across and beyond cultures and disciplines.

I firstly introduce the background of transdisciplinarity and the philosophy of dialogue, then the context of the two teaching experiences.

1.2.   Transcultural and transdisciplinary approach: Preliminary research

As indicated by its Latin prefix *trans*, transculturality concerns that which is "between," "across" and "beyond" each individual culture (Nicolescu 1985). Transcultural dialogue describes the dialogue between cultures according to a transdisciplinary approach.

The term "transdisciplinarity" was proposed for the first time in 1972, by Jean Piaget, Swiss philosopher and psychologist (Apostel et al. 1972). The transdisciplinary approach was developed, starting from 1985, by Basarab Nicolescu, Romanian physicist, together with other scholars of different disciplines and countries, including Edgar Morin, French sociologist, and Lima de Freitas, Portuguese painter and writer. Nicolescu, together with Morin and de Freitas, co-authored the *Charter of Transdisciplinarity*, which was adopted by the participants of the First World Congress of Transdisciplinarity (1994, Convento da Arrábida, Portugal) (Nicolescu 2008). In 1987, Nicolescu founded the International Centre for Transdisciplinary Research (CIRET), a non- profit organization located in Paris, counting today over 150 members from 26 countries and dedicated to the coordination of research, literature, and education on this topic. Transdisciplinarity is defined in CIRET's moral project:

> Transdisciplinarity takes into account the consequences of a flow of information circulating among the various branches of knowledge, permitting the emergence of

unity amidst diversity and diversity through unity. Its objective is to lay bare the nature and characteristics of this flow of information and its principal task is the elaboration of a new language, a new logic, and new concepts to permit the emergence of a real dialogue between the specialists in the different domains of knowledge.

If it is possible to build bridges among disciplines, toward a unity in knowledge, it may also be possible to apply a transdisciplinary method also to different cultures, in particular, for this case study, to a multicultural academic context. Article 10 of the *Charter on Trandisciplinarity*, infact, says: "No single culture is privileged over any other culture. The transdisciplinary approach is inherently transcultural." This suggests that transcultural dialogue needs transdisciplinary dialogue to be realised. Furthermore, dialogue among cultures may be the basis for dialogue among disciplines, as I started to describe in two studies based on my teaching experience in an Italian philosophical-theological faculty (Mangano, 2010a, 2010b).

The findings in transcultural dialogue academic teaching suggested to me that it is possible to find a ground for dialogue based on human experience, a space which enriches cultural identity and builds bridges among cultures, rather than merely displays their common elements. Thus, the transdisciplinary method provides the ground for dialogue between, across and beyond each culture.

1.3. Philosophy of dialogue at a glance

The philosophy of dialogue is a branch of contemporary philosophy founded by Martin Buber, Austrian Jewish philosopher and theologian, theorised in his essay *I and Thou* (Buber 1937). According to Buber, the word pair I-You (in this paper I will focus on this pair, without mentioning the other, "I-It") is at the basis of a relationship between individuals. His conviction that existence is an encounter between "I" and "You" governs his thinking and is expressed in the essay as follows (Buber 1937):

> The *Thou* meets me through grace. It is not found by seeking. But my speaking of the primary word to it is an act of my being, is indeed the act of my being.

> The *Thou* meets me. But I step into direct relation with it. Hence the relation means being chosen and choosing, suffering and action in one.

Buber declares his intent also graphically, with the hyphen between "I" and "You" instead of the conjunction "and," to suggest the link between them, and with the capital letters for both, to indicate the same importance of individuals. "I" cannot exist without "You" and vice versa:

> The primary word *I-Thou* can be spoken only with the whole being.

> I become through my relation to the *Thou*; as *I* become *I*, I say *Thou*. All real living is meeting (Buber 1937).

Buber proposes a space for the relationship between the word **pair** I-You. This space does not belong to only one part (I or You), but it is between them. The relationship starts in this space, which Buber calls "the sphere of between" (Friedman 1955). The space between I and You is where dialogue may occur.

Two other philosophers, Emmanuel Lévinas, Lithuanian-born, and Jacques Derrida, Algerian-born, focused their research on the relationship with the other and among individuals.

Lévinas centred his thinking above all on otherness, "alterity." My interest is particularly in his contribution to the meaning of meeting the face of the other (Lévinas 1969) and its implications. This stance offers an anthropological approach to dialogue (among cultures and among disciplines) in terms of the need for a face-to-face encounter as the answer to the other's call (Lévinas 1969).

Derrida's main contribution to my study on the reciprocity between a transcultural and transdisciplinary approach to dialogue, in relation with the philosophy of dialogue, is found in the meaning of hospitality. In particular: who is the stranger; what is the difference between the other and the foreigner, and between the host and the guest; what does it mean to give hospitality to all of them; and how do we choose to meet the other (foreigner, guest or host) as a basic part of our existence (Derrida 2000).

I take inspiration from the contributions of Buber, Lévinas and Derrida in my teaching experience, as they have much in common: they spent the majority of their life out of their country home and had to work in a non-native language. They described this existential condition of "exiles" as the necessary requirement to understand the need of the other. Furthermore, all of them were close to Jewish culture and religion (especially Buber and Lévinas) in addition to ancient Greek and Latin. Their philosophical approach may be considered transcultural, even if they did not know this term, because it required them to work between, across and beyond their cultures, religions and beliefs, education, and sensibility.

1.4. Context

The first context of the study draws on my teaching experience during two six-month courses on transcultural dialogue at a philosophical-theological institute in Italy. This institution seems made for practicing dialogue: among cultures and disciplines, and between lay and religious people. There are almost twenty cultures, from a total of two-hundred students; more than eighty disciplines, as the bachelor's degree program requires two years of philosophy followed by three years of theology, plus a preliminary year, that precedes studies at the institute, especially for non-Italian students, the majority, who come from non-European countries to start their training as priests, nuns and missionaries.

Each course I held consisted of twenty-six hours of lectures: one course was dedicated to the preliminary year, the other was for the students of the first and second year of philosophy.

There were five students in the preliminary year and sixteen in the philosophical class. The students in the first course came from Zambia; those in the second course came from the Dominican Republic, Poland, South Korea, Zambia, and Italy. All the students of the preliminary year and twelve of the philosophical class started their religious training to become friars, missionaries and priests; the remaining four were lay students.

The second context consisted in three intensive schools of Communication of Scientific Research (CSR) for young scientists: doctoral students, post-doctoral fellows and professionals from public or private research institutes who crossed more than twenty scientific disciplines (including physics, genetics, pharmacology, oncology, cellular biology and biotechnology).

The CSR schools, conducted in different Italian towns, consisted of eight hours of lectures every day for four to five days. There were fourteen participants in the first and in the third schools, and four in the second one. The students were all Italian with the exception of one from Germany who had been living in Italy for twenty years.

The courses and the schools were conducted in Italian. The students in the preliminary year had been in Italy for only a few months and were learning Italian. We sometimes used English in class.

I proposed to the students of the philosophical class also philosophers of their cultures, when possible, with contents in English, French, and Spanish. I found the materials online and suggested to the students to make further research on their own. I asked also to Italian students, who already knew one of these languages, to study the same texts and to do additional research on them, to share the same effort of their colleagues who approach philosophers of a different culture and in a non-native language.

I present the method, including key words and materials; the findings, and their implications for my proposal of dialogue as space where cultures and disciplines may meet.

2.   Method

Both in the philosophical-theological institute and in the CSR schools, I proposed to the students the same approach to dialogue: a space between, across and beyond cultures and disciplines. This implied to teach them how to dialogue, and to understand the difference between it and a discussion, a conversation, or a sharing. It also meant to teach them to become aware of the other and to analyse one another's behaviour during dialogue in class. I had started to describe this approach to dialogue in my initial transcultural dialogue courses (Mangano 2010a, 2010b). I proposed to the class four steps on how to be prepared to dialogue, taking inspiration from two students' contribution that emerged in their group work during my initial study. These steps were: save time for the meeting; do not impose your own idea (aim, strategy, tools); compare all the elements (study, context, members of the group); keep a space for dialogue without dominating the ideas and contributions of the other.

2.1.   "CSR method": Life and Study Together

In CSR schools the transdisciplinary approach to dialogue is enriched by the intensive time that students and professors spend together, which often becomes the occasion for deeper dialogue. It may be defined as the "CSR method": the opportunity to meet the other for the whole day, by following lessons, cooking, eating, and spending free time together. It implies that life and study become one thing, in a location generally far from where they live and work, so they can concentrate in deepening dialogue and meeting the other. The participants become aware of their own and other's behaviours and communication. It leads to improved understanding and interaction among them, especially during the practice of written and oral communication which follows the theoretical lessons.

I also invite speakers from different scientific and humanistic backgrounds (philosophy of science, ethics and sociology of science and scientific marketing) to present their cultural and professional backgrounds at after dinner meetings. These informal presentations offer further occasions for interdisciplinary dialogue.

2.2. Transcultural and Transdisciplinary Teaching

The proposed approach to dialogue is based on human experience rather than on cultures or disciplines. It involves providing basic information on each student's culture and discipline. In courses and CSR schools I introduce some keywords and use similar teaching materials.

2.2.1 Keywords

As I previously described (Mangano 2010a, 2010b), in lectures at the philosophical-theological institute, I firstly define terms explaining their ancient Greek and Latin origins, from which Italian and European cultures derive. Then I present the same terms from the cultural point of view of non-European students. For most of these students, their countries, and cultures had been colonised by Europeans for centuries. The historians and thinkers who had studied these cultures were mostly European. This Eurocentrism may create a cultural burden in a transcultural approach to dialogue. Hence, I believe it is important to introduce each keyword in different cultural perspectives and also in the native language of the students, with their contribution.

In the preliminary year I introduce the terms "dialogue," "culture" and "civilisation," then "Western," "Eastern," "African," "American" and, finally, "person" and "individual." In the philosophical class I furthermore add: "interdisciplinarity," "transdisciplinarity," "transcultural dialogue" and "complexity." Then I propose three terms, which may be considered three steps toward the discovery of the other. They are mutually linked and connected to the philosophers on whom I focus more during the course: otherness (Lévinas 1969); hospitality (Derrida 2000); reciprocity between I and You (Buber 1937).

In CSR schools I define some terms of semiotics to introduce the basics of the theory of communication applied to scientific research (Mangano 2008). I propose three verbs starting from their etymology: "to communicate," "to educate" and "to seduce" (Petrosino[1] 2008). I present two meanings of "to communicate," derived from the Latin *cum munus* and *cum moenia*. The first means to put in common, to present a gift to the other. The original sense of *munus* was a gift, implying an exchange. It indicates a reciprocity, at the basis of the term "community," a group of people who have goods to exchange, from which "communication" derives.

The etymology of *moenia*, instead, means obstacle, barrier. Therefore communication indicates to build a defence, to protect the message rather than share it.

The verbs "to educate" and "to seduce" have the same Latin root, *ducere*, with two different prefixes, *ex* and *se*: *ex ducere* means to bring out something (information, content, but also values, ideals) from someone (the one who is educated). Hence education is a process which involves knowledge, culture, and the sensibility of the educator and student. To educate does not necessary imply to communicate.

Se ducere means to lead away, in the sense of draw away, make a change in one's direction, or persuade. It assumes, in semantic evolution, a meaning close to its contemporary usage, that is to attract, engage, but in the introdution to the theory of communication we refer to the etymology, like for the term "education" (Petrosino 2008).

Communication may be considered a balance between education and seduction (Cacciari & Petrosino 2009), a bridge between them. Therefore the message may be a *munus* or a *moenia,* may educate or seduce the receiver of the message, the other. It depends on what the other means for the sender of the message, the value of the other. Hence also, the basic information for written and oral communication may be an introduction to the encounter with the other.

2.2.2 Teaching materials

As I previously described (Mangano 2010a, 2010b), I prepare notes and slides for each lesson of the courses at the philosophical-theological institute. They include keywords and the main topics of the philosophers I introduce, with references of texts they can find at the institute library and link to websites and papers. All the materials are available online on a free open source e-learning platform (Moodle, Modular Object-Oriented Dynamic Learning Environment) accessible through the institute's homepage, reserved for students and professors.

At the CSR schools I use the *Handbook of Communication of Scientific Research* (Mangano 2008). I also prepare slides of all the lessons, which introduce the main issues of written and oral scientific communication research that I present in the *Handbook.*

I ask all students to enrich the contents with written and oral contributions derived from their culture, life experiences, research and study, which complement my own teaching materials. These tasks require students from the preliminary year to practise Italian and the meeting with the other, as they have to share in class aspects of their culture and listen to other's presentations.

For the students of the philosophical class it implies also an input to learn to write, conduct research and present contents in an academic context. This learning is developed during the course in work consisting of three written compositions (two individual and one in intercultural group) and three oral presentations in class. This work is the principal element I use for the evaluation of each student at the final exam. In addition to it, I also collect indications from their contributions during lessons and to online forums. They consist in written inputs on what we share in class, their findings in research and study, from their cultural perspective, related to the content of each lesson, in addition to their doubts and questions. Therefore at the end of the course I have several elements to evaluate the students and the final exam is still focused on dialogue, more than a formal written or oral examination. In the final lesson I present to the students what I will ask them at the exam: they will evaluate, in an oral presentation of 10-20 minutes, their personal effort in the following tasks and in this order, which I described as transcultural evaluation criteria for the exam (Mangano 2010a, 2010b). They are: disposition to meet the other, to go out from themselves to dialogue with the other; comprehension and knowledge of contents, ability to study, to write and to make research at academic level; contributions during lessons and on forums; knowledge and use of Italian and informatics skill to create an oral presentation. I also ask to the students to propose the mark they might deserve, to test also their aptitude to evaluate themselves critically.

At the CSR schools, I ask the participants to give a ten minute presentation of themselves to their classmates on the first day: who they are, their background and current position, reasons and objectives for participating in the school. I also invite the participants to bring examples of written and oral work, which they present to the class as their contribution to teaching materials. They have to be written or prepared by themselves: for example a scientific paper, the index of their Ph.D. thesis and its presentation, for those in their final year, a poster, and/or an oral presentation for a meeting or for the final year report. These materials are corrected during the practice of written and oral communication, which follow theoretical lessons, and the students offer their contribution to dialogue also from their own disciplinary point of view.

3.   Findings

I now present the findings from the two teaching experiences, first in the philosophical-theological institute, and then in the CSR schools. The findings illustrate how the students demonstrate dialogue as a space between, across and beyond cultures and disciplines through the teaching/learning process.

3.1.   Courses at the Philosophical-Theological Institute

The five students in the preliminary course still needed time and effort to become involved, mainly because they had started to learn Italian only a few months before. The written compositions helped them to improve their Italian, but their oral and written communicative level was still too elementary to provide a notable contribution to this case study. Therefore, I focus on the experiences of the 16 students in the philosophical class.

I noted a growing involvement of many students regarding an awareness of the other and his/her culture during the course. The students' initial approach to transcultural dialogue was influenced by their choice of life, as religious and lay students: they were all Christians of the Catholic denomination. This perspective implies an attitude to look at the other as "the neighbour," according to the Gospel and based on humanity, rather than on taking a philosophical perspective beyond religion to also include life style and culture. Several students initially considered the other and the neighbour synonymous and related otherness to the care for the poor and the sick.

Many students were also influenced by their native culture. For the Zambian students initially the other meant "the stranger," still associated with the white man, like in many African cultures dominated by Europeans for centuries. The other was an identical to "the diverse" who may be considered dangerous, and therefore, better not to host. Similarly, the Korean students demonstrated this attitude toward the Japanese, and the Polish toward the Russians. Therefore, the transcultural approach to dialogue required many students to reconstruct and renegotiate their interior perspectives, that is, their values and beliefs, and even stereotypes and prejudices.

Several students still had difficulties understanding Italian, therefore it took them time to comprehend the contents on transcultural dialogue and to prepare written compositions. Generally, students had little understanding of the notion of a transdisciplinary approach. Only a few developed awareness of the connection between theory and the practice of dialogue among cultures: they first had to study what I proposed in class to understand how to prepare their written compositions; their individual and workgroup texts were necessary to comprehend what they were studying. The interaction embodied in this learning required an increasing responsibility toward themselves, the other and the course, as some of them noted. For example, Marc, a second year Zambian missionary, described his progressive awareness in encountering the other in his third composition:

> At the beginning of this course I did not understand what transcultural dialogue meant. I considered it useless, but it was for a fear to meet the other. After the lessons and the study, especially of Buber and Socrates, I discovered that the other helps me to define myself. I do not lose my cultural identity in the I-You relationship, I find it.

The main effort for him was the discovery of a new meaning of otherness, which influenced his existence, in addition to his approach to dialogue. At the end he felt "happy to be reconciled with the hurts caused by history on his culture," as he said at the exam.

Giovanni, a mature religious Italian student of the first year, immediately recognized the potentialities of a transdisciplinary approach. He continuously helped the other students to become aware of the course's contents. During the exam, he said: "I was impressed by the audacity of philosophers of dialogue. I would never have imagined that a thinker could propose such an uncommon and revolutionary approach to the other. I felt brought by them to unbelievable peaks of mountains."

Many students found the effort of meeting the other in the workgroup a challenging task, especially in learning how to work together. Some of them felt this experience as the first step toward the awareness of dialogue as a space of relationship.

Jean, a second year Dominican Republic religious student, stated in the examination: "It was a very hard course. But it taught me a lot, useful for life. I also have to thank Rosella [a mature lay Italian student of the second year] who taught me what giving hospitality means. She was a home for me."

Some students discovered the other also in the authors they studied. Tiziana, a mature Italian first year lay student, wrote in her last composition: "I can say to *have met* the author, Tanella Boni. She *crosses* me, like M. Buber, I could really feel their suffering and love for mankind, as a result of the relationship and reciprocity."

Tiziana was impressed by Tanella Boni, an Ivorian poet, writer and philosopher, whose focus on research is the practice of tolerance in relationships among individuals. She decided to study Boni's work more deeply for the last written composition. Therefore, Tiziana had to research herself, using French texts (as Boni's writings are not published in Italian). She knew French and contacted the author by e-mail to ask for more information about her work.

Similarly, Caterina, a mature Italian second year lay student, conducted independent research in Spanish, presenting an Argentinean thinker, Enrique Dussel, in her last written composition. Although we had not discussed Dussel in class, Caterina was fascinated by his perspective on otherness. As she wrote, she wanted to introduce to the class "the meaning of hospitality according to the Argentinean perspective, which felt like a guest at home for centuries, because of the European domination."

The half of the class took seriously my proposal of a personal evaluation of their effort at the exam, and suggested a mark they would deserve which was very close to the one I thought for each of them.

These findings offer an idea of dialogue as a space where cultures may meet, the ones of the students and also of the philosophers they studied. Furthermore, these findings indicate the connection between dialogue and relationship: creating spaces of relationship makes possible the ground for dialogue and, at the same time, the space for dialogue may be granted by the relationship.

3.2.   CSR schools

The three CSR schools were intense experiences of living and studying. The majority of participants were highly motivated: many had covered the fees autonomously, as their faculties could not support them, and they used their holidays to attend.

At the outset I invited them to consider the school as an occasion for dialogue and the meeting of the other, in addition to content on the communication of scientific research. Many participants accepted this proposal immediately and put it into practice. As the course proceeded, most students understood that the course content was mutually linked to what we were living and that the space among disciplines needed their individual contribution.

Francesco, Clara and Michele prepared a short video to summarise the experience of each edition of the CSR school in which they participated. It was a way "to thank everybody in a communicative way," as Clara said.

At the end of the summer school, Fabio suggested that I organize a CSR school in his region, in Northern Italy, as he felt the need to "start to build a bridge between private and public areas of scientific research." This particular programme is the third school presented in this case study. Fabio offered to help me with the logistics: identification of sponsors, and location of the school and accommodation, as "a further occasion to meet the other in a concrete way," he added. In addition, the biotech company where he was employed sponsored the participation of three young researchers in addition to himself and his colleague.

Some participants decided to join other iterations of the CSR school: in addition to Fabio, also Michele and Benedetta. I suggested them to introduce part of the theoretical and practical lessons dedicated to written and oral communication. Fabio and Benedetta participated in the summer and winter schools, "to feed the need of the other which the summer school had ignited and which risks to be extinguished by everyday life," as they said. Also Michele participated in two CRS schools. He said to the class the second time: "I returned because I knew the *CSR method* and, as I appreciated it the first time, I was sure it would work this time."

At the last CRS school presented in this case study, Gianni proposed to the other participants to analyse their oral presentations from the first day. These reflections provided an occasion for dialogue between, across, and beyond our disciplines and an opportunity of encountering the other, as Teresa observed:

> I could never have imagined that I could talk about myself in such a way. I am shy, I have hardly ever made speeches and I was convinced to have only to analyse the technical aspects of my presentation. I think that this is dialogue, as each of you is enriching me and I feel free to speak. I have to thank all of you.

Also these findings indicate what dialogue as a space of relationship means. In this case, relationship between, across, and beyond disciplines, instead of cultures, like the previous analysis of teaching experience. Moreover, it is a further evidence of the reciprocity between dialogue among cultures with dialogue among disciplines, which I earlier started to describe (Mangano 2010a, 2010b).

4. Conclusions

The two teaching contexts presented in this case study, the transcultural dialogue courses and CRS schools, were experiences of dialogue as space of relationship between, across and beyond cultures and disciplines, as the findings indicate. They also show the connection between dialogue and relationship, as suggested in the proposal of research.

The majority of students felt "changed inside" after studying and working together, as Paul and Rosella said during the exam of transcultural dialogue and Marta, Judy and Emilio commented at the end of the CSR schools. For all participants, the dialogic experience represented an intellectual change, which included an awareness in understanding content from other cultures and perspectives, doing research at academic level, and approaching new philosophers, sometimes in a language different from their native one. It was also a cultural change, resulting in a new comprehension of terms like otherness, hospitality, and reciprocity, for the students of the theological-philosophical institute, and dialogue and relationship, for students of the CSR schools. The result was, often, an interior change which meant an increasing awareness of dialogue as encounter with the other. These changes made the students "consumed, exhausted," as one participant said, but "made the difference," as others added, between their knowledge of dialogue before the course and the CRS school, and what happened during and after these programmes.

The academic knowledge and experience gained by students in these programmes indicates the importance of dialogue in achieving knowledge and familiarity with content. More importantly, the study points to the value of insight mediated by dialogue, as the result of "a common ground between individuals" (Lonergan 1992). The insight mediated by dialogue which leads to the truth of knowledge is also described by Plato in *Letter VII,* as "a result of continued application to the subject itself and communion therewith" (Plato 1966). Hence, according to Plato, study and life together are the basis for dialogue, which leads to knowledge. This condition, knowledge mediated by dialogue, "does not exist, nor will there ever exist" (Plato 1966), it may happen only with relationship, "communion therewith" (Plato 1966), which requires and is created by dialogue. The need of the relationship to develop dialogue, as a necessary condition, reminds me of Buber's I-You word pair, which "is not found by seeking" (Buber 1937). It implies that relationship between I and you, between individuals, but also between (across and beyond) cultures and disciplines, the aim of this case study, needs a ground to be developed and established. A space which "does not exist" or "is not found by seeking," because it is created by dialogue. Dialogue becomes a space between, across and beyond the I-You relationship, moreover, the hyphen between I and You, their connection, what makes linked and united I and you, "the other" and "the stranger," "the guest," and "the host" (Derrida 2000) one's "face" with another one (Lévinas 1969), and also, the cultures and the disciplines. In such a way dialogue may become "an act of my being," as Buber defined the word I-You (Buber 1937), an existential condition, which may be at the basis of everyday life. Dialogue may become a "lifestyle," a call to build spaces of relationship between (across and beyond) cultures and disciplines, but also between individuals. It has been the experience of some students of the two teaching contexts I presented in this chapter: Tiziana defined the transcultural dialogue course as "a school of dialogue, of reciprocity and otherness, where I learnt also to study, to write and to present an oral contribution." And Lorenzo, Giacomo, and Irene talked about CSR school as a "school of life, where you learn to be, more than to do or to communicate."

Acknowledgements

I firstly wish to thank the students of the two courses of dialogue between cultures and of the CSR schools. Without their enthusiastic contribution, the dialogue among cultures and disciplines would not be possible. I am grateful to Prof. F. Salvatore Currò and to Prof. Sergio Rondinara for having introduced me to the philosophy of dialogue and transdisciplinarity, respectively. Special thanks to Prof. Prue Holmes, who followed with particular attention and competence every step of this chapter and to Marion Weber, who read and corrected it.

References

Apostel, L, Berger, G., Briggs, A. & Michaud, G. (Eds.). (1972). *L'interdisciplinarité – Problèmes d'enseignement et de recherche.* Paris: Centre pour la Recherche et l'Innovation dans l'Enseignement, Organisation de Coopération et de développement économique.

Buber, M. (1937). *I and thou.* (R. G. Smith, Trans.). Edinburgh, Scotland: T. and T. Clark.

Cacciari, M. & Petrosino, S. (2009, January–February). Educare nella modernità: dialogo con Massimo Cacciari e Silvano Petrosino [Education in contemporary times: a dialogue with Massimo Cacciari and Silvano Petrosino] *Didascalie [Captions]* 1–2, 18–32. Retrieved from: http://www.vivoscuola.it/c/document_library/get_file?uuid=df453b18-8d16-4504-a123-fc4ecbfc8e99&groupId=10137

Charter of Transdisciplinarity (1994). Retrieved from: http://basarab.nicolescu.perso.sfr.fr/ciret/indexen.html

Derrida, J. (2000). *Of Hospitality.* (Rachel Bowlby, Trans.). Stanford, CA: Stanford University Press.

Friedman, M. S. (1955). *Martin Buber: The life of dialogue.* Chicago, IL: University of Chicago Press.

Lévinas, E. (1969). *Totality and infinity: An essay on exteriority.* (A. Lingis, Trans.). Pittsburgh, PA: Duquesne University Press.

Lonergan, B. J. F. (1992). *Insight: A study of human understanding.* F. E. Crowe & R. M. Doran (Eds.), Collected Works. vol. 3. Toronto, CA: University of Toronto Press.

Mangano, M. F. (2008). *Manuale di comunicazione della ricerca scientifica* [Handbook of Communication of Scientific Research]. Trento, Italy: Ed. Uni-Service.

Mangano, M. F. (2010a). Passi verso la scoperta dell'altro: esperimenti di dialogo transculturale [Steps toward the discovery of the other: experiments of Transcultural Dialogue]. In: A. Bissoni & L. Di Sciullo (Eds.), *Identità e accoglienza. Tra limite e desiderio* [Identity and hospitality. Between the limit and the wish] (pp 87–99). Turin, Italy: Ed. Elledici.

Mangano, M. F. (2010b). Kültürler arasındaki diyalog disiplinler arasındaki diyalogun temeli olunca: İtalya''daki bir felsefe-teoloji fakültesindeki kültürler ötesi diyalog deneyi [When dialogue between cultures is the basis of dialogue between disciplines: Experiments of transcultural dialogue in a faculty of philosophy-theology in Italy]. In Z. Karahan Uslu, & C. Bilgili, (Eds.), *Medya Eleştirileri 2010 Kırılan Kalıplar - 2: Kültürlerarası İletişim, Çokkültürlülük [Media Critics 2010, Broken Frames 2: Intercultural Communication, Multiculturalism]* (pp. 45–75). Istanbul, Turkey: Beta Publishing House.

Moral project (1987). Retrieved from: http://basarab.nicolescu.perso.sfr.fr/ciret/english/projen.htm

Nicolescu, B. (1985). *Nous, la particule et le monde* [Us, the particles and the world]. Paris, France: Le Mail.

Nicolescu, B. (1996). *La transdisciplinarité.* Monaco, Germany: Le Rocher. *Manifesto of Transdisciplinarity.* (2002) (K. C. Voss, Trans.). New York, NY: SUNY Press.

Nicolescu, B. (2001). *Meaning through transdisciplinary knowledge*. Retrieved from: http://www.metanexus.net/essay/meaning-through-transdisciplinary-knowledge

Nicolescu, B. (Ed.) (2008). *Transdisciplinarity—Theory and practice*. Cresskill, NJ: Hampton Press.

Petrosino, S. (2008). *L'esperienza della parola. Testo, moralità e scrittura* [The experience of the word. Text, morality and writing]. (2nd ed.). Milan, Italy: Vita e Pensiero.

Piaget, J. (1972). *L'épistémologie des relations interdisciplinaires* [The epistemology of interdisciplinarity]. In Apostel, G. Berger, A. Briggs, & G. Michaud (Eds.), *L'interdisciplinarité— Problèmes d'enseignement et de recherche. Centre pour la Recherche et l'Innovation dans l'Enseignement*. Paris, France: Organisation de Coopération et de développement économique.

Plato (1966). *Plato in Twelve Volumes*. Vol. 7. (R. G. Bury, Trans.). Cambridge, MA: Harvard University Press.

Endnotes

1. Silvano Petrosino is an Italian thinker who teaches *Theories of Communication and Philosophy of Communication* at the Catholic University of Milan and Piacenza. His focus on research is, above all, the contributions of J. Derrida and E. Lévinas and he translated into Italian some of their works. I took inspiration from his lessons at the course of theory of communication which I followed in academic year 2000–2001 and from his studies on Derrida and Lévinas related to the value of the other and their implications on communication.

6

Developing *Cosmopolitan* Professional
Identities: Engaging Australian and
Hong Kong Trainee Teachers
in Intercultural Conversations

Erika Hepple

Key Words

- ► Intercultural conversation
- ► Cosmopolitan identities
- ► Teacher education

1. Introduction

School classrooms have become increasingly culturally and linguistically diverse, making it imperative for teachers to develop more *cosmopolitan* professional identities, demonstrating globalised perspectives and being able to communicate and relate interculturally. Intercultural education should therefore be an essential component of teacher education programs, assisting trainee teachers to become accomplished intercultural communicators, able to build relationships and mediate difference (Byram & Fleming 1998; Byram 2009). Unfortunately, however, intercultural education tends to lack a discipline-based core within the structures of teacher education, and hence, teachers often lack the necessary conceptual grounding and skills in intercultural communication (Cushner & Mahon 2009). This was the impetus for bringing together a group of domestic and international trainee teachers to engage in structured intercultural conversations as part of their teacher education studies at an Australian university. The Australian trainee teachers were in the second year of their bachelor of education degree program at the Queensland University of Technology (QUT) in Brisbane, Australia. Their conversational partners were postgraduate teacher trainees from Hong Kong who were participating in a short study abroad professional program at the same university. This research was framed as a case study exploring the affordances of this curriculum intervention. The research question guiding this case study was: "Does engaging international and domestic trainee teachers in structured intercultural conversations help them develop more cosmopolitan professional identities?"

What are the features of *cosmopolitan professional identity*? Cosmopolitan teachers are envisaged as able to "work, communicate, and exchange—physically and virtually—across national and regional boundaries with . . . cultural others" (Luke 2004, 1439). A cosmopolitan identity is characterised as having "dual affect," the ability to maintain local/global viewpoints at the same time, understanding the world from another's as well as one's own perspective (Goldstein 2007). Such a stance allows teachers to avoid stereotypes and understand cultural identities as "individually emergent and expressive" and with their own "individual cultural trajectories" (Holliday 2011, 66). Being intercultural involves challenging one's existing cultural practices and assumptions by experiencing other dimensions of human diversity. By interacting with culturally and linguistically different individuals, we are paradoxically made more aware of our own socialisation into particular cultural view points with expectations and normed ways of being and doing. With this heightened awareness, teachers are better able to consciously position themselves at a meeting place of cultures, sometimes termed the 'third space,' avoiding cultural stereotypes and 'either/or' dichotomous cultural viewpoints (Alexander 2008; Kramsch 2009).

Both Australia and Hong Kong need more cosmopolitan teachers to work productively with their culturally and linguistically diverse school populations. In Australia, an example of linguistic diversity is found in the more than 100,000 Australians aged between 5–19 years who communicate in Arabic, Vietnamese, or Cantonese at home (Clyne 2008). However, in contrast to diversity in student demographics, the profile of trainee teachers is becoming more homogeneous: predominantly Anglo-Australian and middle-class, and "with limited or no experience with persons from another ethnicity or social class" (Mills 2008, 267). These trainee teachers need to be able to communicate and relate interculturally with diverse children learning through the medium of English as an Additional Language (EAL) in mainstream classes (Miller, Kostogriz, & Gearon 2009). In Hong Kong classrooms, increasing numbers of children from Mainland China have been enrolled following the 1997 reunification. These students need scaffolding to adjust to learning through the medium of Cantonese rather than Putonghua, and to also learn English as an Additional Language (Rao & Yuen 2007). In addition, meeting the educational needs of ethnic minorities—children from India, Indonesia, Japan, Nepal, Pakistan, Philippines, and Thailand—continues to be a cause for concern in Hong Kong (Connelly, Gube, & Thapa 2013; Kapai 2011).

Intercultural conversations are seen as one way to ameliorate this lack in the teacher education curriculum, by offering opportunities for dialogic interaction with cultural others, supported by a process of guided reflection. *Dialogic* here is used in the Bakhtinian sense as the interaction of multiple voices and viewpoints, which come together in collision and combination, and through which individual understandings are being continually shaped and clarified (Bakhtin 1986). Dialogism offers a sociocultural perspective of knowledge being formed dynamically in and through interaction (Marchenkova 2004). From this perspective, engaging in intercultural conversations can help trainee teachers to begin to articulate, problematise, and de-centre from familiar social practices and cultural norms (Holmes 2006; Holmes & O'Neill 2010). This makes it possible for trainees to develop a position of "outsideness" leading to more creative intercultural understanding (Bakhtin 1981). This is complex and unsettling work, and yet it is through the dissonance generated that shifts in intercultural understanding are gained (Tang & Choi 2004). This was the rationale for implementing a curriculum intervention to bring together Hong Kong and Australian trainee teachers to engage in intercultural conversations as an integral part of their respective teacher education programs.

2. Background to the Study

The fifteen Hong Kong participants in this research were attending a professional study abroad program at the Queensland University of Technology (QUT) in Brisbane, sponsored by the Hong Kong government. For the Hong Kong trainees, these conversations were an opportunity to interact and exchange with intercultural peers, and increase their knowledge of the Australian education system, adding richness to the comparative understandings afforded by the study abroad experience (Bodycott & Crew 2001).

The seventy-nine Australian participants were all enrolled in a core primary curriculum unit on literacy teaching at the same university in Brisbane. The literacy unit prepares trainee teachers to plan programs of explicit reading and writing instruction for linguistically, culturally, and socially diverse groups of trainees, including learners of English as an Additional Language. By engaging in these intercultural conversations, the Australian trainees were aiming to refine their understandings of the cultural background and the linguistic needs of Hong Kong learners they may encounter in their future teaching in Australian classrooms.

The difference in participant numbers from the two groups reflects the different enrolment in their respective study programs. To accommodate this situation, the intercultural conversations were organized in small groups, with approximately five Australian trainees partnering one Hong Kong student. Whilst conversations are often construed as involving interaction between just two partners, in fact there is no such constraint in reality. The small group conversational context afforded the participants sufficient scope and impetus to generate a range of significant intercultural insights, as the findings from this study show. Flexibility in organization of the intercultural conversations is an inevitable necessity when including participants from study abroad programs, where enrolments fluctuate and scheduling of programs often occurs outside the usual semester dates. The intercultural conversations were incorporated into the curriculum and assessment in both the literacy unit and the Study Abroad program.

The intercultural conversations comprised three key elements: Preparation, Contact, and Reflection.

2.1. Preparation

For all participants, the preparation phase began one month prior to the first face-to-face intercultural conversation and focused on extending cultural and linguistic understandings. The Australian trainees, in their literacy tutorials, focused on expanding their understanding of language variation, the linguistic needs of English as an Additional Language learners, and some information about education in Hong Kong. The preparation phase for the Hong Kong trainees focused on orienting them to their forthcoming stay in Brisbane, via Internet resources on Australian language, culture, and lifestyle, and through e-mail contacts with the program organizer in Brisbane. On arrival in Brisbane, the Hong Kong trainees were also introduced to some of their partners' literacy coursework, so that they had some understanding of the educational issues of concern to their Australian peers.

E-mail contact between the two groups was set up two weeks before the arrival of the Hong Kong trainees so participants could start to get to know each other and for professional dialogue to begin. This initial e-mailing was useful as an ice-breaker and a way of extending the time available for communication between the two groups. It also highlighted the Australian trainees' uncertainty about how to communicate in the intercultural context with an unknown peer, inappropriately assuming shared familiarity with Australian social life and Australian expressions. The writing of the e-mails to the Hong Kong trainees was discussed and analyzed as a whole group process in class by the literacy lecturer, who used this opportunity to begin explicitly questioning the trainees' assumptions about effective intercultural communication.

2.2. Contact

Face-to-face contact between the two groups took place in the first week of the Hong Kong participants stay in Brisbane. The intercultural conversations were organized in small groups consisting of approximately five Australian trainees and one Hong Kong student, maintaining the same groupings that were established for the e-mail exchanges. Questions were prepared by both sets of participants before the face-to-face meetings to facilitate discussions. The participants met for two intercultural conversations, each lasting one hour, within the allocated class session time. Available meeting time on campus was constrained by the timing of the study abroad program toward the close of the semester.

2.3. Reflection

Integral to the structuring of the intercultural conversations was engaging participants in reflection on these intercultural experiences. The importance of reflection in developing professional identity has been discussed at length in the literature on teacher education (Bain et al. 2002; Korthagen 2010; Korthagen & Vasalos 2005; Schon 1983). Research has also demonstrated that richer insights accrue from a process of guided reflection, with input by a lecturer or mentor, to help trainee teachers unpack the significance of their intercultural experiences (Hepple 2012; Scoffham & Barnes 2009). Guided reflection was therefore embedded within the intercultural conversational process from the outset. As part of the preparation, reflection on emergent cultural understandings arose in tutorials through analyses and critique of course materials and the writing of the introductory e-mails. In addition, each intercultural conversation was followed by a reflective feedback session within each program schedule, exploring the content and process of the small group dialogues.

3. Analyses of Intercultural Conversations

Participant feedback was gathered through face-to-face interviews (Australian participants) and written feedback (Hong Kong participants), using a set of eight interview questions (see Appendix A). (The difference in data collection method arose through the ethical requirement to wait until the completion of all assessment in each program before gathering feedback from participants. By this time, the Hong Kong trainees had returned home and were not available for interviews with the researcher.)

Twenty Australian trainee teachers were invited to provide their individual reflective feedback on the intercultural conversations, through one-to-one interviews lasting thirty minutes, with the co-researcher for this study. Seventeen trainees (eleven females, six males) gave their informed consent to take up this opportunity. The selection of these Australian participants was made via purposeful 'typical sampling' (Creswell 2012) on the basis that these participants represented the broad range of perspectives expressed in class discussions following the intercultural conversations. All fifteen Hong Kong participants (eleven females and four males) gave their informed consent to provide their reflective feedback via written responses to the same eight interview questions. Data were transcribed and coded following a grounded approach (Glaser & Strauss 1967), with recursive readings and finer-grained coding of the participants' feedback until central themes emerged. In the reporting of data and in accordance with ethical requirements, pseudonyms have been used to protect the identity of participants. The three key emergent themes are described and discussed in the following pages: communicating interculturally through English; complexities in exchanging cultural information; and becoming cosmopolitan teachers.

3.1.   Communicating Interculturally through English

One of the key aspects of becoming a more cosmopolitan teacher is the ability to communicate and exchange with cultural others. The use of English as the medium of communication was one of the most frequent points of feedback from the Australian trainee teachers, who were impressed by the high level of English language competence demonstrated by the Hong Kong trainee teachers: "I was amazed by how good her English was—I hadn't expected that" (Paul). The Australian trainees noted making some slight adjustments to their speech: "thinking about the level of language to use as I spoke" (Jane), and using "a better class of English, less colloquial for example" (Christine). They had anticipated communication through English to be problematic with the Hong Kong trainee teachers and had some accommodation strategies ready, such as: "to speak slowly and articulate clearly and use lots of hand movements, but we didn't need to" (Susan). From the frequency of such feedback, it seems that one of the outcomes of the intercultural conversations is that the Australian trainees now have a broader view of the linguistic capabilities of speakers who use English as an Additional Language. Their comments also suggest that their stereotypical expectations of language weakness were immediately challenged through these face-to-face encounters with the Hong Kong trainees.

As the Hong Kong trainees' fluency in English generally allowed the conversations to flow freely, the Australian trainees became aware of more subtle pragmatic factors involved in the dialogic exchange. Despite a positive attitude and being aware that body language is part of the communication, Australian trainees found it difficult to interpret meanings across cultures, as one student observed: "I expected to have to use body language cues (looking to see if what I was saying was going in) but I couldn't tell what her cues meant—she leant forward a lot and smiled—she was so bubbly and keen but I don't know if she was really understanding" (Sam). Such comments from the Australian participants indicate a willingness to be intercultural speakers, but that they need more strategies to draw on to negotiate meanings when talking with intercultural peers. A number of the Australian trainees concluded that it would have been helpful to have discussed politeness formulae in Hong Kong, before meeting their Hong Kong partners. This increased pragmatic awareness, acknowledging the gaps in their understanding of the intertwining of language and culture, is a significant outcome of these conversations.

By contrast, the Hong Kong participants did not foreground the use of English as the medium of communication as particularly noteworthy or problematic in their feedback on their intercultural conversations. Only two Hong Kong trainee teachers made any mention of English language proficiency in their feedback. One individual noted he had "a pronunciation problem" (Tak-Wah) when trying to explain the Hong Kong education system to Australian peers, and the other participant noted that one of the gains from these intercultural conversations was "improvement in spoken English" (Mei). Apart from these two comments, the Hong Kong participants' comments were not focused on their own language proficiency or the particular language use of their Australian partners. This may reflect the fact that they had multiple opportunities in their study abroad program, prior to giving feedback on their intercultural conversations, where they discussed their own use of English as an Additional Language and specific features of Australian English. Therefore, the Hong Kong trainee teachers may not have felt the need to use this feedback as a forum to discuss issues of communicating through English in the Australian context. However, it may also reflect a notably different perception of having English as a lingua franca—*a shared means of communication*—as a positive attribute. As one of the Hong Kong participants observed: "We all speak English" and he was citing this as an example of shared common ground (Chi Wai). This is in sharp contrast to the initial concerns of the Australian trainees that in conversation with second language users, the English language would constitute a possible barrier to communication.

Concerns about using English as the medium of communication were not voiced by the Hong Kong participants but by native-speaker Australian trainee teachers. It was the domestic participants who expressed uncertainty about whether their language use would be intelligible to their Hong Kong partner and whether they would have to adjust their speech to get their message across. As one of the Australian participants explained, the Hong Kong peers "had been in the country, out and about, and were used to the Australian dialect. And we knew he could understand. A lot of people [Australians] were put off by the fact that *they* had to change *their* speech" (Ian). This is an unusual twist on the general assumption that intercultural conversations necessarily offer most linguistic challenges to the visiting international trainees.

While the HK participants were described as "accomplished" and "very good" in their use of English, which is their second or third language, a number of Australian participants saw this as a point of negative contrast to their own skills in second language learning: "I was impressed by the fact that she speaks 3 languages—if you're Australian, hardly anyone speaks more than one" (Jane). However, in this group of trainee teachers nine of the seventeen respondents had experience of learning at least one other language, which included: Norwegian, Italian, German, French, Indonesian, Japanese, Spanish, and Mandarin. The individual who had learnt Mandarin in school noted that:

> as a foreign language you learn segments of language as distinct from learning a conversation—like my experience of learning Mandarin. I could have ordered a lobster in primary school and said that it was hot, but I could not have had a conversation (Crystal)

Having made this comment, it is unsurprising that this trainee teacher did not choose to communicate with her intercultural peers in Mandarin, even though most of the Hong Kong trainees were proficient Mandarin speakers. This Australian student's stated inability to have a conversation in a language other than English raises a larger question about how trainees' intercultural communicative needs are catered for in foreign language learning classrooms (Scarino & Crichton 2008). This can be seen as one of the contributing factors to these participants using solely English as the medium of communication in these conversations.

3.2.   Complexities around Exchanging Cultural Information

The key focus for participants in the intercultural conversations was increasing their knowledge of each other's educational context, to learn more about how English language is taught and learnt in Hong Kong and Australian classrooms. The Hong Kong participants sought information about the differences in educational provision in different Australian states; features of private and public schooling; and mainstream approaches to teaching literacy. In turn the Hong Kong trainees described the system of Chinese-medium and English-medium schooling in Hong Kong, and also explained how English language is taught as a compulsory subject from the first year of primary school onwards. Discussing language learning experiences with their Hong Kong peers made the Australian trainee teachers aware of how challenging the learning of English as an Additional Language is: "when you are an English speaker you expect others to know English—you don't really think about how much work it takes to learn—so this was surprising" (Joanna). As these trainee teachers are very likely to have EAL students in their future classes, this appreciation of the complexity of the language learner's task is an important starting point to inform their teaching.

Difficulties in answering questions about one's own educational processes were experienced by both Australian and Hong Kong participants. For both partners, it was a chance to begin to see familiar structures and practices from an outsider's perspective: "it was interesting that things that seemed so ordinary to us would be so interesting to someone else" (Susan). Other participants with prior intercultural experience took a more comparative stance: "Because I lived in other countries, I know that school systems are different and know that you have to think carefully when explaining things" (Grace). However, giving careful explanations is not easy, as it involves describing taken-for-granted routines: "to explain why things happen as they do—it's easy to explain *what* but not *why* because in my experience that's just the way it has always been" (Joanna). They all commented on the realization that they needed to have a deeper knowledge of their own education systems. Australian trainee teachers commented: "In just trying to explain the Australian system… you realized that you really don't know the details of the Australian system yourself" (Steven). One of the Hong Kong participants summed up these feelings succinctly, noting it was "hard to explain something I have taken for granted to somebody who doesn't share the same knowledge as I do" (Chi Wai).

Being positioned as 'cultural representatives' within their intercultural conversations, both Hong Kong and Australian trainee teachers voiced concerns about creating positive impressions of their home culture: "I wouldn't want her to think negative things about education in Australia. I wouldn't want to accidentally create misinterpretations" (Debra). This awareness of creating positive or negative interpretations was taken a step further by a Hong Kong trainee teacher who reflected on the importance of maintaining a positive view of his educational system to enhance his own teaching in the future. During the IC he had become aware of his: "negative perception towards my own education system and this would certainly affect my mood of teaching in the future. I'd better look at the credits of my own education system rather than the defects" (Kwok-Wing). His commentary here is indicative of how shifts in understanding occurred through reflecting on their representations of their own cultural and educational practices during the intercultural conversations.

Participants' concerns about how they explained and represented their cultural practices to others were not only in dialogues between Australian and Hong Kong partners. Australian trainees mentioned feeling uncomfortable at times taking on an 'expert' role when expressing their professional knowledge in front of other Australians: "If the Hong Kong trainees didn't understand, the Australian trainees were uncomfortable about changing it and repeating. There was a lot of terminology that we were using. We only have a surface understanding of the terminology ourselves . . . This might be why the Australian trainees were uncomfortable speaking in front of each other. There might have been a fear of being uncovered" (Julia). The participants' feedback reveals their discomfort in being positioned in this unfamiliar role of 'expert,' thus exposing a more *vulnerable self* (Holmes & O'Neill 2010) and providing the provocation for reflective professional identity work.

There was also a perceived imbalance in the level of cultural knowledge between the two groups, in that the Hong Kong trainee teachers were deemed to have more understanding of Australian social and educational practices than the Australian trainees had of Hong Kong ones. One of the Hong Kong participants expressed this as the Australian trainee teachers needing deeper cultural knowledge if they were to understand the educational context in Hong Kong:

> They may not be able to understand when a certain topic is difficult for Hong Kong trainees. I need to explain more about the Chinese language system to the B.Ed. trainees. Besides, they may need to understand the Chinese culture so as to have a better understanding of why things happen in Hong Kong classrooms (Yingying)

As well as needing to understand more about Chinese language and culture, Hong Kong participants perceived the Australian trainees as uninformed about the differences in education systems in Hong Kong and Mainland China: "the schooling system in Hong Kong is different from that of Mainland China but the Aussie trainees seem don't get the concept" (Mei Ying).

By contrast, the Australian trainee teachers assumed, rightly or wrongly, more shared knowledge when describing their educational system to their Hong Kong partner: "the Hong Kong trainees were more familiar with Western culture than we were with Hong Kong culture—I felt she understood and so didn't have to go further" (Jane). This confident assumption of familiarity with both Australian culture and English language variation is surprising given the fact that the Hong Kong students had only been in the country for a total of two weeks when these intercultural conversations took place. Such a perspective is also significant in that the comparison equates Australian culture with Western culture generally, indicating that implicit in this discourse is a stereotypical division between Western and Eastern cultures that, in this instance, was not explored further.

3.3.   Becoming Cosmopolitan Teachers

One of the central characteristics of a cosmopolitan teacher is the desire and ability to communicate and exchange with cultural others (Luke 2004). The majority of participants found their shared professional interest in teaching helped them establish points of connection: "We both are enthusiastic about teaching and we value the chance to know more about each other's culture" (Yingying) and "Compared to being a tourist, being a fellow student was different . . . that's where we could connect and relate" (Debra). In their reflective feedback, all but one of the thirty-two respondents deemed their engagement in the conversations to have been a positive intercultural learning experience. One Australian trainee gave a negative evaluation of the interaction noting "I did not bring much out of those meetings" (Harry).

For the majority of participants, this chance to relate interculturally was appreciated for providing insights into "the ways they think or perceive the world; how they talk to each other; what topics they usually talk with" (Chi Wai). Getting to know their intercultural partner allowed more global identifications to emerge:

> I felt like I was talking to a peer in the field—I was blown away by commonalities...
> [it] reinforced for me the global scale of our lives—in this day and age, there's a lot
> of travel potential—we're not tied into a rural job in Queensland—personally, this
> excites me about being a teacher (Josh)

Josh's reference to his Hong Kong partner as "a peer in the field" and a horizon beyond his home state of Queensland indicates a more cosmopolitan perspective in which both Australian and Hong Kong trainee teachers belong to a global professional community. The immediate goal for both sets of participants had been to increase their professional understandings of each other's educational context, in particular the pedagogies for developing English language competence in Hong Kong and Australian classrooms. Engaging in the intercultural conversations helped many participants begin to consider English language teaching from different cultural perspectives. For the Australian trainees this involved seeing the learning of English language from the viewpoint of someone for whom this is not their first language:

> as a result of what the student said I changed my assignment, focusing on sounds
> that might be difficult to articulate. I learned about this in the discussion... although
> I had done preparation it was only during the discussion that it came together
> (Jane)

In turn, Hong Kong trainees remarked on the range of interactive teaching activities mentioned by their Australian peers and commented: "a new approach of English teaching is learnt from the Australian students . . . I think Hong Kong classroom can try the Australian style of learning and arouse the students' interest in learning English" (Fengyi).

Another Australian student, Julia, wanted to teach in China: "so this experience was very helpful for me because I realize that I will have to adjust my ways of doing things" (Julia). The insights that participants gained from these relatively short intercultural conversations were appreciated as a rare opportunity to build global perspectives: "When I think of teaching I don't think only of teaching in Australia because I want to travel and learn in different cultures. But in our course we only get content for Australian cultures and curriculum studies . . . More of the units could be taught about different cultures" (Julia). Such feedback indicates that curriculum in teacher education programs need to be focused beyond the local, to meet the global aspirations of trainees.

4. Conclusions

The research question framing this study was: "Does engaging international and domestic trainee teachers in structured intercultural conversations help them develop more cosmopolitan professional identities?" From the feedback it can be seen that the Australian participants in particular are developing their linguistic awareness through these intercultural conversations. The Australian trainees, particularly monolingual speakers, wrestled with uncertainties about how to negotiate meanings with their intercultural partners as they were not accustomed to questioning or adjusting their use of English as their first language. They also became more sensitive to the interplay of language and culture, noting the need for more pragmatic knowledge to guide their understanding of their intercultural partner's words and gestures.

By contrast, the Hong Kong trainees, as very competent bilingual/multilingual speakers were used to having to negotiate meanings through English as a second or third language and saw the sharing of English language as a point of connection rather than a problem. These findings highlight the value of holding more intercultural conversations specifically to help domestic trainees extend their intercultural communication skills, learning a new flexibility in their use of English to mediate cultural and linguistic differences. This is an interesting shift from the dominant focus in much of the research literature where intercultural communication has been largely seen in terms of international students making cultural and linguistic adaptations to the host context (Lin 2008; Turner 2009).

Engaging in the intercultural conversations can be seen to be building stronger professional awareness among both the Australian and Hong Kong trainees, making visible their own taken-for-granted educational structures and practices, and highlighting the gaps in their knowledge of these, as well as their lack of knowledge of other culture's educational systems and values. All participants acknowledged the complexity of trying to exchange cultural information and mediate differences without shared discourses, noting that they have much yet to learn about effectively communicating interculturally. This common need to develop more competence in intercultural communication argues the importance of providing specific programs addressing this within teacher education. Given the fact that these Australian and Hong Kong trainee teachers will be teaching increasing numbers of culturally and linguistically diverse school children in their future careers, it is of great importance that they continue to build on the insights gained from these intercultural conversations. As one student explained: "they're not that different . . . there's a lot of people that need to realize this . . . it's a small world—you've got to learn to deal with it—you're not the only person in the world" (Susan). Susan's comment demonstrates her expanded intercultural awareness and her adoption of a more active personal role in deconstructing cultural chauvinism. As Holliday (2011, 147) notes:

> Imagining Self in relation to Other . . . is at the heart of the issue of cultural chauvinism . . . [and] responsibility has to be taken for it by everybody at every level. It underlies everything that takes on the presence of neutrality in cultural difference, and attempts to solve this difference."

Tackling such complex issues as cultural chauvinism, in order to engage productively with cultural and linguistic diversity, is a fundamental aspect of teacher education programs. In order to address these issues, there is a need to embed intercultural communication and intercultural competence within the curriculum. Curriculum interventions which engage domestic and international trainee teachers in focused intercultural conversations are one way of working toward this goal.

Acknowledgment

I would like to thank Dr. Karen Dooley for her substantial contribution to this study in her capacity as co-researcher in this project. However, the views expressed in this chapter are my own.

References

Alexander, R. (2008). *Essays on pedagogy*. London and New York: Routledge.

Bain, J. D., Ballantyne, R., Mills, C., & Lester, N. C. (2002). *Reflecting on practice: Student teachers' perspectives*. Flaxton, Queensland: Post Pressed.

Bakhtin, M. M. (1981). *The dialogic imagination*. Austin, TX: University of Texas Press.

Bakhtin, M. M. (1986). *Speech genres and other late essays*. Austin, TX: University of Texas Press.

Bodycott, P., & Crew, V. (2001). *Language and cultural immersion: Perspectives on short term study and residence abroad*. Hong Kong: Hong Kong Institute of Education.

Byram, M. (2009). The intercultural speaker and the pedagogy of foreign language education. In D. K. Deardorff (Ed.), *The Sage handbook of intercultural competence* (pp. 321–333). Thousand Oaks, CA: Sage.

Byram, M., & Fleming, M. (1998). *Language learning in intercultural perspective: Approaches through drama and ethnography*. Cambridge: Cambridge University Press.

Clyne, M. (2008). Australia's unrecognized resources boom—Language for Australia's future. Retrieved from http://www.arts.monash.edu.au/language-and-society/--downloads/languages-for-australias-future.pdf

Connelly, J., Gube, J., and Thapa, C. B. (2013). Hong Kong's ethnic and linguistic minority immigrant students: An evaluation of educational support measures. In E.L. Brown & A. Krasteva (Eds.), *Migrants and Refugees: Equitable education for displaced populations* (pp. 191–214). Charlotte, North Carolina: Information Age Publishing.

Creswell, J. (2012). *Educational research: Planning, conducting and evaluating quantitative and qualitative research* (4th ed.). New Jersey: Prentice Hall.

Cushner, K., & Mahon, J. (2009). Developing the intercultural competence of educators and their trainees: Creating the blueprints. In D. Deardorff (Ed.), *The SAGE Handbook of Intercultural Competence* (pp. 304–320). Thousand Oaks: SAGE.

Glaser, B., & Strauss, A. (1967). *The discovery of grounded theory*. Chicago: Aldine.

Goldstein, T. (2007). Educating world teachers for cosmopolitan classrooms and schools. *Asia Pacific Journal of Education, 27*(2), 131–155.

Hepple, E. (2012). Questioning pedagogies: Hong Kong pre-service teachers' dialogic reflections on a transnational school experience. *Journal of Education for Teaching: International Research and Pedagogy, 38*(3), 309–322.

Holliday, A. (2011). *Intercultural communication and ideology*. Thousand Oaks: Sage.

Holmes, P. (2006). Problematising intercultural communication competence in the pluricultural classroom: Chinese trainees in a New Zealand University. *Language and Intercultural Communication, 1*, 18–34.

Holmes, P., & O'Neill, G. (2010). Autoethnography and self-reflection: Tools for self-assessing intercultural competence. In Y. Tsai & S. Houghton (Eds.), *Becoming intercultural: Inside and outside the classroom* (pp. 167–193). Newcastle upon Tyne: Cambridge Scholars.

Kapai, P. (2011). *Education of ethnic minority children.* Submission from the Centre for Comparative and Public Law, Faculty of Law, University of Hong Kong to the Meeting of Legislative Council Panel on Education 12 December, 2011.

Korthagen, F. (2010). How teacher education can make a difference. *Journal of Education for Teaching, 36* (4), 407–423.

Korthagen, F., & Vasalos, A. (2005). Levels in reflection: Core reflection as a means to enhance professional growth. *Teachers and Teaching: Theory and Practice, 11*(1), 47–71.

Kramsch, C. (2009). Third culture and language education. In V. Cook & W. Li (Eds.), *Contemporary applied linguistics: Language teaching and learning* (pp. 233–254). London & New York: Continuum.

Lin, J.-H. I. (2008). *Transferring cultural capital: Narratives of international students' transition into an Australian University.* Paper presented at the Australian Association for Research in Education (AARE) Conference.

Luke, A. (2004). Teaching after the market: From commodity to cosmopolitan. *Teachers College Record, 106*(7), 1422–1443.

Marchenkova, L. (2004). Language, culture, and self. In J. K. Hall, L. Marchenkova, & G. Vitanova (Eds.), *Dialogue with Bakhtin on second and foreign language learning* (pp. 160–178). Abingdon: Lawrence Erlbaum.

Miller, J. M., Kostogriz, A., & Gearon, M. M. (Eds.). (2009). *Culturally and linguistically diverse classrooms. New dilemmas for teachers.* UK: Multilingual Matters.

Mills, C. (2008). Making a difference: moving beyond the superficial treatment of diversity. *Asia-Pacific Journal of Teacher Education, 36*(4), 261–275.

Rao, N., & Yuen, M. (2007). Listening to children: Voices of newly arrived immigrants from the Chinese mainland to Hong Kong. In L. Adams & A. Kirova (Eds.), *Global migration and education* (pp. 139–150). New York, NY: Routledge.

Scarino, A., & Crichton, J. (2008). Why the intercultural matters to language teaching and learning: an orientation to the ILTLP program. *Babel, 43*(1), 4–6.

Schon, D. (1983). *The reflective practitioner: How professionals think in action.* New York: Basic Books.

Scoffham, S., & Barnes, J. (2009). Tranformational experiences and deep learning: the impact of an intercultural study visit to India in UK initial teacher education students. *Journal of Education for Teaching, 35*(3), 257–270.

Tang, Y. F. S., & Choi, P. L. (2004). The development of personal, intercultural and professional competence in international field experience in initial teacher education. *Asia Pacific Education Review, 5*(1), 50–63.

Turner, Y. (2009). "Knowing me, knowing you," Is there nothing we can do?: Pedagogic challenges in using group work to create an intercultural learning space. *Journal of Studies in International Education, 13*(2), 240–255.

Appendix A

Questions to Participants

1. What did you learn about the teaching of English from the Hong Kong/Australian trainee teachers?

2. What insight did you gain from the process of explaining your education system to a trainee teacher from another culture?

3. What difficulty did you find in explaining and describing English teaching/classroom culture to a person from another culture?

4. What information about the other person's lifestyle impressed or interested you?

5. What common ground did you find through meeting with these trainees twice?

6. Have you kept in contact with the trainees?

7. For future intercultural conversations, what do you feel would be most useful as preparation for the first meeting with the other trainees?

8. Beforehand, what were you hoping to get from these conversations? What did you gain from them?

7

Challenges in International Baccalaureate Students' Intercultural Dialogue

Gertrud Tarp

Key Words

- ► Grounded theory
- ► Student voices
- ► International network
- ► Spaces of interaction
- ► Situated English

1. Introduction

The aim of this study is to clarify and understand how international baccalaureate (IB) students experience intercultural dialogue in an IB educational context. It is an attempt to illuminate student attitude, dialogue, and interaction. To give further meaning to the data links are drawn to relevant sociological theory, which will give an understanding of student behaviour in the different spaces of interaction and their participation in intercultural dialogue.

The IB is a world-wide, two-year school program using English as a lingua franca (ELF) in the transition years between late high school and the first or second year at university. IB schools exist in a large number of countries, and the IB examination gives access to universities all over the world. The IB context enables an investigation of students engaging in intercultural dialogue. It also makes it possible to study how a variety of different cultures and nationalities, subject to the same educational conditions, experience intercultural dialogue.

2. Intercultural Dialogue and English as a Lingua Franca

Since the concept of "intercultural dialogue" underpins this study, I describe it here, along with ELF, the concept applied to the language used in an IB context. According to the Council of Europe (2008) "Intercultural dialogue is understood as a process that comprises an open and respectful exchange of views between individuals and groups with different ethnic, cultural, religious and linguistic background and heritage, on the basis of mutual understanding and respect" (17). Intercultural dialogue entails an exchange of views between individuals or groups requiring that participants listen to one another, but not that they end in agreement.

The importance of understanding intercultural encounters and processes as constitutive of dialogue is emphasized both by Byram (2009) and Ganesh and Holmes (2011). According to the Council of Europe, intercultural dialogue is increasingly seen as one of the ways to promote mutual understanding, better living together and an active sense of European citizenship and belonging. The Council (2008) emphasizes that "only dialogue allows people to live in unity and diversity" (16). However, the competences necessary for intercultural dialogue to succeed are not automatically acquired in everyday life. They need to be learned, practiced, and maintained throughout life. Intercultural dialogue also needs specific spaces to succeed. The Council (2008, 2010) states that providers of education can play a crucial role in the pursuit of these aims (i.e., competences and spaces). Given the nature of the IB learning context, it is possible to expect that students, to varying extents, engage in intercultural dialogue in their everyday interactions.

ELF is part of the more general phenomenon of 'English as an international language' or 'world Englishes' (see Jenkins 2003; McArthur 1998; Melchers and Shaw 2003). It is essentially conceived as "a 'contact language' between persons who share neither a common native tongue nor a common (national) culture, and for whom English is the chosen foreign language of communication" (Firth 1996, 240). In the context of IB education in Denmark, English is the usual means of communication among students from different language backgrounds and across linguacultural boundaries.

Since English is the basis of intercultural interaction and dialogue among these IB students, it is useful to mention briefly some of the discussions in the literature concerning ELF. The concept of ELF also raises the question whether ELF develops into a specific version of English not accepting standard norms and not related to a specific culture. The version of English being used is of importance since, to some extent, it influences student intercultural interaction and dialogue.

3.   Case Study Rationale

Locating a study of intercultural dialogue in an IB school is desirable given its pluricultural/plurilingual student body. Further, the growth of IB schools, since their foundation in Geneva, Switzerland, in 1968, has been between 10 percent and 20 percent each year. There are already 2,447 IB schools in 131 countries with more than 668,000 students (www.ibo.org/diploma/curriculum/group1/ - 2008, December 1 and 2010, May 12). This development emphasizes the interest in and the importance of international education and intercultural dialogue.

The IB curriculum, as adopted by this Danish IB school, is international in its focus, and it allows IB students to experience intercultural dialogue in a way that is constructive to their development as world citizens.

The IB curriculum emphasizes the concepts of "an international perspective, intercultural understanding and an understanding of another culture." It is described as a hexagon consisting of six major subjects: First and Second Language, Individuals and Societies, Experimental Sciences, Mathematics, and The Arts. It is compulsory for students to study their mother tongue. Subjects other than languages may be taught and examined in English, French, or Spanish. Studying the literature of the student's first language, including the study of selections of world literature, is seen as important in providing the student with an international perspective and the development of intercultural understanding. The aim of studying a second language is to promote an understanding of another culture. In addition, a large range of modern languages are available plus two classical languages, Latin and classical Greek (www.ibo.org/diploma/curriculum/group1/ - 2008, December 1). In this IB school a significant part of teaching and learning in the IB curriculum is carried out in English. Thus English is an important language of communication for students both in and outside the classroom.

4.   Methodology

The methodology applied to understanding students' intercultural dialogue experiences is grounded theory in order to inductively generate theory from those experiences. The aim of grounded theory is to develop a theory about the phenomenon studied on the basis of the empirical data, and to be open to new impressions and contexts. A grounded theory approach emphasizes the researcher's theoretical knowledge and theoretical sensitivity in order to compare the generated theory with existing theories to further illuminate the findings (Glaser as cited in Strauss & Corbin 1990, 46). The importance of listening to agents, in this case study, the students, is emphasized by their active role in generating the data (through their intercultural dialogic experiences) (Strauss & Corbin 1990; Tarp 2006, 2011). Therefore, the question guiding this study is: How do IB students experience intercultural dialogue in a Danish IB school?

5. Design and Data Collection

The full study behind this case study is among others inspired by Stake (2000), and I was involved as a researcher in the whole process. The case comprises twenty-seven participants from eleven different countries, and the data collection took place in English. It took four years and included the same group of students attending a pre-IB, an IB first year, and an IB second year class. In addition four post-IB students were interviewed. The first part of the data collection included semi-structured written narratives. On the basis of the narratives a retrospective questionnaire with student statements was prepared and given to the students. The final part of the data collection included one-hour focus group interviews. The focus groups discussed the answers to the retrospective questionnaire.

6. Data Analysis

The continuous interaction between data collection and data analysis resulted in the discovery of student categories and emergent themes. The participants can be divided into EFL (English as a foreign language) students from abroad, ENL (English as a native language) students, and Danish EFL students.

6.1. EFL Students

EFL students having English as a foreign language come from different countries such as China, Greenland, Poland, Russia, and Vietnam. An example is a Vietnamese student:

> I figure out that to make people understand me clearer, it is very useful when I use some of my body language to express what I mean. However, English is still a huge problem for me now; I still can't roll my tongue when I pronounce some difficult words so it could lead to a new word with different meaning. I practice my English when I socialize with the other students because for me, that is how I get my English much better. When I am with other students, especially with someone close to me then I feel more comfortable to talk to them because I know that they will listen, try to understand me and help me pronounce the correct way of that word (Vietnamese, M).

The Vietnamese student seems to choose the space for learning where he is able to cope and where he can improve his English (i.e., outside class). For him there are two different spaces: in class and outside class. He is aware that he can form a network outside class. In this way he can improve his language skills and get a better chance of managing in class.
Some EFL students comment on dominance in class:

> As my experience, there seems to be and they always tend to have one student as the major speaker to run the discussion—and it always seems to be either the

one who speaks most fluently in English or the one who is the best in this subject among those students (Chinese, M).

Thus dominance in class requires either language skills in English or academic knowledge. The importance of language skills is also mentioned by another EFL student:

> In conclusion I would say that English is a quite simple language to learn on the basic or intermediate level, but many people have not mastered it sufficiently to communicate beyond a "commercial" level. This is disturbing, and in the case of Denmark for example, gives a false image of how apt and able local people actually are. Nevertheless, I encountered more positive situations than negative ones, and it is always an amazing feeling, connecting with someone in a common language that is not the mother tongue of either of us (Hungarian, F).

The statement emphasizes the importance of communication but also of having a common language, which enables intercultural communication and dialogue.

These findings suggest that EFL students especially take part in intercultural dialogue outside class with the purpose of improving their language skills. Academic knowledge and language skills seem to be essential to succeed in class.

6.2.   ENL Students

ENL students having English as a native language comment on the workload in terms of assignments and exam papers. A Welsh student mentions that she has no problems turning in all the assignments and living up to the exam standards. At the same time she mentions her lack of networks and socialization outside class:

> The IB is quite demanding and most Danish students complain about the workload mainly because they are used to less work. The workload is not beyond what people can do, but you need to have some grasp of languages. You have to stay on top of everything. (. . .) I did not really do anything to socialize (Welsh, F).

The example shows that the ENL student knows how to cope in class, but she does not really feel the need to do anything to socialize outside class. She complains about the language used:

> The English you develop becomes a different kind of English. I have to regain my British English when I go back to England. It becomes international English or social English or a simplification of the English language. You cannot really associate it with any culture (. . .). Sometimes I have problems understanding the Danish teachers speaking English because they use Danish examples (. . .). There is a lot of language switch (Welsh, F).

So for her the IB education is a way of improving her academic knowledge but not her language skills or access to intercultural dialogue.

The challenges experienced in connection with the use of non-standard English are also mentioned by an American male student saying "My classmates had a pretty good grammar but a poor knowledge of words." He states that it took him a year to adapt to and figure out what the non-native English speaking students meant when using ELF. For instance he did not understand the question "Are you smoking?" meaning "do you smoke?" Not until later did he understand a different version of English.

Thus, ENL students often experience lingua franca English as nonsense and feel frustrated when trying to interpret and construct new meaning. They are not necessarily very effective communicators in intercultural encounters and intercultural dialogue. However, they are effective when studying textbooks and writing exam papers, but not always outside class.

6.3. Danish EFL Students

Danish EFL students having English as a foreign language seem to form a special category of students because they are familiar with the school surroundings and feel at home. They mention the feeling of togetherness. At the same time they complain about foreign students' attitudes:

> IB students from abroad do not take a step to be completely involved. Certainly, there is a language barrier, and they have a hard time not during lessons but after class. For instance we have in class a Chinese student. He does not want to participate in group work. He is always concerned about himself and his needs. When it is a question of group work, he leaves and tells us that he is tired. But people get used to other cultures' weaknesses (Danish, F, Anne).

Most Danish students emphasize the advantages of using ELF and of being able to communicate with foreigners:

> My overall experience of using English as lingua franca is very positive, and I find it wonderful that I'm able to communicate with so many different people all over the world (Danish, F, Bodil).

Some students mention the problem of deterioration when English is used as ELF, so being with other ELF students might not improve their English:

> It really is a "world language," although obviously it is spoken with very different accents in very different ways and on very different levels. The latter can be disturbing, as it might lead to the deterioration to the individual's level of language (...) an environment that is not stimulating or challenging can lead to forgetting words or getting used to wrong expressions or pronunciation (Danish, F, Cecilie).

In addition, the use of ELF might lead to confusion and misunderstanding due to different connotations:

> These differences between British and American English also cause minor problems sometimes when using English as common lingua franca. Last I have noticed that different cultures have different connotations to the English words. This can sometimes cause a bit of confusion (Danish, F, Dorthe).

These findings indicate that the students express a certain kind of cultural and linguistic awareness, which is pointed out by a post IB student saying "I learnt to be culturally aware." However, the same student says "My network is Danish. I have no contact with former IB students" (Danish, F, Elin).

The statements show lack of interest in being active in intercultural dialogue and building up an international network.

Foreign EFL students complain about the Danish attitude to language "Try to only keep it in English" (Hungarian, F) and socialization "Danes can be too much involved in classes, so that non-Danish speaking students might have problems" (Vietnamese, M).

In general Danish EFL students seem to have special conditions due to their nationality. The result is that they tend to switch to their mother tongue and focus on their national network instead of taking part in intercultural dialogue.

7. Theoretical Considerations: Student Access to Intercultural Dialogue

The analysis shows two major spaces of interaction where intercultural dialogue can take place: in class (student/student/teacher) and outside class (student/student). In these spaces successful intercultural dialogue will depend on language skills, academic knowledge, cultural background, and attitude. In addition the analysis shows that IB English is a special version of standard English situated in the specific context.

To give further meaning to the findings, lines are drawn to sociological theory. The IB class is an example of a cultural meeting where students interact, and where intercultural dialogue can take place. Social interaction can be described by means of Bourdieu's concepts of field, capital, and habitus:

> In analytical terms, a field may be defined as a network, or a configuration, of objective relations between positions. These positions are objectively defined, in their existence and in the determinations they impose upon their occupants, agents or institutions, by their present and potential situation in the structure of the distribution of species of power (or capital) whose possession commands access to the specific profits that are at stake in the field (..) We can indeed, with caution, compare a field to a game (..) To be more precise, the strategies of a "player" and everything that defines his "game" are a function not only of the volume and

structure of his capital, but also (..) of the dispositions (habitus) (Bourdieu & Wacquant 1992, 96–99).

According to Bourdieu and Wacquant (1992), the social space is divided into fields where people compete about the capital in the field. And their chances to win or gain a profit depend upon their habitus (i.e., the habits they have developed over time). The competition for its capital means that in a social field there will be both "winners" and "losers." In the case of the IB class, students will be "winners" or "losers" in the social field. They will be more or less successful in participating in intercultural dialogue (i.e., in exchanging views and listening to each other) (European Council 2008). Thus their success will depend on the habitus they have developed in the field or bring to the field.

The reason for calling the IB class a field is that students have something at stake. Field exists in terms of the IB space. There are different agents with different kinds of habitus (what students do). Student habitus will decide whether they can build up capital (what students gain) in the field. Capital is divided into symbolic capital (academic knowledge, language) and social knowledge (social competence) (Bourdieu 1998, 19–30). It is a field where students can play a game, accept the rules, invest, take chances, and lose. Consequently it is a question of either winning or losing symbolic and/or social capital.

The analysis shows two fields: in class and outside class. In class students compete over symbolic capital in terms of academic knowledge with high grades. Outside class they compete over social capital in terms of international social networks. Some will be successful and some will be less successful depending on their habitus. In class linguistic habitus or academic knowledge is important since knowledge is communicated by means of English. Outside class what is needed is social habitus and the willingness to communicate with foreigners in a form of English situated in the context. Habitus outside class is built up through communication in the form of intercultural dialogue.

7.1. Field: Class

Students who are able to build up symbolic capital in class are ENL students but also EFL students with suitable habitus in terms of thorough academic knowledge and sufficient language skills and study techniques. An example is the Welsh student stating that "You have to stand on top of everything. The workload is not beyond what people can do, but you need to have some grasp of languages" (Welsh, F).

EFL students try to get suitable habitus to cope in class, especially by improving their English "(. . .) and help me to pronounce the correct way of that word" (Vietnamese, M). But also by being willing to communicate in English, "Nevertheless, I encountered more positive situations than negative ones, and it is always an amazing feeling, connecting with someone in a common language that is not the mother tongue of either of us" (Hungarian, F). The Danish EFL students seem to be divided between those having suitable habitus and those without. An example is their attitude to speaking English. Some students are aware of language deterioration and challenges: "An environment that is not stimulating or challenging can lead to forgetting words or getting used to wrong expressions or pronunciation" (Danish, F, Cecilie), whereas others switch to Danish, "Try to only keep it in English" (Hungarian, F), and do not benefit from the intercultural mixture in class.

Thus ENL students become successful in class whereas some EFL students become less successful.

7.2.   Field: Outside Class

Students who build up social capital are those who socialize with the other students outside class. Most Danish EFL students are not interested in socializing with foreign students and building up international social capital. This appears from their statements "My network is Danish. I have no contact with former foreign IB students" (Danish, F, Elin). The same applies to the ENL students "I did not do anything to socialize" (Welsh, F). Students being successful outside class are especially EFL students realizing the importance of socialization and intercultural dialogue "When I am with other students, especially with someone close to me then I feel more comfortable to talk to them because I know that they will listen, try to understand me and help me to pronounce the correct way of that word" (Vietnamese, M).

Students who are willing to take part in intercultural dialogue will become successful outside class. Intercultural dialogue enables them to build up social capital. However, EFL students do not necessarily build up international social capital. It requires an effort and willingness to take part in intercultural dialogue. Of course, providers of education can play a crucial role in creating the right spaces for intercultural dialogue to take place for instance by means of the IB-activity CAS (Creativity, Action, Service) aiming to let the student experience the importance of life outside school. Thus different factors can facilitate student access to intercultural dialogue.

8.   Theoretical Considerations: Situated English and Intercultural Dialogue

There are arguments pointing at ELF being situated in the specific context. Furthermore there are studies showing that it might not be an advantage being a native speaker in an ELF context for intercultural dialogue to succeed "native speakers of English may actually be at a disadvantage because—probably for that very reason—they tend not to be very effective communicators in intercultural encounters" (Seidlhofer 2010, 364).

The statements given by ENL students support the above arguments concerning native speakers of English and indicate that it is not only a question of language skills in order to cope in the IB field and participate in intercultural dialogue. IB students develop their own version of English, created, negotiated, and situated in the social interaction between the users/the agents in a specific context and functioning as a contact language and language of communication. This resonates with the statement given by the Welsh, female student:

> The English you develop becomes a different kind of English. I have to regain my British English when I go back to England. It becomes international English or social English or a simplification of the English language. You cannot really associate it with any culture (Welsh, F).

It also resonates with a statement given by an American professor in the IB school: "In certain situations English develops into a specific language, which is understood by the users but not by those having English as a native language."

Brutt-Griffler (as cited in Seidlhofer 2001) states that we need to acknowledge the vital role and authority of ELF users as "agents of language change" (138), which is the case for IB students. They develop a localized and situated version of English, adapted to the specific context and depending on their communicative codes, native languages, and level of English. The version developed can either be considered as non-standard English or give rise to rethinking of language in relation to changing global relations. This supports the view that ELF requires an understanding of language that seeks neither national nor international framings of English, but instead incorporates the local, agency, and context in the users' complex interactions (Pennycook 2010, 684–685). Consequently, successful intercultural dialogue among IB students depends not only on their English language skills but to a great extent on their willingness to participate in intercultural dialogue.

9. Conclusion

The aim and objective of the case study was to examine a space where intercultural dialogue takes place, in this case, an IB context in Denmark. The study shows different student groupings, depending on their language skills, academic knowledge, cultural background and willingness to participate in intercultural dialogue. Seen in relation to Bourdieu's concepts of field (IB spaces: in class, outside class), capital (what students gain) and habitus (what students do), students become "winners" or "losers" (i.e., more or less successful, depending on their ability to build up symbolic capital (academic knowledge, language) and social capital (social competence) in the two different fields: in class and outside class).

EFL student are successful outside class since they are willing to take part in intercultural dialogue and thus build up international social capital. Their academic knowledge and language skills will decide whether they are successful in class. ENL students are successful in class since they are able to build up symbolic capital in terms of academic knowledge. However, they may be less successful outside class because they may not be interested in taking part in intercultural dialogue. Some Danish EFL students are less successful in class due to their lack of language skills and academic knowledge. They may also be less successful outside class if they are not willing to build up international social capital. Consequently, high gain in one space does not necessarily mean high gain in another space.

Some IB students seem to be aware of obstacles such as linguistic obstacles (pronunciation, grammatical mistakes, different connotations, vocabulary) giving rise to confusion and misunderstanding. The most important opportunities mentioned by students are related to improved access to foreign cultures, intercultural dialogue, and education. The study raises the question whether ELF develops into situated English with a cross-cultural foundation and without any institutional framing—a language which is developed in the specific context, and which might be difficult to understand for ENL students. Being an ENL student speaking standard English does not necessarily result in successful intercultural dialogue. Student willingness to communicate with foreigners and the specific spaces of interaction seem to be of great importance for intercultural dialogue to take place. Thus lingua franca English and intercultural dialogue seem to be complex phenomena depending on student attitude, background, language, and space. Successful intercultural dialogue among students in terms of exchanging views and listening to one another requires awareness among educators and students. Educators need to be aware that their roles as educators comprise not only language education but also focus on student background, attitude, and competences. For intercultural dialogue to succeed, different spaces of interaction and listening to student voices are also important aspects for educators to pay attention to.

References

Bourdieu, P. (1998). *Practical reason.* Cambridge: Polity Press.

Bourdieu, P., & Wacquant, L. J. D. (1992). *An invitation to a reflexive sociology.* Chicago: The University of Chicago Press.

Byram, M. (2009). Intercultural competence in foreign language education. In D. Deardorff (Ed.), *The sage handbook of intercultural competence* (pp. 321–332). Thousand Oaks, CA: Sage.

Council of Europe (2010). Speaking across borders: The role of higher education in furthering intercultural dialogue. *Council of Europe Higher Education Series, 16.* Strasbourg: Council of Europe Publishing.

Council of Europe Ministers of Foreign Affairs (2008). *White paper on intercultural dialogue "Living together as equals in dignity."* Strasbourg: Council of Europe.

Firth, A. (1996). The discursive accomplishment of normality. On "lingua franca" English and conversation analysis. *Journal of Pragmatics, 26,* 237–259.

Ganesh, S., & Holmes, P. (2011). Positioning intercultural dialogue—theories, pragmatics, and an agenda. *Journal of international and intercultural communication, 4.*2, 81–86.

International Baccalaureate (n.d.). *Diploma programme curriculum.* Retrieved from www.ibo.org/diploma/curriculum/group1/

Jenkins, J. (2003). *World Englishes.* London: Routledge.

McArthur, T. (1998). *The English languages.* Cambridge: Cambridge University Press.

Melchers, G., & Shaw, P. (2003*). World Englishes.* London: Arnold.

Pennycook, A. (2010). The future of Englishes. One, many or none? In A. Kirkpatrick (Ed.) *The Routledge handbook of world Englishes* (pp. 673–687). New York: Routledge.

Seidlhofer, B. (2001). Closing a conceptual gap: The case for a description of English as a lingua franca. *International journal of applied linguistics, 11*(2), 133–158.

Seidlhofer, B. (2010). Lingua franca English. In A. Kirkpatrick (Ed.) *The Routledge handbook of world Englishes* (pp. 355–371). New York: Routledge.

Stake, R. E. (2000). Case studies In N. L. Denzin & Y. S. Lincoln (Eds.) *Handbook of qualitative research* (pp. 435–454). London: Sage Publications.

Strauss, A., & Corbin, J. (1990). *Basics of qualitative research. Grounded theory procedures and techniques.* London: Sage Publications.

Tarp, G. (2006). Student perspectives in short term study programmes abroad: A grounded theory study. In M. Byram & A. Feng (Eds.) *Living and studying abroad. Research and practice* (pp. 157–185). Clevedon: Multilingual Matters.

Tarp, G. (2011). *Listening to agent agendas in student exchanges—A grounded theory study.* Saarbrücken: Lambert Academic Publishing.

PART IV

Building Dialogue Through Arts and Media

8

Bollywood in the City: Can the Consumption of Bollywood Cinema Serve as a Site for Intercultural Discovery and Dialogue?

Ruma J. Sen

Key Words

- ► Bollywood
- ► Performance of identity
- ► Global capitalism
- ► Media consumption

1. Introduction

Bollywood's new "coolness" (Banker 2001) creates the space for what Clifford calls "political struggles to define the local as distinctive community" (Clifford 1994, 308)—a space distinctly evident in the New York metropolitan area. This is made possible particularly by the post-globalized Indian film industry that has reconstructed its representations to provide a "legitimate" and acceptable image of India, and Indians, for a welcome consumption and recuperation of these images by current generations of Indian Americans—in direct contrast to the image of South Asians floating in Western consciousness since 2001. At the same time, and particularly observable in the New York metropolitan area, the consumption of Bollywood music is no longer exclusive to the Indian American community. New York lounges frequently cater to Bollywood music, the "Masala Bhangra workout" is the hottest item on the fitness circuit, and Bhangra rap and Bollywood music are now synonymous with contemporary Indian music for the average listener. Another significant aspect of the Bollywoodization of the New York metropolitan area has been the immense popularity of Bollywood cinematic heartthrobs performing live to stadiums packed with diasporic and mainstream audiences. This marks a visible shift in Bollywood content from being evocative of nostalgia and desire for "home" to a form of consuming "India" by mainstream audiences.

As part of this research project, I spent several years collecting ethnographic data in the New York–New Jersey metropolitan area. This data comprised of field notes from cultural programs and Bollywood events that I attended, interviews conducted with those attending such events, notes collected from casual conversations I had while watching films with both Indian and American audiences, and finally, extensive interviews with selected participants. A necessary part of this data is comprised of the textual analysis of the films discussed during these interviews and/or viewed as part of the ethnographic process. Drawing from this varied research data, this chapter addresses questions related to both the consumption of Bollywood within the global media economy, and the evolution of a Bollywood cosmopolitan aesthetic emerging in the West. In particular, how do such sites create or facilitate potential intercultural encounters, both as learning and a reflection process. Some of the questions that will be addressed include, what is the currency that Bollywood is able to cash on in recent times that make it an attractive cultural product? What has caused the recent spate in "Bollywoodization" of global pop culture, specifically that of Hollywood and American popular culture? In the process, the paper examines the transnational politics of identity underlying Bollywood's coming of age in Hollywood/USA. Additionally, it explores the politics of visibility of "Indian" culture in the US given the rapidly growing popularity of Bollywood in America.

2. Bollywood Enters Global Consciousness

In the past fifteen years, the Asian American population in the United States has doubled, reaching a total of 12.3 million (14 million if mixed Asian Americans were included). At the same time, emerging trends in the fashion and cultural industry have reinforced the status of Bollywood as "the new cool." The last decade witnessed several milestones in the emergence of the Bollywood aesthetic in the West. For instance, the movie *Bend It Like Beckham* was a surprise hit in theaters, Nicole Kidman's Indian-inspired earrings made headlines at the Golden Globes, and Ashton Kutcher got a little Kama Sutra at New York's K lounge. Thus, the content of the margins have now come emerged to occupy center-stage. For instance, in summer 2005, the American small screen sizzled with Indian movies—Turner Classic Movies screened a twelve-film festival dedicated to Bollywood, described in *USA Today* as "India's colorful, over-the-top film genre." The Sundance Channel gave Indian cinema a showcase with the series "Bollywood Boulevard" July 18 to 20 (9:00 p.m. ET/PT). On July 13, 2005, National Public Radio featured a story on this new America that needs to acknowledge the growing influence of Asian Americans on American pop culture market.

In 2007, the first 24-hour English language American television network for South Asians called American Desi was launched as part of the DISH network. Soon afterward, MTV Networks announced the launch of MTV World, with separate channels targeted at South Asian Americans, Chinese Americans, and Korean Americans. These major developments occurred primarily in response to this trend described above, and a testament to the increasingly diverse and multi-cultural nature of the US, as described by Judy McGrath of MTV Networks. Explaining their own initiative of launching MTV2's channel targeted at South Asians, MTV Desi, McGrath explains this endeavor as "the next logical step for MTV Networks, delivering customized programming that reflects the identities of these audiences, not to mention providing another platform for all the great talent from these communities" (Rajghatta, 2004). In the words of Nusrat Durrani, chief of MTV Desi at its inception, "we are at a moment in time where young Asian Americans want to see themselves on television . . . we want this platform to be a mirror for them." Speaking of making it accessible to a mainstream audience, he comments, "we do want these channels to be windows to the rest of America into these fascinating cultures and we are working towards that very deliberately to make these accessible to whoever is interested" (Syndell 2005).

I must acknowledge here the overtly kitschy and essentialized nature of much of these representations—such remonstrations continue with *The Namesake* in 2007, Brad Pitt and Angelina Jolie experience an Indian summer shooting for *A Mighty Heart*, and the Imaginasian Theater in New York City provides movies from South Asia as a staple for NY moviegoers. None of these ventures however mark an acknowledgment of the breadth of Indian diasporic experiences; instead they mark an Indian consciousness that is still tinged with the element of the exotic. For those like Durrani and others from the Indian American community this serves as an unequivocal approval of a multicultural America that is in equal parts culturally enlightened and politically apathetic, or blind.

2.1. Music and Dance as Conduits for Cultural Exchange

Bhangra (a cultural practice involving music and dance) is part of a rich cultural tradition of Punjab in northern India and is historically associated with the harvest festival. However, in its current iteration Bhangra is symbolic of the global flow of a local tradition that has gained immense popularity as the hybrid music produced in Britain by British Asian music producers through mixing Punjabi folk melodies with western pop and African/Caribbean dance rhythms.

Bhangra has been a cultural staple of Indian immigrant communities globally, particularly in the large Punjabi communities in the UK. However, in recent times, with hybridization and influences from hip-hop, rap, and other musical genres, Bhangra has found a prominent place in the international music scenes. As such, Basement Bhangra (popularized by DJ Rekha, Basement Bhangra is the New York version of contemporary British pub music) is no longer a phenomenon exclusive to clubs, parties, and weddings, but reaches homes in the form of workout videos and weekly doses of televised Indian programming every Saturday morning. Most importantly, Bollywood Nights, or concerts of enormous proportions are a staple of every season in and around NYC, the most famous of them being the Bollywood Awards nights held in Atlantic City and concerts featuring megastars like Shah Rukh Khan, one of the most recognizable faces in the world.

The transformative power of music in recreating social spaces is most evident through the ever-rising popularity of what is generally known as "desi" music. Desi music provides young Indian Americans, both first and second generation, with a self-affirming and empowering bond of commonality, and a public statement of their place in mainstream American youth culture, and allows them to create their own "cool pose." Drawing on Lavie and Swedenburg's (1996) concept of "third time-spaces" this transcultural consumption of Bollywood allows second generation Indian Americans to create a space that is both distinctly their own and yet "consumable" by mainstream audiences. The sought-after nature of Bollywood thus allows the Indian American youth to position themselves as brokers of this cultural commodity, and the spaces within which Bollywood is consumed (like the multiplexes and theaters where movies and concerts are staged) become their own third time-space. Thus, Bollywood's new coolness creates the space for what Clifford calls "political struggles to define the local as distinctive community" (Clifford 1994, 308). This is made possible particularly by the post-globalized Indian film industry that has reconstructed its representations to provide a much more "legitimate" and acceptable image of Indian Americans, for a more welcome consumption and recuperation of these images by the current generations of Indian Americans.

While most consumption of Indian music by mainstream America, including second generation Indians is still largely dominated by Bhangra rap, Bollywood music is making its inroads into this market, due to the rapid proliferation of the market for remixes of old and new Bollywood music by DJs. Introduced largely once again in cities like NYC by highly popular DJs like DJ Rekha and DJ Suhail (whose popularity now overshadow any single Bollywood album or song, singer, or songwriter), this version of music allows, as Dietrich writes, for young Indians in Chicago to create "a self-affirming and empowering bond of commonality, and a public statement of their place in mainstream American youth culture." (1999)

I would like to briefly mention "the world tour" organized a few years ago titled *Temptations 2004* featuring none other than Shah Rukh Khan (internationally recognized Bollywood icon, the reigning superstar of Hindi cinema) and a host of other big names from Bollywood. While I attended this event with the expectation of being surrounded by my fellow desis, the sheer volume of attendees and the range of communities and ethnicities represented at the filled-to-capacity auditorium astounded me. The profound experience of watching Bollywood megastars sitting next to a group of Hispanic women who knew the lyrics of the latest SRK songs left an indelible impression in my mind of the far-reaching consequences of the mainstreaming of Bollywood. I was most curious about the visible shift in the target audience for Bollywood as being consumed largely by first generation Indian Americans as evocative of nostalgia and desire for "home" to a form of consuming "India" by mainstream audiences.

Since then, there have been several such events (although none with the reigning superstar) but interestingly titled, Rockstars 2006—particularly interesting since these rock stars can only lip-sync, and Incredibles 2007. The Incredibles 2007 tour included actual musical stars, but garnered a lot less hype reinforcing the mythical or cult status of some Bollywood megastars. While these concerts or mega events are promoted largely to South Asian audiences, interestingly enough mainstream (mostly white) audience continue to throng these shows, either by virtue of having been exposed to Bollywood through friends or some other source of pop culture.

2.2. Shah Rukh Khan—A Cross-Cultural Phenomenon

"The Big Apple was a big hit in Bollywood's latest blockbuster!" claims a press release on the New York City Mayor's Office website. Referring to local news items, the Mayor's website states that the film *Kal Ho Na Ho* (*Tomorrow May Never Come*, 2003) is the first Indian film to be archived in the library of the Academy of Motion Picture Arts and Sciences. Quoting the director of the film Nikhil Advani, who considers the city of New York to have actually been presented as "the fourth character in the love story" the website lists the locations used in this film that include the Fulton Ferry Landing, Union Square Park, Columbus Circle, Brooklyn College, and the Regent Hotel. It also mentions the phenomenal box office success of this film as well as the awards won at Indian and international festivals. The fourth character of the film is referenced not just in the locales, but in the popular images of Indian restaurants dotting the Manhattan skyline, Jackson Heights or any other Asian Indian ethnic enclave in the boroughs of New York. The characters of this film weld seamlessly to reinforce the image of an Indian walking the streets of NYC as inherent, assumed, and even essential.

Bollywood megastar Shah Rukh Khan is one of the main protagonists of this film. The image of him with outstretched hands (the one that is featured on the Mayor's Office website and on the cover of the DVD) is perhaps the most recognizable association for Indians with the Brooklyn Bridge. It will not be an exaggeration to say that Indians are a lot more likely to recognize the bridge as a backdrop for SRK/KHNH than they may have otherwise been prior to this film. However his face has been a familiar feature in the city long before this film. He is not just the leading superstar in India, but for Indians everywhere, and as recent studies and news reports reveal, his iconic status crosses national boundaries and affects Indians everywhere.

His growing popularity among New Yorkers of all colors, denominations, and ethnicities has been fed by several factors: his films run to packed houses at the Loews in Times Square, he regularly performs at "Bollywood shows" in the city, he is even spotted around town every so often promoting either a film, or sometimes simply himself! The second-generation Indian American population's growing contact with, and affinity toward Bollywood films and music has over time, fueled this frenzy. They consume Bollywood as an affirmation of their hyphenated identity; in turn, they introduce their American counterparts to this cultural phenomenon, thus contributing to its surging popularity within the mainstream population.

It is therefore not a surprise that during my weekly dose of "desi" TV on Saturday morning, I hear the following words coming from a blonde female on screen: "My name is Jennifer but my friends call me Jaswinder. I LOVE Punjabi culture and I love Bhangra..." She continues confidently, "I think I can easily pass off as a Punjabi in Punjab." She is asked by the VJ, "Have you been to India?" "Yes, to Bombay . . ." and asked whether she has a boyfriend, "possibly someone in Bombay!" (AVS show, September 2009)

In a recent visit to Afghanistan, an American colleague had an interesting encounter with Bollywood. She and her partner who is an Afghan-American were in the country shooting a film about an Afghan-American's return to the war-torn country. She describes vividly her interview with a Mujahideen fighter as she finds him surrounded by AK-47's and other guns, and a tiny television playing the latest Bollywood blockbuster. What follows is an incredible experience in identity mediation; where the Mujahideen fighter speaks of his affinity to Bollywood particularly due to the leading actor, Shah Rukh Khan, whom he believes to be of Afghan origin! Alongside, there is the unique moment of nostalgia created for the filmmaker who is visibly moved by the sight of the Brooklyn Bridge—a recurrent image in that film set in New York City: *Kal Ho Na Ho* (*Tomorrow May Never Come*, 2003). She is overwhelmed with homesickness as she sees New York City and tearfully misses "home."

In this moment Bollywood generates a new kind of rendering of home/nation, no longer limited to the Indian diaspora elsewhere but for a traveling American in Afghanistan! The global and the local intersect in multiple ways to construct new forms of mediated identity. Bollywood thus transitions into forming a discursive site where identities are performed, cultural understanding is negotiated, and most of all a global ethos of cultural consumption is standardized.

2.3. Icons, Spectacles, and the Performative in Bollywood Films

Visual representations of the West are no longer essentialized into distinct dichotomies of good and evil. West is no longer simply synonymous with all that is decadent and amoral as it was in the movies even as recently as the nineties. Today, as Bollywood increasingly caters to a transnational audience, particularly the diasporas, visual and textual representations of the West which is now more "familiar" than "foreign," provide the framework for identity construction that is both global and local at the same time, Indian in spirit and transnational in character. Therefore, increasingly, the main characters in these films occupy that middle ground and perform these disjunctured identities and legitimate this new in-betweenness. Just as in such re-reading of the self and other, home and nation are also re-evaluated and re-presented.

Whether in the use of flags (both Indian and American) as symbolically marking a diasporic identity (*Kal Ho Na Ho*, 2003), or the elements of the earth—presented in a box of spices—as representing an Indian's connection to the homeland (*Swades*, 2004, or even the national anthems used both as background and central element (*Kabhi Khushi Kabhi Gham*, 2001), each of these films strategically use visual and textual elements to mark the dichotomies and tensions that influence identities in disjuncture. In turn, these elements also effectively construct homes and nations, and mark the scope for multiple identities. Such complexities in identity construction reveal the potential for multiple readings of the dichotomies for audiences, and in turn provide the space for Indian, diasporic, and global mainstream audiences to engage with Bollywood films.

Bollywood has made a significant shift in its representation of East-West in recent years, moving beyond the frame of East/home equals all that is good and familiar, and the West/other equals negative and strange. West is no longer strange, it is now presented as a place that allows one to be comfortably both Indian and Western (more specifically, British or American). It is important to note that despite such acknowledgment of the power of diasporic audiences and changing times, these films continue to preface tradition over modernity, and equate the ideal with constructs such as "good moral values," usually (re)presented on the body of the woman.

Whether in *Kabhi Khushi Kabhi Gham* (2000) or in *Kal Ho Na Ho* (2003) markers of a western lifestyle (London, New York City) are presented as blending seamlessly with Indian cultural traditions of weddings, religious festivities, and the family that is most important of all. It must be noted here that both visual cues (such as the song and dance sequences) and the textual messages (presented through the dialogues) are most significant in their references to being "Indian" and "American" or "Western" that are presented in limited and limiting forms—invariably affluent, inevitably or obliquely Hindu. Therefore, at their core such representations affirm "tradition" over all else.

In *Kal Ho Na Ho* (*If Tomorrow Never Comes*, 2003) the film opens with images and description of New York through the voice of the female protagonist—not just as a place but as a fourth main character of the film. Each main character is introduced, so is New York City (NYC). In fact, NYC is the first character to be introduced, through visually compelling images that both construct NYC as a place where Indians seek to belong ("Every fourth face here is Indian"), and as a space that is universal and can hold multiple meanings for those viewing the images—of the Brooklyn Bridge, the yellow cabs, Times Square, and Central Park. Subsequent scenes include: Wall Street's famous bronze bull, Water's Edge restaurant, Union Square station, Fulton Ferry landing, Columbus Circle.

Such markers of this global space evoke a range of emotions, and semiotically construct for audiences and characters alike, being both Indian and American. Following this opening, there are several recurring images—Brooklyn Bridge and Brooklyn Bridge Park, Central Park, Times Square, and the yellow cab—these images are used so frequently because they are the most recognizable images for the Indian diaspora everywhere and for Indians "back home."

Through song lyrics, dialogues, and images all cultures are caricatured and stereotyped, albeit fondly. While Indian boys come to the US to marry women to get Green Cards, they also bring with them the "good luck" and kind benevolence of "back home." What is remarkable is the effortless ease with which these images and lyrics offer Bollywood's reading of Indian life in New York (in this instance), where break-dancing youth join in on a Bollywood-style dance set that includes a gospel choir! Such song sequences are representations of desire and imagination—ingredients that appeal to audiences transnationally, and are therefore able to overcome linguistic and cultural barriers.

After the milestone of *Kal Ho Na Ho*, how does the trend move forward? In more recent films, the diaspora is no longer being showcased nor are the locations exalted. The diaspora is now made commonplace and so are its locations. In *Kabhi Alvida Na Kehna* (*Never Say Goodbye,* 2009) the story is set entirely in the US—New York and Philadelphia—no longer as exotic locations but as an integral part of the story and woven into the development of the characters. It is important to note here that it is no longer just the big banners like Dharma Productions and Yashraj Films, but many of the smaller production houses use the same landscapes and similar plots that pivot on a range of diasporic experiences. Now the story takes center-stage where infidelity and extra-marital relations get a treatment that is given the diasporic/"western" edge—no longer ensconced within the framework of morality (as in Bollywood movies of even a few years ago).

Noteworthy is the seeming lack of taxi drivers, sweepers, maids, and dishwashers of Indian origin from the cinematic frames of any such "diaspora oriented" films. This raises an important question about diasporic audiences and what they seek to consume of the Indian cultural industry. The focus has now shifted to a more mature, sophisticated treatment of struggles in diasporic life; however this is exclusive to the affluent community. This exclusive focus on the rich Indian diaspora is significant because of what is absent from this discussion—the working class within the diaspora—the invisible element in the diasporic rubric—an invisibility that is as pronounced in the mainstream culture and media's lens on the South Asian diaspora, as it is a marked absence from any looking-glass representation of the diasporic self. This raises a question significant to exploring the diasporic audience as living with blinders and the role of the American Dream in this equation.

Another interesting factor with diasporic audiences is the apathy toward films made by upcoming critically acclaimed directors who focus on socially relevant issues particularly in India. The diasporic audience is eager to experience the "fantastic realism" of Bollywood films as evident in the box office returns of recent films. Some of the films under the Yashraj

Banner and Dharma Productions manage to garner more revenue in the US and UK than even in India. In contrast, some recent critically acclaimed films like *Black Friday* (Anurag Kashyap, 2007), *Life in a Metro* (Anurag Basu, 2007) barely register on the diasporic radar.

2.4. Consuming Bollywood: From Diaspora to Mainstream Audiences

Consuming Bollywood makes one "authentic" Indian—the diasporic struggle for authenticity in identity and in-betweenness is heightened for second generation Indian Americans through their contentious relations with Bollywood. One of the most visible outcomes have been the recent proliferation of Indian Americans who now produce, direct, even act in films that are typically caught in the angst of the duality of their identities. Often these films are also spoofs of Bollywood films, which in turn only reinforce the iconic quality of Bollywood. Bollywood films have thus taken on a life of their own; the film mania has created a demand for the cultural industry itself, spawning Bollywood inspired fashion endorsed by the elite of Hollywood, subsequently adapted for mass consumption by Bloomingdales and Marshall's alike. Not surprisingly then, last year witnessed the launch of Earth-NYC. Its claim to fame was the ethnic interior design conceived by one of the leading Bollywood fashion designers, Manish Malhotra, who was commissioned to specifically infuse Bollywood into the interiors of what is now one of the most hip and upscale night-spots in Chelsea, NYC!

As Bollywood continues to grow in its popularity within the diaspora, and in mainstream America, there are some outcomes that are heartening just as there are other negative consequences. In Passaic County, New Jersey, public schools were closed in November 2005 to celebrate the Hindu festival, Diwali. National and regional newspapers, including *New York Times* covered local celebrations of Diwali on their front pages. However, as has been addressed in previous research (Ram 2008), much of these celebrations are enactments of scenes from the latest Bollywood blockbuster. Bollywood films have made their way into a Trivial Pursuit style board game as well.

Bollywood abroad is therefore no longer the fiefdom of migrant Indians. Mainstream (White, Latino, African, Caribbean) audiences in the US actively participate in the consumption of this cultural industry. Besides the experience of sitting next to Latino women at the Temptations concert while they sang all of Shah Rukh Khan's songs, as part of my ethnographic experience, more recently I have watched Bollywood films in the company of many non-Indian colleagues and friends. Some typical comments include, albeit with vociferous declarations of love/adoration of Bollywood, that these films are "unabashedly melodramatic, sentimental, and unrealistic" "over-the-top kitchy" "cheesy" and my favorite, "it's just so strange." The key question is: what is it that they seek to consume in the name of Indian movies/Bollywood and why? What do Bollywood movies serve up that Hollywood fails to supply—for instance, the ability to romanticize and fantasize about love and life—formalism/fantasy versus realism.

2.5.   Bollywood as a Discursive Site

Bollywood texts have thus long served as sites for cultural dialogue, understanding, and exchange. From its inception, Bollywood has remained inspired by western cinema, and Hollywood in particular, and the former masters of Bollywood have unabashedly copied stories, plotlines, themes, and locations from films as broad-ranging as the wild Western to the slapstick comedy genres. However, the "romantic" in Bollywood is unique to its own cultural constructions of being Indian and the associated aspirations of a young, dynamic, simultaneously modern and traditional, "authentic" Indian. Desai and Dudrah (2008) refer to Bollywood as "a mode of production, a way of producing culture within a national and global context that is inextricably linked to the Indian nation-state and the postcolonial economy of liberalization" (2).

Bollywood is made synonymous with Indian cinema for audiences outside India, despite films being made in thirty different languages and dialects. The "portability and mobility of song and dance sequences outside of the film itself" into other forms of media (ex., radio, video, television, digital media, live performance, etc.) is an important aspect of not only the success of Bollywood films to move through cultural and linguistic barriers, it is also critical to the development of media and cultural technologies in South Asia that facilitate this portability through websites that cater to all kinds of audiences (Desai & Dudrah 2008, 11). According to Amit Khanna of Plus Channel, non-Indian audiences are attracted to Indian movies for their "feel-good, all-happy-in-the-end, tender love stories with lots of songs and dances" (Rajadhyaksha 2008, 23).

In their seemingly uncomplicated cross-fertilization of an Indian ethos and sensibility with Western stories and themes, Bollywood films have long provided for western audiences, what an avid Caucasian American viewer of such films in the New York metropolitan area calls "guilty pleasures of watching mindless moralistic stories that are full of fantasy and make-believe, handsome hunks and gorgeous women" (Interview Participant, 2009). It is interesting to consider—within the context of cultural learning—what exactly is learned here about both India and an "Indian" reading of the West. Yet again, there is according to Daya Thussu, still hope in the future. As he rightly observes, "in an era of the Pentagon-declared "long war" against "terrorism," Indian cinema and its culture may emerge as an important corrective to the excesses of Hollywood's representation of the Islamic "other"" (2008, 111) as evidenced in films like New York, *My Name is Khan*, and *Kurbaan*, to name a few Bollywood films that address these issues.

One of the most coveted and awarded "feel-good" films of last year, *Zindagi Na Milegi Dobara* (ZNMD, 2011, trans. *Life does not always give you second chances*), triumphed at the box-office and garnered rave reviews from critics. Indian and mainstream audiences flocked to see Bollywood actors in a road-movie perform alongside Maria del Mar Fernandez, a Spanish flamenco singer in the song titled "Senorita." Filmed extensively in Spain, this film could easily serve up as a promotional video for Tourism Espana as towns across Spain and their festivals such as the La Tomatina festival and the Encierro (Running of the Bulls) were presented as visual and cultural treats. While the film remains an example of the immense and lasting impact of globalization on Bollywood film content and style, it serves also as a reminder that through filmic composition appreciation of other cultures can occur, and the strange can be made familiar. At the same time, the film serves as a reminder that the margins of global popular culture like Bollywood can fold into the center of mainland Europe where flashmobs can dance to the Senorita song in Barcelona, and Shah Rukh Khan can draw frenzied mobs in Amsterdam. It also makes possible the imagination of a world where the center-margin dichotomy itself can be disrupted—a world where the New York premiere of *The Great Gatsby* finds Amitabh Bachchan—the living legend of Bollywood—drawing larger crowds and more hysteria than the likes of Leonardo DiCaprio. India has now become fashionable on the global screen, and Bollywood is without a doubt "the new cool."

3. (Re)presenting India to the World

Not everyone is thrilled that India is fashionable today. The inevitable concern is: everything that is cool today fades into oblivion tomorrow. "I'm a person, not a fashion statement," Parminder Nagra of *Bend It Like Beckham* fame commented in an interview in 2003. "For me, being Indian is just a label. It honestly makes me cringe if people think it's trendy to be Indian, and tomorrow it's all over" (Nagra, as quoted in Freydkin, 2003). What began as Madonna's cache in the nineties has grown exponentially in recent years, but what happens to this new hip India when things Indian are no longer hip. In the meantime however, Bollywood continues to determine how India and being Indian gets constructed for the average American.

Perhaps the most precarious consequence of this trend is the construction of India as a Hindu nation, with Hindu people celebrating Hindu traditions. While Diwali continues to be celebrated in India in its most secular representations, Bollywood has co-opted it into a mediated representation that is essentialist in its religiosity. Consequently, a secular reading of India becomes increasingly untenable within the mainstream just as much as it is rare today among Indians in the United States. Besides conflating a Hindu-Bollywood with a Hindu India, such constructions of India erase the scope for all other forms of being Indian, particularly in relation to social class, social mobility, and hierarchies, both in India and within the Indian diaspora. Consequently, a secular reading of India becomes increasingly improbable, as alternative or competing discourses to the ones floated by Bollywood do not exist in the global consciousness. There are no points of entry for the historically significant discourse of India as secular in the popular consciousness of today—a national identity borne out of a postcolonial struggle drawn on the lines of factionalism and religious separatism. Contemporary relevance of such a secular identity is particularly significant in a post-9/11 world, one that Indians have acutely felt across the globe. However, in the past few decades Bollywood films have made mainstream an essentially north Indian Hindu identity, as noted by several recent books (Dudrah & Desai 2008; Kavoori & Punathambekar 2008).

This essay has thus far explored the transcultural consumption of Bollywood cinema across global urban spaces as a "site" to study intercultural discovery and dialogue. According to the Council of Europe Ministers of Foreign Affairs (2008), "Intercultural dialogue is understood as a process that comprises an open and respectful exchange of views between individuals and groups with different ethnic, cultural, religious and linguistic backgrounds and heritage, on the basis of mutual understanding and respect. It requires the freedom and ability to express oneself, as well as the willingness and capacity to listen to the views of others. Intercultural dialogue contributes to political, social, cultural and economic integration and the cohesion of culturally diverse societies." (17). More recently, popular art and cultural forms have served very effectively as sites where intercultural exchange can occur, through sharing and learning about diverse cultural norms and practices. However, the quality of this exchange is tempered or influenced by those participating in these sites.

In the case of Bollywood serving as a site for intercultural exchange, what gets exchanged is a convenient consumption of culture and cultural artifacts, regardless of any reflection on the political, economic, or social consequences of such consumption, both for those who consume and in whose name these products are produced. A global capitalist consumerist economy is maintained, and culture is subsumed within the overwhelming structural limitations of a revenue-driven industry. While other forms of regional/national cinema like that from Iran, China, Italy, or France circulate in the form of "film as culture" Indian cinema (now conflated with a specific form like Bombay cinema, or Bollywood) is consumed as a cultural commodity, as part of a globally circulated Indian cultural industry. Therefore, the value of what constitutes as Indian cinema moves from the realm of cinema as a sublime art form to kitschy, consumable pop culture.

References

Akhtar, Z. (Director). (2011). *Zindagi na milegi dobara* [Film]. Mumbai: Excel Entertainment.

Banaji, Shakuntala (2006). *Reading 'Bollywood': The young audience and Hindi films*. New York: Palgrave Macmillian.

Banker, A. (2001). *Bollywood*. London: Oldcastle Books.

Clifford, J. (1994). Diasporas. *Cultural Anthropology, 9*(3): 302–338.

Council of Europe Ministers of Foreign Affairs (2008). *White paper on intercultural dialogue "Living together as equals in dignity."* Strasbourg: Council of Europe. Desai, J., & Dudrah, R. (2008). The essential Bollywood. In R. Dudrah & J. Desai (Eds.), *The Bollywood reader* (pp. 1–20). New York: Open University Press.

Dietrich, G. (1999). Desi music vibes: The performance of Indian youth culture in Chicago. *Asian Music* 31, 35–61.

Dudrah, R., & Desai, J. (Eds.) (2008). *The Bollywood reader*. New York: Open University Press.

Dudrah, Rajinder K. (2006). *Sociology goes to the movies*. New Delhi: Sage Publications.

Freydkin, D. (June 4, 2003). India spicing up American fashion, movies. *USA Today*. Retrieved from http://usatoday30.usatoday.com/life/2003-06-04-india_x.htm

Gowariker, A. (2004). *Swades: We, the people* [Film]. Mumbai: UTV Motion Pictures.

Johar, K. (Producer & Director). (2001). *Kabhi Khushi Kabhi Gham* [Film]. Mumbai: Dharma Productions.

Johar, K. (Producer & Director). (2003). *Kal Ho Na Ho* [Film]. Mumbai: Dharma Productions.

Johar, K. (Producer & Director). (2006). *Kabhi Alvida Na Kehna* [Film]. Mumbai: Dharma Productions.

Juluri, V. (2003). *Becoming a global audience: Longing and belonging in Indian music television*. New York: Peter Lang Publishing.

Lavie, S., & Swedenburg, T. (1996). Introduction: Displacement, diaspora, and geographies of identity. In S. Lavie & T. Swedenburg (Eds.), *Displacement, diaspora, and geographies of identity* (pp. 1–26). Durham, NC: Duke University Press.

Kavoori, A. P., & Punathambekar, P. (Eds.), (2008). *Global Bollywood*. New York: NYU Press.

Punathambekar, A., & Kavoori, A. P. (2008). Introduction: Global Bollywood. In A. P. Kavoori and A. Punathambekar (Eds.), *Global Bollywood* (pp. 17–40). New York: NYU Press.

Rai, A. S. (2009). *Untimely Bollywood: Globalization and India's new media assemblage*. Durham: Duke University Press.

Rajadhyaksha, A. (2008). The "Bollywoodization" of the Indian Cinema: Cultural nationalism in a global arena. In R. Dudrah and J. Desai (Eds.), *The Bollywood Reader* (pp. 190–200). New York: Open University Press.

Rajghatta, C. (2004, December 15). Now, watch desi TV in America. *The Times of India*. Retrieved from http://timesofindia.indiatimes.com/world/Now-watch-desi-TV-in-America/articleshow/959947.cms

Ram, A. (2008). Bollywood and globalization: Reassembling gender and nation in Kal Ho Na Ho. In M. Meyers (Ed.), *Women in popular culture: Representation and meaning* (2nd Ed) (pp. 137–150). New York: Hampton Press.

Syndell, L. (2005, July 13). MTV promotes Asian pop music in U.S. *NPR Music*. Retrieved from http://www.npr.org/templates/story/story.php?storyId=4751394

Thussu, D. K. (2008). The globalization of Bollywood: The hype and hope. In A. P. Kavoori and A. Punathambekar (Eds.), *Global Bollywood* (pp. 97–116). New York: NYU Press.

9

Storms, Lies, and Silence: Notes towards a Non-Dialogic Mode of Intercultural Contact

David Gunn

Key Words

- ► Intercultural contact
- ► Silence
- ► Experience
- ► Moments of misunderstanding
- ► Art
- ► Participation

1. Preamble

"Yes, we understand"

Pov Punisa, Khmer musician in conversation with the English author

Sitting on the floor of a Phnom Penh studio, the conversation stumbling in a no-mans-land between English and Khmer, Punisa and I both trying to "make ourselves understood," and enthusiastically claiming to understand the other. So caught up in this urge to communicate that we did not recognize that our attempts at understanding were creating a barrier. Failing to understand that there was something of value here beyond understanding.

The observations contained within this paper emerge from my own experience as the director of Incidental, an interdisciplinary organization that has spent the last seven years working on cultural projects that combine aspects of experimental sound, new media, community activism, and participatory artwork. Although diverse in format, these projects share a commitment to explore forms of creativity that are either ignored or sidelined within more traditional gallery-based art exhibitions, installations, and performances. This work has taken place in a range of geographies and contexts—including documentary sound projects in Manila City (Philippines) and Manchester's Moss Side (UK), artistic interventions within deprived community housing projects in Phnom Pehn and participatory new media work in the South Wales valleys and the Lower East Side of Manhattan (USA).

This paper is not written by an academic theorist or researcher, but by a practitioner with more than a passing interest in both direct experience of and theoretical approaches to participation and collaboration. Accordingly the chapter does not seek to develop a finished conceptual model or framework, but rather to document the process of my own thinking as it has evolved in response to the experience of particular projects. In particular, it focuses upon my own experiences of the frictions within and resistances to dialogue-based models of intercultural projects. To begin, I seek to consider in some detail the assumptions contained within the phrase "intercultural dialogue," and to question the extent to which intercultural contact must be conceived as a process of dialogue. I then go on to explore how the complex assumptions within this phrase are manifested within the arts, before exploring how we might conceptualize forms of intercultural creative experience that resist conventional models of communicative exchange.

2.   Contact Situations

When undertaking creative projects that have an intercultural dimension the spectre of understanding is never far away. In moments where we come into contact with those who exhibit different linguistic patterns or worldviews to our own, the desire to establish common areas of understanding and exchange seems a very basic human urge. Tacitly, such contact situations are routinely perceived and evaluated according to the degree to which communicative exchange is achieved—to what extent do we understand, and are we able to make ourselves understood? Although most obvious at an individual level, such common and apparently natural assumptions are also echoed at a range of institutional and cultural levels—with vast programs of work devoted to the fostering of dialogue and understanding between cultures and geographic regions.

But to what extent are such assumptions inevitable? When exploring the dynamics of intercultural dialogue, should we not first question why dialogue itself is seen as the pre-eminent form of inter-cultural experience? Is it possible to conceive of other forms of such experience? What qualities might they have? And what forms of personal and inter-personal experience might be eclipsed and overshadowed by our obsession with dialogue?

In order to examine such questions, it quickly becomes necessary to challenge the very use of the phrase "intercultural dialogue"—since such a phrase clearly establishes linguistic models as the primary means by which to frame and evaluate intercultural experiences. Accordingly, throughout this paper we use a more neutral concept of "intercultural contact," by which we simply mean a moment when individuals from different cultural backgrounds come into contact with one another. The degree to which such contact experiences can or should be explained according to linguistic models of dialogue is one of the key concerns of this paper.

Although this paper is concerned primarily with the limitations of experience under-stood within the framework of dialogue, it is worth acknowledging that the notion of an "intercultural" experience itself is open to question. For me, it is a word that reverberates with the values and experiences of a previous age, with images of structured contact between coherent groups, shadows of Cortés on the beach of Veracruz, or the ghost of Malinowski exploring the Trobriands in starched whites. Such mental models of firm boundaries and borders may be less than helpful for both practitioners and theorists in a world where complex and multiple forms of diversity both surround and exist within us all. In my own experience, moments of profound and stark difference have occurred as frequently upon my own doorstep as they have in foreign lands. In the inaugural pages of Hau journal, David Graeber proposed a way in which modern anthropology might depart from its original function as a means through which the West sought to understand (and frequently subjugate) other cultures and traditions. For Graeber, a twenty-first century anthropology will operate not only to foster understanding of an unfamiliar Other, but will use this understanding as a means to turn the gaze back upon itself, recognizing that which surrounds the reader in their own everyday life as unfamiliar and strange (Graeber et al. 2011). This paper is written with a similar intention in mind. For although we are concerned initially with ideas of intercultural contact, the themes I explore will be shown to be equally relevant for other forms of interaction. As I consider both the undervalued and unrecognized qualities of intercultural contact, I intend to do so in a way that provokes a more general re-evaluation of "contact experiences" of all kind.

3. The Speech Situation

Before returning to such themes, I'd like to consider the phenomena of "intercultural dia-logue" itself in some detail, a phrase patterning that appears so frequently in contemporary literature that its terms appear almost inseparable, with each mention of "intercultural" followed inevitably by words such as dialogue, exchange, understanding. It seems our notion of intercultural contact is almost ineluctably understood within terms of linguistic dialogue, a dialogic exchange that results in an enriched understanding of the Other. Why is this the case?

At least part of the reason for this may be that as a whole, the broader context of the social sciences within which intercultural studies exists abounds in models of dialogue, from Habermas' neoplatonic "ideal speech situation," an emphatically fictive "ideal form" of interpersonal dialogue where meaning is exchanged without distortion (Habermas 1987), to Gadamer's framing of dialogue as the negotiation of difference, a means to map the edges of our own preconceptions, "to test out prejudices" and achieve "fusion" of our horizons with those of another (Gadamer 1989). Repeatedly, linguistic exchange remains the metaphorical and conceptual touchstone of inter-personal contact, of co-presence itself. Everything seethes with communicative intent, even when linguistic communication is absent—every inaction is understood to be a latent form of resistance or non-conformism, each silence or aporia revealed to be an articulate site of communication. In the work of Bohm, Factor, and Garrett (1991), the exchange of logos is explicitly contrasted with other forms of physical and musical contact between individuals, with these latter forms seen as secondary, ephemeral. Reflecting on the fundamentals of contact between diverse groups, they state:

> "they can sing, dance or play together with little difficulty but their inability to talk together about subjects that matter deeply to them seems invariably to lead to dispute, division and often to violence. In our view this condition points to a deep and pervasive defect in the process of human thought." (Bohm, Factor, & Garrett 1991)

An inability to talk is a defect. Non-verbal acts of co-presence like singing and dancing are seen as impoverished forms of the speech act, stunted modes of communication that cannot heal social divisions. As so often in the Western canon, we perceive the tense contours of a world founded upon the division of Dionysus and Apollo: on one side looms unruly and unmanageable chaos and on the other stands order, form, and language. In the fabric of Bohm's text, acts such as singing, dancing, and playing slide almost imperceptibly into division and violence and it is only logos that can repair this rift, that can forge order from chaos. Difference is seen not only as the defining characteristic, a "fatal flaw" of human consciousness, but a characteristic that must be overcome by language. In the beginning was the word.

Such assumptions run deep in the Western historical consciousness, and it is not surprising that the reliance upon linguistic models for contact extend to our understanding of the form and function of social and collective experience such as the arts. To take one example, the Council of Europe's Declaration on Intercultural Dialogue states:

> Intercultural dialogue is a process that comprises an open and respectful exchange or interaction between individuals, groups and organisations with differ-

ent cultural backgrounds or world views. Among its aims are: to develop a deeper understanding of diverse perspectives and practices; to increase participation and the freedom and ability to make choices; to foster equality; and to enhance creative processes. (Council of Europe 2008)

Although the emphasis here is different from that of Bohm et al., the trace of logos and its intimate connection to the creative process is once again clear—intercultural dialogue enhances creative processes. Elsewhere, we find its mirror opposite, with creative processes seen as a means to enhance dialogue—from the brash "instrumentalisation" of the arts as a tool to promote cultural dialogue (of which more later) to more subtle examples such as Daniel Barenboim and Edward Said's Weimar Workshop, a utopian act that brought together classical musicians from across the Middle East, and composed of "an orchestral rehearsal every day . . . and at night, several days a week . . . discussions about music, culture, politics" (Barenboim & Said 2004). In this example, music is used as a means to prepare for dialogue and clearly envisaged as a means, however small, to effect change in the world at large.

Although differing in emphasis, the viewpoints of Barenboim and Said (2004) and that of the Council of Europe exist on the same vector, establishing a connective tissue between art and dialogue. Borrowing terms from the work of Frazer (1922), in contemporary Western societies we see art invoked as a form of "imitative magic" to effect enhanced social dialogue, or dialogue presented as a form of "contagious magic" by which to improve the arts. Art enriched by or seeking to attain an ideal speech situation. In either model, the conceptualization of art and dialogue are intimately interlinked and mutually reinforcing.

Such assumptions seem entirely natural, entirely normal. Things are better when people understand each other. An artistic product is judged by what it communicates. And yet, as I undertook and reflected upon a range of our projects, I could not escape the feeling that this idea of a symbiotic, mutually reinforcing relationship between art and dialogue often simply did not provide a useful critical architecture through which to understand or approach our direct experiences on the ground. And this is not to invoke a notion of the "ineffability" of the arts, but simply to note that within my own experiences of intercultural contact, there was something left untouched and ignored in each of these discourses.

4. A Khmer Storm

Cambodia, early May 2009. In the middle of a six-week long international residency undertaken by Incidental in collaboration with one of Cambodia's foremost cultural organizations, Cambodian Living Arts (CLA). The project itself consisted of a series of loose improvised sessions by myself and four classically trained Khmer musicians, culminating in a live performance at the *Centre Culturel Français*, and the subsequent commercial release of the album "Krom Monster" (2011) based upon recordings from these sessions.

There we were one particular morning, sitting on the floor in the humidity of CLA Studio, exploring ways to juxtapose traditional Khmer instrumentation with electronics and improvisation. Three of them spoke no English, one a handful of words and phrases. My Khmer almost completely non-existent and certainly insufficient to the task in hand. I was hoping to experiment with "freer" improvisation, but just couldn't get this idea across, my explanation unnecessarily complex, opaque . . . we were all frustrated. As we paused, I absent-mindedly started previewing a series of recordings on my hard drive, including one recording of storm and rain I had made a few weeks earlier during a thunderstorm. One of the other musicians made a comment I didn't quite understand . . . in trying to respond I explained where the recording came from . . . this explanation itself was met with confusion . . . Then, a sudden flurry of enthusiasm from my Khmer counterparts. I didn't quite follow what was happening—until Punisa translated for me—"Ok, we get it. We need to be the storm! The Gong can be the thunder . . . Tro Sao can be the wind . . . Ksae Diew can be the frogs, and Roneat can be the rain." Not really what I was trying to say—but much more interesting. So they started playing, exploring for the first time in our sessions a very natural and quite beautiful form of collective performance. I did not play along, but left the rains and drones continuing underneath them. Happily, this performance was recorded, and was included almost untouched in the Krom Monster debut album.

That this piece features excellent playing between the Khmer musicians is true, but the core of what matters to us here is simple: that in the exact moment Punisa claimed to "understand" what was being said, she did not—but it was precisely the lack of understanding that made this moment possible. When considering the notion of intercultural dialogue, value is often placed upon lucid exchange of ideas and the ability to communicate. But I am both haunted and energized by moments such as this—instances of profound misunderstanding that stand at the heart of the creative and social experience—something we couldn't have done without. Although inter-cultural projects place a value on moments of exchange and understanding, throughout the Krom Monster project it was frequently these mis-steps, the slippages of meaning in our constant to-and-fro between English and Khmer that were the defining moments—where the collapse of meaning offered a crucial flexibility of action, and an opportunity to step away from the burdens of communication. This was a project that was explicitly focused upon contact between two very different groups and traditions. And yet, where we might expect this to mean an emphasis on dialogue, the moments that mattered most occurred when meaningful signification failed, where language was at its limit, creating an aporia that did not lead towards a resolution, but remained simply "a gap in things." Or to state things more simply—our words did not make sense to each other and that was what made things interesting.

I am aware that these experiences could themselves be instrumentalised by communication theorists, that these silences could be forced to speak. One might suggest that the initial misunderstanding marked a "horizon of understanding" that was then overcome, or constituted the basis of a communicative exchange. This was not the case. Attempts at communication failed. What emerged was a kind of co-presence that did not require understanding. One may seek to impose a communicative model upon music performance, to assert that we were speaking to each other through music. But to what extent can such a sentence itself be understood as anything other than metaphor? And should we not recognize that metaphor itself is perhaps the defining operation of language? To what extent could this sentence be anything more than the imposition of a linguistic model upon what was an emphatically non-linguistic experience? And is not the real problem here that accounts of intercultural contact are too often written by those whose discipline is grounded in a complete faith in the act of writing itself?

In this paper, I have termed experiences like the one I experienced in Cambodia as moments of silence—moments where linguistic operations and communicative exchange collapse or fall away. Such experiences map out a territory that seems foreign to most accounts we have read of inter-cultural dialogue, accounts which remain grounded in a conceptual model of linguistic communication, where the value of events can be assigned precisely according to the degree to which they may be made to "mean" something. In seeking to understand or at least approach moments that step away from this model, Gadamer (1989) and Bohm's (1991) rhapsodies of communication remain entirely silent.

4.1. The Lies I Have Told

In my experience, such moments of silence have not been restricted to moments of contact between individuals who speak different languages. A few months after the completion of the Krom Monster project, I found myself in the north of England, experiencing a very different form of cultural contact, and a very different version of silence. The cultural landscape in the UK during this period was complex and controversial, with arts funding often used to legitimize ambitious schemes of regeneration and gentrification. The arts frequently operated at the vanguard of aggressive urban regeneration, with artists colonizing low-income areas of a city to be swiftly followed by commercial investment. At the same time, the arts also acted as a kind of apologist for these processes via a proliferation of community arts projects that sought to "give voice" to such communities precisely as they were being slowly displaced and destroyed. During this time the arts not only paved the way for the reterritorialisation and gentrification of poorer areas, but also operated to "denude" public critique and discussion about these very processes (Murphy 2012). We should note that it was precisely during this period that funding bodies and artists themselves placed a renewed emphasis upon collaborative and participatory techniques within the creative experience, and the role of the arts to promote self-expression became a zeitgeist encapsulated in works such as Anthony Gormley's Fourth Plinth project "One and Other," which claimed to offer "A living portrait of the nation. A voice for the voiceless" (Gormley 2010).

As an arts organization active in the UK during this time, we struggled with our own complicity in such processes. In one instance, we found ourselves working in Sheffield, negotiating the cultural complexities of working with communities from a very different cultural background to our own, collecting firsthand narratives of local residents upon the site of a recently demolished garden city development. And whilst as an organization we have on several occasions worked with ideas of testimony and remembrance, it is important to recognize that the prevailing emphasis on "real stories" has an ambiguous function. Often seen quite genuinely by practitioners, funders, and audiences as a means to give voice to vulnerable or under-represented groups, the invitation to collect "real stories" also frequently operates to impose identity, with apparently open forms of inter-personal dialogue being used to tacitly reshape the presentation of minority groups and to establish what kinds of narrative and history are understood to be an appropriate representation of a particular area or issue.

In this particular project, we responded quite simply by inviting those we met to speak about their own memories of the area, with the proviso that they could tell the truth or, if they so wished, to tell us complete lies and fabrications. The change this wrought within the project and its internal social dynamics was instructive. Where previous moments of "invited participation" had often felt stilted or problematic, these moments built upon a foundation of lies and mistruths quickly became animated and energized. Participants would lie enthusiastically, overlaying science fiction or fantasy scenarios upon their local environment, or constructing prosaic and credible yet entirely false histories or events set in their community. On occasion, an individual might use a lie to make a clear didactic point. This latter type of lie is certainly the most appealing to communications theory, but during this project it was the exception rather than the rule—and one that obscures the fundamental role that lies seemed to fulfill in this process. For as we progressed, it became clear that for most participants, the lies were not a mode of communication but a tactic of departure. The substance of each lie was less significant than the simple fact of lying itself, the way in which it offered a means to step away from the hegemony of communicative exchange. To step away from the kinds of self-dramatisation and self-narration that vulnerable communities are often asked to engage in by institutions and community artists. A stepping away from the structures of power embodied and enacted in these requests. And perhaps, a stepping-away from the assumption that communication itself should be the pre-eminent goal of community arts. Almost by chance, a door opened to show us that sharing a moment of intercultural contact need not be a moment of dialogue or exchange and indeed could be all the richer for it.

4.2.   Dll rrrrr beeeee bö rrrremarks

The examples from my own practice examined in the previous sections are modest, and deliberately so—these were not large programs of work explicitly designed to challenge traditional forms of intercultural exchange or creativity. Instead, they were moments occurring within relatively conventional structures of intercultural artistic practice—accidental occurrences that suggestively challenged the universality of those very structures. Such moments open out into a territory explored more methodically by a handful of individuals operating at the fringes of contemporary literature over the last century, and concerned specifically with aspects of silence, the collapse of sense and meaning itself in both culture and language. Such writers are a mongrel crowd, writing on the borderlines of gnosis and nihilism—from George Bataille's quest for the inexpressible summit that leads him to state "all communication participates in suicide" (Bataille 2004), to the insistent and perhaps not-altogether serious intent of William Burroughs to "rub out the word" (Burroughs & Gysin 1978), or the incantatory non-sense of Kurt Schwitters' *Ursonate*:

> Fümms bö wö tää zää Uu,
> pögiff,
> kwii Ee.
> Oooooooooooooooooooooooooo,
> dll rrrrr beeeee bö
> dll rrrrr beeeee bö fümms bö,
> rrrrr beeeee bö fümms bö wö,
> beeeee bö fümms bö wö tää,
> bö fümms bö wö tää zää,
> fümms bö wö tää zää Uu:

Even within the scope of a more conservative discipline like literary criticism, we might recognize a kindred spirit in Bloom's dense and allusive "The Anxiety of Influence," as he seeks to challenge models of artistic influence based upon sympathetic understanding with his explosive assertion that great literary works were often forged in processes of misunderstanding, blindness, misprision, swerve, and absence (Bloom 1997).

Although quite distinct in their political and aesthetic frameworks, each of these writers sought to challenge the way in which their societies understood and evaluated ideas of language and the creative experience. Just as I found myself in moments of inter-personal experience that derived no value from the notions of communicative exchange or the "ideal speech situations" of Habermas, Bohm, or Gadamer, these writers explicitly sought to document and to invoke moments where language gives way. *Ursonate* remains one of the more extreme examples in this field, as Schwitters created an auditory and textual experience that remains almost entirely resistant to traditional forms of linguistic or literary analysis. When asked to explain the philosophy behind his own practice, Schwitters wrote:

> "Meaning is only essential if it is to be used as one such factor. I play off sense against nonsense. I prefer nonsense, but that is a purely personal matter. I pity nonsense, because until now it has been so neglected in the making of art, and that's why I love it." (Schwitters 2000)

In other words . . . there are other truths. Even as writers, individuals such as Schwitters, Bataille, and Burroughs display a fundamentally equivocal relationship to writing and to language. Their works are filled with the knowledge that language conceals as much as it communicates, and obfuscates as much as it conveys. And it is because of this deep-seated suspicion that such authors provide a valuable counterpoint to the other theorists discussed in this paper. Bohm and Gadamer remain writers fatally dedicated to the fact of writing, dedicated to the written page as a means to achieve the ideal speech situation. By contrast, these poets and philosophers offer a new approach to the notions of human experience precisely because of the way in which they retain a fundamental sense of ambiguity to the words they speak, using and abusing language as a way to reach beyond language itself, to access other forms of experience.

4.3.   Cave Paintings and the Construction of Silence

Whilst a more comprehensive analysis of these writers remains outside the scope of this paper, such work raises important questions not only about the role of language within contact experiences, but even the origins and purpose of art itself. For some, such origins quickly became an explicit part of their work—seeking out alternative forms of cultural consciousness implicit in Paleolithic cave painting (Bataille 2005) or the numerical cosmologies of the Maya (Burroughs 1992). And indeed, it is not only poetic projects on this theme that offer a provocative perspective upon the relationship between art and dialogue. In his analysis of Paleolithic cave painting, David Lewis-Williams (2002) posits a vision of creative processes and inter-cultural contact that differs radically to those implied in documents such as the Council on Europe's declaration on intercultural dialogue. In his research, Lewis-Williams became fascinated by the fact that some of the key locations of Paleolithic cave art also occurred in areas where there was archaeological evidence of Neanderthal and Homo sapiens living in close proximity. Exploring the possibilities of social contact between both groups, and the disparity between the Neanderthal and Homo sapiens' cognitive capacity for prototypical artistic activity such as the creation of cave painting and portable art, Lewis-Williams (2002) concludes:

> As a result of the type of social relations that developed during the Middle to Upper Paleolithic Transition between Neanderthal and anatomically modern communities . . . mental imagery acquired a new and special layer of significance [amongst Homo sapiens communities] . . . it now became important for those people to fix their images of another world . . . which was one of the key traits that distinguished them from the Neanderthals . . . they created a new kind of society, a new set of social distinctions. Socialized altered consciousness, cosmology, religion, political influence and image-making (the fore-runner of art) all came together in the sort of society that we consider fully modern. Individual people could now use esoteric resources to fashion their personae in relation to their followers. Those resources could be guarded and could thus become a controlled mechanism of social diversity, stratification and exploitation . . . [art in the caves] provided controllable topological templates for mental and social distinctions.

In essence, we have what might be considered the earliest example of "inter-cultural dialogue," occurring contemporaneously with the "birth of art" witnessed by creative projects like *Chauvet cave* and *Les Trois Frères*. In Lewis-Williams' analysis, creative processes themselves were not inherently vehicles for dialogue and exchange. In fact, they were, at their essence, something else entirely. The very "birth of art" may be understood itself as a tool for the creation of otherness, a sharp delineation of difference, a form of creative expression valued precisely not for its opportunity for dialogue, but for the way in which it provokes silence and incomprehension in the Paleolithic Other.

In contrast to contemporary perspectives upon inter-cultural contact that see the arts as a conduit for dialogue and harmony, the Paleolithic experience forces us to consider its opposite: that the creative experience can also operate as a construction of difference, a process of violence and complicity. Or as Walter Benjamin caustically asserted, "there is no document of civilization that is not at the same time a document of barbarism" (Benjamin 1999).

5.   Towards a Beginning

Where does this leave us? At the beginning of this paper, we reviewed a range of sources to demonstrate the ways in which the concept of dialogue remains the predominant way in which intercultural contact is both understood and evaluated, before going on to document how this is manifested within discourse regarding the arts. I then proceeded to review two examples from my own practice that seemed to point towards another way of understanding and experiencing cultural contact. During the Krom Monster project in Cambodia, I marked a moment at which dialogue collapsed to release something that would have otherwise remained hidden, where speech gave way to other forms of inter-cultural contact that did not rely upon linguistic frameworks of communicative exchange. In a second experience, this time within the UK, I colluded in a situation where speech itself was used to collapse meaning, to create forms of verbal exchange that were almost entirely meaningless. Seen in a certain light, these two operations appear to be one and the same—both the misunderstanding and the lie seem to us to be processes by which a diverse group of individuals approach a sharing of (literal or metaphorical) silence—an emptying out of meaning, a form of collective presence that does not only avoid but actively rejects communicative exchange in favour of something altogether more rich and strange.

This essay has been focused upon those elements that are excluded in the prevailing formulations of inter-cultural dialogue, but this should not be read as an outright rejection of the values of intercultural dialogue. Indeed, as part of our ongoing work in Cambodia and the UK we are engaged with other projects that are founded quite directly upon notions of dialogue, exchange, and communication. However, it is important to acknowledge that this is far from being the only approach available to us, and to recognize the conceptual short-circuit so prevalent within the inter-cultural sphere, the synaptic jump that effortlessly connects "intercultural" to "dialogue/exchange" without a moment's pause.

We need a few more pauses. Indeed, increasingly, I have come to see my professional practice as a series of opportunities to create such moments of pause—and this paper is one such opportunity. Just as Schwitters (2000) sought to celebrate those aspects of experience he felt were neglected within poetry, this paper has sought to create spaces for forms of experience that are neglected within the current models of intercultural dialogue. As we formulate or experience moments of intercultural contact, we must learn to embrace those aspects which are resistant to linguistic models and structures, to learn how to value the emotional, social, and creative power in co-present non-dialogue. We must learn to both understand and share moments of silence.

References

Barenboim, D., & Said, E. (2004). *Parallels & paradoxes—Explorations in music & society*. New York, NY: Vintage.

Bataille, G. (2004). *On Nietzsche*. (B. Boone, Trans). London, UK: *Continuum*. (original work published 1954).

Bataille, G. (2005). *The Passage from animal to man and the birth of art*. In *The cradle of humanity*. (S. Kendal & M. Kendall, Trans). Brooklyn, NY: Zone Books. (original work published 1953)

Benjamin, W. (1999). *Theses on the philosophy of history* (Zorn H., trans). In W. Benjamin, *Illuminations* (pp. 245–255). London, UK: Pimlico. (original work published 1950)

Bloom, H. (1997). *The anxiety of influence—a theory of poetry*. New York, NY: Oxford University Press. (original work published 1973)

Bohm D., Factor D., & Garrett P. (1991). *Dialogue: A proposal*. Retrieved from http://www.david-bohm.net/dialogue/dialogue_proposal.html

Burroughs, W. (1992). *The soft machine*. New York, NY: Grove Press. (original work published 1966)

Burroughs W., & Gysin B. (1978). *The third mind*, New York, NY: Viking Press.

Council of Europe. (2008). White paper on intercultural dialogue: "Living together as equals in dignity." Retrieved from www.coe.int/dialogue

Frazer, J. G. (1922). *The Golden bough: A Study in magic and religion*. New York: Macmillan.

Gadamer, H. G. (1989). *Truth and method* (2nd ed.). (J. Weinsheimer & D. G. Marshall, Trans.). New York, NY: Crossroads.

Gormley, A. (2010). *One & other*. London, UK: Jonathan Cape.

Graeber, D., & Da Col, G. (2011). The return of ethnographic theory. *HAU: Journal of Ethnographic Theory 1*. Retrieved from http://haujournal.org/

Habermas, J. (1987). *The theory of communicative action: Vol. 2. Life world and system: A critique of functionalist reason*. (T. McCarthy, Trans.). Boston, MA: Beacon Press.

Krom Monster, Krom Monster (2011). CD release, London, UK: Incidental.

Lewis-Williams, D. (2002). *The mind in the cave: Consciousness and the origin of art*. London UK, Thames and Hudson.

Murphy, S. (2012). *The art kettle*. Winchester, UK: Zero Books.

Schwitters, K. (2000). *Consistent poetry art*, as quoted in "I is Style." Rotterdam, the Netherlands: NAI Publishers. (original work published 1920)

PART V

Building Dialogue In/Through Research

10

Anthropology as Intercultural Critique: Challenging the Singularity of Islamic Identity

Tabassum "Ruhi" Khan

Key Words

- ► Native ethnography
- ► Gender
- ► Islamic identity
- ► Indian Muslims

1. Introduction

Anthropology's investigative focus has been on understanding cultural differences (Abu-Lughod 1991). Hence, even as critics point out that anthropology as a discipline has been primarily a study of the non-Western "other" by the Western "self" (Abu-Lughod 1991), constructing a divide between "the West and the non-West" and sustaining an iniquitous equation between the two (Said 1979), the field is rife as a site of complex intercultural dialogues. As the reflexive turn in anthropology opens up to scrutiny the hierarchies and power relationships structured into anthropological approaches and scholarship (see Crapanzano

1980; Fabian 1983; Clifford & Marcus 1986), this paper argues that the concerns of the discipline have been brought closer to those in the field of intercultural communication studies, which is invested in facilitating equitable and just dialogues across cultural divides.

Given the heightened sensitivity to power equations within dialogic processes, this paper focuses on native ethnographers' dialogues with their own communities. While acknowledging the way native ethnographers' (situated in Western-power-knowledge networks) investigations of their own (mostly third-world) communities have contributed to more egalitarian knowledge (see Abu-Lughod 1991), it also questions native ethnographers' assertions of a priori knowledge based on ethnic, religious, or gendered affiliations. Pointing to the polar opposite contexts of first world academia and the third world social and economic churnings, it argues that native ethnographers and their informants are products of very different "habitas" or social, economic, and political living conditions. Therefore, it proposes that these interactions be explored as a case of intercultural dialogues. The highlighting of difference between native ethnographers and their informants is intended to not only illustrate that "the self is split, caught at the intersection of systems of difference" as feminist critics have argued (see Abu-Lughod 1991, 140)[1]. It is also to draw attention to the way varying socio-economic contexts[2] as well as access to different languages create grounds for miscommunications and even failed communications between members who deem themselves as belonging to the same community.

The case study that I contribute to this collection of intercultural dialogues is my experience as a Muslim woman of establishing my authority among my informants—young Muslim women residents of an exclusive Muslim enclave in New Delhi, India. I begin with foregrounding my assumptions that I was best positioned to translate their experiences because of the commonalities of religion and gender that we shared. I then contrast my assumption with my experiences in the field to show how they were both simplistic and deeply problematic. As Chandra Mohanty (1991/2012) has argued, just as gendered affiliations cannot simply be assumed based on shared biological or sociological constructs of gender, so also religious affinities cannot be supposed in negation of differences in material and social realities that exist between those doing the investigation (in this case, the ethnographer) and the informants in the field, the young Muslim women.

In this paper I scrutinize the performance of a religious ritual, constructing the core of Islamic identity, to show the diversity in the internalizations of religiosity, and to argue that native ethnographers, in overlooking the complex layers of experiences shaping a religious identity, can also be guilty of perpetuating homogenizing and totalizing narratives. The stress on how native anthropologists must constantly acknowledge different intersecting vectors shaping selfhood furthers discussions on reflexive ethnography, the workings of power, as well as the concern in intercultural communication to facilitate just and equitable communication across self and other. In essence, my argument is that mindfulness and appreciation of differences and a recognition of the essential intercultural nature of dialogues creates rich, nuanced, and more egalitarian conversations and bodies of knowledge.

2. The Native Ethnographer's Authority

My fieldwork was in the exclusive Muslim enclave to which I am intimately connected, even as I am situated within a very different context of Western academia through a complex web of relationships which problematizes the classic notion of "return" of native ethnographer and also the narrative of "dramatic entry" claimed by classical anthropologists. This is because neither do I belong to this community, but nor is this an unfamiliar site. Rather, I have come to be associated with the area, referred to as Jamia with its various subdivisions and clusters, by virtue of being a student at the higher education institution and university that lies at the heart of this enclave and is one of the main reasons for the settlement of this community. The Jamia University, which was set up by a group of Muslim intellectuals in the early 1920s, was part of the larger Indian freedom struggle from British colonial rule. It was an endeavor to indigenize education, endorsed by Gandhi himself, which drew to this area (on the banks of river Yamuna that flows through the city of Delhi) prominent Muslim intellectuals from Indian states of Uttar Pradesh and Bihar, as well as students and other settlers. However, after India's independence and the partition of the Indian subcontinent into the nation states of India and Pakistan, the area's growth has been attributed more to the endemic fear psychosis engendered among Indian Muslims who had chosen not to migrate to Pakistan, but have nonetheless been held responsible for the division of the subcontinent, and viewed with suspicion and disdain by the dominant Hindu community. According to Baig Sahab (personal communication July, 2007), a long-time resident and founder of the communities around the Jamia University, Muslims migrated here because this region was close to water. They were deeply apprehensive that, in the eventuality of a communal riot, becoming increasingly common in post-independence India, they could be subject to most inhumane conditions if their water supply were shut off. However, now, although the fear of violence is still an endemic feature, the area's growth is attributed to other reasons. Today improved prospects for higher education attract new migrants to the area. The university, after being included in the federally supported centers of excellence in 1989, and offering a range of professional and highly rated courses in engineering, architecture, journalism, and even medicine, has become even more central to Muslim ambitions. But as the marshlands disappear and are replaced by rows upon rows of closely constructed homes, the area is not only gaining the semblance of a ghetto but is also referred to as such by other residents of the metropolitan city of New Delhi.

My associations with the Jamia enclave, which first began when I was enrolled in Jamia University's journalism program, have continued even after my migration to American academia. I drew on this connection to recruit informants for an investigation of emerging subjectivities of Muslim youth in an age of relentless globalization. In the initial phase of my research, I felt sure of my claims to an insider status, not only because, as an Indian Muslim I shared with the residents their North Indian Islamic cultural heritage, language, food, and dress, but also because in post 9/11, due to circumstances of acute Islamophobia, our common religious identity has taken on a new perspective. Today, state surveillance forces, which had once targeted mainly the poor and the disempowered, profile all Muslims as suspects, regardless of socio-economic, class, or educational status. An unintended consequence of this surveillance has been a sense of enhanced affinity among Muslims across class and other divides. Therefore, not mindful of any distance which may have been created by my moving away to the United States, I felt particularly bolstered by arguments such as Bourdieu's (1977) that insiders are better able to understand the community's social life because an outsider's stance can often affect its "(mis)understanding." I was sure that I could empathize with the Muslim youth and present a picture of how globalizing forces, which have created seismic shifts in Indian social, cultural, and economic landscapes, were also informing Muslim populations, who have been largely under-represented in this academic debate.

My experiences in the field soon exposed the inadequacies of such assumptions of unqualified access. I became aware that I could not presume to speak for the Muslim youth or Muslim women even if my claims as a native ethnographer had been greatly strengthened by circumstances not of my own making. Though Abu-Lughod (1991), argues that native ethnographers based in Western academia or "halfies" have problematized the distinction between self and other that have historically defined the field of anthropology, leading to more sympathetic and democratic construction of knowledge, the fact is that even "halfies" who stand on shifting grounds between two worlds must confront "the dubiousness of maintaining that relationships between self and other are innocent of power" (141). Indeed, they must confront how a native ethnographer's presumed ability to speak for his/her community is greatly complicated (even compromised) by his/her situatedness in the West. The native ethnographers must address the way their position in Western academia not only confers on them greater social and economic capital as compared to their compatriots in their native lands, but also how it implicates them within institutional pressures and other political imperatives to study the "other" in a fashion not dissimilar to the motives guiding traditional anthropology. Therefore, even if native ethnographers render unstable difference between self and other, they are also positioned in a hierarchical power equation that cannot be ignored. But this is not to negate native ethnographers' ability to create an empathetic and insightful representation of their community. Instead, references to the working of power, even in this most sympathetic of contexts, helps undermine assumptions of coherence which often underline representations of cultures. The recognition of power inequations as well as socio-economic and cultural differences between native ethnographers and their native informants would create a multi-layered and meaningful intercultural dialogue. This would be a particularly effective strategy for what Abu-Lughod (1991) refers to as "writing against cultures" or deconstructing notions of Islam as singular and monolithic and essentially opposed to modernity (see Huntington 1993 and Rushdie 2004).

What is also important to maintaining transparency and objectivity in ethnographic accounts is the understanding of the "halfies" investment in their own community. The strategy for "writing against cultures" inherent in the heightened awareness of diversity was especially important to me as a Muslim and as an Indian, given the stigmatization about Islam, and my own situatedness in these discriminatory contexts. The systemic marginalization of Indian Muslims, which has reduced them to an inward-looking, depressed, and a suspect minority, existing within crowded exclusive enclaves, is a painful reality that I, as Indian Muslim, wish to overcome. Hence even as my academic endeavor was to address gaps in scholarship, which has analyzed the transformation of Indian society from a socialist nation to a thriving free-market economy and to point out that the attendant changes in public consciousness have been investigated only from the perspective of the dominant Hindu middle class communities, I was also trying to foreground a minority population's claim to equal citizenship. Moreover, in calling attention to Muslim women's internalization of the protean visions of selfhood and feminine agency, I was struggling to present Muslim community's responsiveness to transformative potential of new modernities as being truly revolutionary. And yet despite my best intentions to foreground the agency of Muslims and to negate false impressions of their inertness, a chance encounter alerted me to the power inequations underlining ethnographic encounters, and made me realize that I was dangerously close to usurping my informants' stories.

Observing the performance of mandatory Friday prayers, which Muslims across the world scrupulously perform as a primary social and religious obligation, with my informants, the young Muslim women, brought into sharp focus the unique interpretations and internalizations that each individual brings even to a religious experience perceived to be universal and therefore identical for all Muslims. It also made me realize the fallacy of being an insider and of perceiving not only Islamic identity as a predetermined political and social sensibility, but also seeing Muslim women as a coherent and preexisting group. In my desire to belong, I was making the same mistake of prescribing to self-explanatory and given categories of gendered and religious identity, a tendency severely critiqued by Mohanty (1991/2012) and not realizing that both these identities are constructed as Mohanty argues by "complex interactions between class, culture, religious, and other ideological institutions and frameworks" (355).

The account that I present is constructed from the point of view of the participant and an observer, and it recounts the ways in which I, as the ethnographer, internalized the experience both as a Muslim in the company of other Muslims and as a scholar. The foregrounding of the existence of the researcher and the believer in the same person and the juxtapositioning of the ethnographer's and the informants' experiences emphasize "the system of differences" of class, education, access, and facilities within which identities are constructed (see Abu-Lughod 1991).. It also brings into sharp relief the intercultural nature of a dialogue, constructed across these intersecting and differentiating vectors, which destroys the essentialist arguments of monolithic religious or gendered identities, and draws attention to identities as a constructed rather than a given reality.

3. Matters of Faith and Assumptions of Shared Experiences

It was on a hot and humid Friday afternoon in the month of August 2007, that I was able to participate in the Friday *zohar* or afternoon prayers with my informants, the young Muslim women. I had been visiting them at university Polytechnic and was sitting and talking to one of them, Ameena, when Shaista, a student of electrical engineering, walked into the staff rest and recreation room where we were sitting, and rather peremptorily asked Ameena if she had said her *namaz*. Ameena looked up, totally confused and taken aback. She had been so busy talking to me that I think she had completely forgotten about the Friday prayers. When she realized that she looked very sheepish and contrite and conscious of her mistake, and sat almost stupefied in her chair. It then occurred to me that I had not given any thought to it either. I was older than all of them by at least fifteen years and yet I had not been mindful about the Friday prayers. I wondered if they would think badly of me and if this lapse on my part would decrease the level of intimacy that I shared with them.

I was struck by how different things were now as compared to the mid-1990s when I had studied and worked in Jamia. It is true that Friday prayers were very important even then, and most Muslim men, employed at the university went to the mosque to pray in a *jamat* as a mark of respect to one of the most important of Islamic traditions. My father used his lunch break to seek a mosque that was closest to his office to offer his Friday prayers, and this is the way of most Muslim men in India. I know of no man in my immediate circle who misses his Friday prayers, though they may not be conscientious about *namaz* at other times. As in Indian Islamic culture, women are not required go to the mosque but offer their prayers, including the very important Friday prayers at home. Hence, women employees and students of Jamia had stayed behind at work. I had never encountered such concern or urgency about offering the Friday prayers before. I also felt very embarrassed with the possibility of transgressing my religious norms by not paying adequate heed to Friday prayers. Ameena finally got out of her stupor and became involved in the search for the *janamaz* or prayer rug needed to offer the namaz. They could not find one, but the confidence with which they went on looking for it seemed to indicate that they had used the staff rest and recreation room on many previous occasions to say their Friday *namaz*. I had not seen a Muslim woman offering her prayers at her work place even in an Islamic university like Jamia, though in private realms they may have been practicing and devout Muslims. Moreover, I, as a working woman in India, never offered the Friday *namaz* although I could have put down my prayer mat in the corner of my office, especially when I was working in Jamia, where there are other Muslim employees as well as Hindu members of staff. I distinctly remember that I was never very keen on proclaiming a different identity from my other non-Muslim and Hindu co-workers. Perhaps, these were the times when the secularism of Indian politics and the strivings of India's first Prime Minister Nehru to keep religion out of public sphere in a very religious country had resonated strongly among educated middle classes, both Hindus and Muslims. Moreover, in the former state controlled economy, Muslims had fewer employment opportunities and as the discriminatory regimes arrayed against them were stronger (see Sachar Committee Report 2006), they had preferred to maintain a subdued public presence in order to ensure their upward mobility. Hence, public performance of Islamic religious obligations was not a routine matter. I suppose things had changed because these young Muslim women had few qualms about public display of their religiosity.

When they asked me to join them in prayer, I was transfixed. I was talking to a different generation who were products of very different times. Within minutes Shaista and Ameena had done their *wazu* (mandatory ablutions) and were ready. There was still that problem of the *janamaz*; there was no prayer mat. They needed a clean space to prostrate and the room was not too clean. In the center of the room was a large table with chairs all around. Shaista suggested that they could pray on top of the table. Ameena hesitated but then could not refuse. Such was their zeal that they ignored the possibility of looking ludicrous. I said that as I was not a student I could not take this liberty and people might look upon this behavior as highly inappropriate on my part. I offered to instead watch the door and recite the *suras* (verses from *Quran*) while sitting in my chair. Both Shaista and Ameena knew that was not necessary as their non-Muslim classmates could have watched the door. While they prayed I could not but help thinking about how a whole amalgam of the "system of differences" that was at work in our very different enactments of our Indian Muslim identity. The most conspicuous at this moment seemed to be a generational difference, which also reflected on the very different socio-economic and political contexts in which we had internalized our religious identity.

There have been many sweeping changes in society since the liberalization and globalization of Indian economy in 1991. A rapidly growing economy and expanding private sector has created increased options for participation in the mainstream Indian economy for a marginalized and discriminated population like the Muslims. These young women were also representatives of the increasing desire among the Muslim youth for finding employment in the growing economy and to emerge in the Indian public sphere as competent consumer citizens. The young women, enrolled in professional courses like electronic and civil engineering, and computer sciences, had definite plans of seeking employment after graduation. This was very different from even a decade ago when most middle class let alone lower middle class women were educated only up to the point of finding a suitable match for them. Muslim women, as members of a segregated community in India, had been doubly withdrawn from Indian society. But these young women had plans of stepping out of their distinct community and yet they were so conscientious about maintaining their distinct Muslim identity. I was amazed at their ease, their lack of self-consciousness and their poise even as they stood atop a table. I wondered could it be that Shaista and Ameena were able to perform their prayers in public so effortlessly because they were used to praying almost five times a day? Or was it that they were so comfortable within the Islamic environs of the college, and so sure that no one would object to their praying on top of the conference table?

Shaista and Ameena reflected a very different generational attitude towards espousing of the Islamic identity, given the extremely changed contexts today as compared to my formative years when "Nehruvian" socialism and secularism were the norm and religion was kept strictly out of politics and public spheres. But today, with the rise of Hindu right-wing nationalism and political parties since the early 1990s, religion has come center-stage in democratic public spheres. This development has on one hand created a hostile environment for other religious populations, especially the Muslims. On the other hand, it has made a religious minority population like the Muslims a lot less self-conscious about asserting their religious and cultural difference in their own spaces like the Jamia University. Moreover, given the extensive spread of satellite television and Internet, Muslims, whose culture and way of life has been smothered by the dominance of majority Hindu cultures in public spheres, now have access to Islamic symbols and ideologies. These young women and many of my other informants were avid viewers of satellite television channels like Peace TV, which are uplinked from Middle-Eastern countries and reflect a new presence of global Islam within contexts of neoliberal globalization.

Even as I reflected on the generational differences aided by socio-economic and political changes in India, I was alerted to the personal differences in the enactment of their religiosity by Swati, their non-Muslim friend who was also watching them pray. She pointed out that Ameena was reciting the verses very rapidly and quite differently from Shaista, drawing attention to an essential difference in performing the exact same postures. Shaista bowed down before a higher reality quite unlike Ameena, who although focused on her performance, completely lacked passion. I tried to make sense of the divergence within the similarities and disparities in the everyday lives of Ameena and Shaista constructed by their family backgrounds and their personal ambitions. I gathered from my conversations that the women in Ameena's home enjoyed greater freedom and control over their lives. Ameena's mother was educated, employed, and happy despite the fact that she had only two daughters. She enjoyed the same respect, which in patriarchal north Indian Muslim society is generally granted to women who have a male child as reflected in Ameena's confidence. She also had a reputation of being hot tempered and was quite famous for giving a "dressing down" to young men who invaded her privacy or bothered her in any way, which was remarkable as most other women in the predominantly Muslim university were shy and withdrawing. Many times I had heard Razia, Ameena's close Muslim friend, scolding her for being too brave and for fighting with the boys for no reason. Shaista's behavior was more subdued. She came from a home where few women worked outside the home and Shaista and her sister were among the first to pursue a professional degree. I believe that in the absence of the support and counsel such as what Ameena could seek from her mother, who was a teacher at a well-known school and therefore more adept at dealing with the world outside the home, Shaista depended more on her inner resources. Her prayers were integrated into her hardworking life focused on achieving new ambitions. Hence, while she did not openly challenge the patriarchal norms of the male centered north Indian Muslim culture, which Ameena resented, Shaista, by training to join the professional workforce as a computer software engineer, was reconstructing the intimate spheres of family and gender relationships in a much more definitive manner. Young women were prescribing to norms of Indian Muslim culture, including the strict prescription to religious obligations in a way that did not apply to me. Even if Ameena appeared to be less constrained, she was not really so, as she expressed concern if she was being viewed by her colleagues as being too loud and aggressive. Her anxiety validates the existence of certain prescriptive norms, which inscribe the life and experiences of Muslim women. These hegemonic behavior codes are also the agglutinating force in a religious and ethnic community.

The differences in my informants' expressions of religiosity indicate that varying socio-economic and cultural contexts influence the internalization of traditional and cultural codes. In the next section, I draw attention to how class differences unsettle assumptions of a community's internal homogeneity and how communications across these differences can be conceived as inter-cultural dialogues. The respect for variance accorded in intercultural dialogue would render the ethnographic encounters more productive, and make the ensuing narrative more egalitarian.

3.1. Class and Gendered Religious Norms

Ameena and Shaista performed the *sajda*, or the act of prostration before God in unique ways. Ameena performed the *sajda* exactly in the same manner as it is performed by men, that is, to go down on your knees and then bow down with arms extended forward and the forehead touching the ground. In this position, the spinal cord is absolutely straight, the feet are curled at the toes, and your seat is raised about half a foot above the ground. However Shaista did not sit on her hunches; rather, she folded her feet beneath her and when she bent forward she kept sitting on the ground. Her back was bent forward in an elegant but uncomfortable manner. She looked more modest as compared to Ameena, whose posture though more natural drew attention to her posterior. Shaista's uncomfortable bending did not draw your eye to any part of her body.

Since I perform the *sajda* as Ameena did, I discussed Shaista's posture with my mother. My mother said that as a young girl even she had been taught to do the *sajda* in the manner that Shaista followed. It was considered immodest to raise your seat above the ground and bend forward like a man. My mother stopped praying like that when she observed that all women in Mecca were bowing down in *sijda* in the same posture as the men. Therefore, she had never taught us the posture, which she had been taught as a child and which she knew from her experience was the way that most north Indian Muslim women prayed.

The act of performing *sajda* in the *namaz* is almost one of utter abandonment. It feels like a moment when you have given up your cares to someone else by the mere act of prostrating before the inevitable. It is common knowledge that in this posture the blood flow to the brain increases; and when the brain is suffused with oxygen there is a moment akin to bliss in human consciousness. But, this moment of bliss was denied to Shaista, because in her unnatural manner of prostrating the blood flow to the brain would not have increased dramatically. And if that was so, then as a woman she had been denied this feeling of bliss. This gender difference struck me as unjust. Why was the act of prostrating before God altered for women? And why were they not allowed to be their natural unconstrained self? I wanted very much to talk to both Ameena and Shaista about it. However, this conversation would not be easy, as it involved navigating myriad small differences that are often over-looked given the salience of homogenous religious identities; but which nonetheless high-light how class and education create internal factions and discrepancies.

3.2. Negotiating Gendered Differences: Across Experiences of Class and Education

Ameena and Shaista were saying only the four *farz* (mandatory) *rakats* (routines), which take about six to seven minutes. But I was getting nervous that someone might come in, and also my position was truly awkward. On one hand, I did not want these young women to think that because I lived in America, I was so far gone from my religion that I did not think twice about missing my *namaz*. But at the same time, I could not offer my prayers so pub-licly. After the four *rakats* of *namaz*, they said a brief *dua* (prayer of seeking grace from God) in a calm and confident way.

According to Abu-Lughod (1991), native ethnographers perform an important political function of undermining the constructs of differences and inequalities that are inherent in the knowledge about third world cultures (what she refers to as the act of writing against cultures) by focusing on "various connections and interconnections, historical and contem-porary, between a community and the anthropologist working there and writing about it" (148). However, my politics, as it is expressed in the deconstruction of this ethnographic encounter, is to highlight the dissimilarities and divergence in the internalization and expression of Islamic religious identity. The "will to knowledge" or the reason for under-standing the self and the other is to counter the simplistic notions about Islam, which make it impossible to relate to the religion other than in essentialist and determinist manner. The difference in the styles of performing the *sijda* facilitated a discussion between Shaista, Ameena, and I as a site for the play of how different socio-economic contexts, family his-tories, personalities, and their interconnected dynamics construct our religious identities.

Thus, the role of class and age are significant in this context, as I felt no hesitation in pointing out to the young women how my mother had taught me to pray. I narrated to them my life in the Middle-East—a place which Indian Muslims tend to associate with an authen-tic expression of Islam, considering that this is the area of its birth, and therefore an associ-ation with this place (by virtue of migration contingent upon higher education and employment) would perhaps also enhance my standing as a Muslim. I explained in great detail that women in the Middle-East prayed like Ameena did. I stressed the many benefits of performing the *sajda* that were denied in the posture which Shaista followed. And to soften my didactic stance I also shared with them that my mother too had prayed in a sim-ilar fashion till she had gone to Mecca, but when she had seen the women praying in the same fashion as the men, she had decided to change her way. Shaista listened to me politely and replied firmly, "mujhe aise hi sikhaya gaya hai. Namaz ladkiyon aur ladkon ke liye alag hoti hai [this is the way my parents have taught me to pray. The *namaz* is different for girls and for boys]. Ameena was praying wrong" (author's translation, original in Urdu, personal communication, December 9, 2007). Ameena did not correct Shaista, rather she said, "Mein aise pad rahi thi, kyunki, my *churidar* was too tight" [I was praying like that because my pants were too tight] (author's translation, original in Urdu & English, personal communication, December 9, 2007). Priyanka, their friend who is not a Muslim and who was overhearing the conversation, interjected and said, "ladkiyon and ladkon mein bahut farak hai Musalmano mein, ladkiyon par bahut limitations hain Islam mein" [there are many differences in Islam among boys and girls. Girls face many limitations] (author's translation, original in Hindi, personal communication, December 9, 2007). Neither Shaista, Ameena, nor Razia commented on Priyanka's observations about Islam or on the restrictions on women's self-expressions. I asked them if they would like to change the way they prayed because it was not fair to deny women the right to be natural. My informants drew a line at this question and they kept silent. I share a very friendly and warm relationship with them; however, they did not allow me to question the implicit rules of their religion. At this point it could not have been clearer to me how fallacious my assumption about speaking for Muslim women was. We shared the same religion, yet it was evident that our individual identities were much more than a question of adherence to a shared ideology. The "systems of difference" of family dynamics, education, travel, specific social, political, and economic contexts in which our lives were being shaped were operational here and I had to tacitly and implicitly understand this. Shaista and Ameena were clearly unwilling to let me translate my religious belief and apply it to their specific life experiences.

Finally, Shaista retorted, "*ladkiyon ke liye har cheez, bahut si cheezen, mushkil hai. Yeh to chooti si baat hai*" [everything, so many things are complicated for women. This is such a small incident] (personal communication, December 9, 2007). Shaista had dismissed the small differences in religious obligations between men and women as immaterial. She implied that it was not important to challenge these issues when the world posed other tougher challenges for women. She was speaking from her very particular position, wherein as a young Muslim woman, her biggest struggle was to acquire the life and professional skills needed to find a good and well-paying job. She had to wage this battle in the face of the discrimination which Muslims had faced and to avail the small window of opportunity that had been opened up to her by economic liberalization. According to Shaista, it was more important for them to focus on pressing issues like becoming better educated in order to secure their dream job. The question of gender equality in religious practices was not a pressing issue at the moment, especially as institutions of religion as well as patriarchy were her allies, wherein one brought her comfort and the other offered her protection.

Shaista was approaching her dream to work as a software engineer for a multi-national corporation with full understanding of her constraints. She was yet to learn to speak English fluently, as an essential qualification for employment in global companies. I watched her struggle to improve her English language skills over the years that I have been acquainted with her. It was a tough battle because she did not attend an English medium school, as the doors of most private and elite educational institutes are not open to middle-class Muslims. In fact she shared with me that she sought my company because I could speak English fluidly and she aspired to reach my level of competence. She did master the language in just a few years, despite her initial nervousness, which she expressed as, "Main nahin soochti kea age kya hai, how will I achieve what I want, kyunki main kuch nahin kar paoon gi" [I don't think too much about the difficulties that lie ahead for me. Or how will I achieve what I want to achieve because if I thought about it I won't be able to do anything. I would get disheartened" (author's translation, original in Urdu, personal communication, December 9, 2007).

It would have been easy to interpret their disagreement with me over question of gender inequalities as lack of agency. But reading their response as rising from particular socio-economic realities of Indian Muslims helped to avoid such simplification and generalization[3]. I understand their rejection of my advice as a deferred decision, but one which is also implicated in the politicization of religion in India in the past two decades. Shaista and Ameena were resisting any attempt (even by another Muslim) to encroach upon their sacred and ideological spaces. Firstly, they saw no immediate need to address this issue, given the other and more pressing struggles. Secondly, the rise of right wing Hindu nationalism has put a minority population on its defensive. I was not welcome to make any comments on their articulations of their religious identity, even if I had presumed I could do so because I too am a Muslim. Taking a leaf from Abu Lughod's (1991) argument to take into account extra local and long-term process as manifest in particular lives and actions of individuals, I had to examine my informants' situated realities in the context of my very different experiences and life setting. Therefore, even if gender inequalities within religious practices rankled me, the researcher situated in the west and well-versed in feminist critiques, and given my age and enhanced social and economic capital, for my informants the inequities structured by religion and tradition were less profound than other discriminations faced by them as a marginalized minority population within highly competitive economic and social spheres. Hence, the questions I raised were not considered to be a matter of immediate relevance. It was only in retrospect, when I was able to comprehend the "systems of difference" structuring the ethnographic encounter which not only dispelled myths about unqualified access and homogenous communities, but also allowed me to write a layered and more incisive account of the evolving gendered Muslim subjectivities.

4. Conclusion

This paper argues that native ethnographers' recognition of encounters in the field even with those with whom they share religious, ethnic, and cultural affiliations as a question of speaking across divides, to which intercultural dialogues are highly sensitive, would create more authentic and democratic narrative. The acceptance of divergence, differences, and disagreements would accentuate how workings of power shape both experience and knowledge. It would thereby contribute to both discussions on the question of reflexivity in ethnographic knowledge construction, as well as on concerns of lucidity and clarity in intercultural dialogues.

This deconstruction of a particular religious performance which is perceived as being integral to Islamic identity has illustrated that religious identities are not monolithic but created at the intersection of shifting and ever fluid conditions created by class, education, and occupational status, and even political awareness of the family members. It has also pointed out that if native ethnographers were more open to the idea that notwithstanding core affiliations with their native community, they were still speaking across to another culture, the stories that they would tell would be more nuanced and capable of unsettling hegemonic notions and attendant power equations.

References

Abu-Lughod, L. (1991). Writing against culture. In R. G. Fox (Ed.), Recapturing anthropology: Working in the present (pp. 137–162). Santa Fe, NM: School of American Research Press.

Bourdieu, P. (1977). *Outline of a theory of practice.* Cambridge: Cambridge University Press.

Clifford, J., & Marcus, G. (Eds.) (1986). *Writing culture: The poetics and politics of ethnography.* Berkeley: University of California Press.

Crapanzano, V. (1980). *Tuhami: Portrait of a Moroccan.* Chicago: University of Chicago Press.

Fabian, J. (1983). *Time and the other: How anthropology makes its object.* New York: Columbia University Press.

Huntington, S. P. (1993). The clash of civilizations. *Foreign Affairs, 72*(3), 22–50.

Jamia University website. http://www.jmi.ac.in/aboutjamia/profile/history/historical_note-13

Mohanty, C. T. (1991/2012). Under the Western eyes: Feminist scholarship and colonial discourses. In M. G. Durham & D. M. Kellner (Eds.), Media and Cultural Studies: Keyworks (pp. 347–364). Maldan, MA: Willey-Blackwell.

Narayan, K. (1993). How native is a "native" anthropologist? *American Anthropologist, 95,* 671–686.

Rushdie, S. (2004). Yes, this is about Islam. In F. J. Lechner & J. Boli (Eds.). The globalization reader (pp. 357–359). Malden, MA: Blackwell Publishing.

Sachar Committee Report (2006). Ministery of Minority Affairs, Government of India. Retrieved from http://www.minorityaffairs.gov.in/sachar

Said, E. W. (1979). *Orientalism.* New York: Vintage Books.

Endnotes

1. In stressing the complexity and multiplicity of vectors which constitute selfhood, reflexive ethnographers' contention is that native anthropologists cannot seek unfettered endorsement for representing their native communities in the most reliable and just manner because the power equations inherent in the construction and representation of the self and the other may have been unsettled by native ethnographers, and they not have been completely erased (see Narayan 1993).

2. Kirin Narayan (1993) argues that native ethnographers, in their endeavors to construct the social life of their communities, have a tendency to highlight affinities between themselves and their native communities, while underplaying differences of class, education, access, and social mobility.

3. Chandra Mohanty (1991/2012) has critiqued the generalization of third world's women's assumed lack of power and will in the first wave feminist scholarship. However, this tendency continues to plague representations of Muslim women across the world due to lack of effective critique.

11

Community Autoethnography: A Critical Visceral Way of "Doing" Intercultural Relationships

Sandra L. Pensoneau-Conway
Satoshi Toyosaki
Sachiko Tankei-Aminian
Farshad Aminian-Tankei

Key Words

- ▶ Intersubjectivity
- ▶ Community autoethnography
- ▶ Intercultural relationships

1. Doing Relationships

We are in intercultural relationships with each other. These relationships are essential to and formative of our identities, which emerge at the complex intersections of cultural, national, ideological, linguistic, and historical politics. We celebrate the complexity with which our relationships develop and from which we attempt to meaningfully theorize intercultural relational dialogue.

"We are in relationships with each other." The "are" connotes an ontological state of being in the present, coming from the relational history and moving towards the relational future. We are not *in*, but rather, we "do" our relationships with each other. This shift from the "state" ("in") to the action ("do") underscores the role of dialogue in theorizing intercultural relationships. Dialogue is the very "doings" of our relationships.

2. Dialogue

Intercultural communication scholars have understood dialogue as a critical opportunity for transformation (Simpson 2008) and a potential site for cultural critique (Strine 2004). Dialogue facilitates the doing of our (intercultural) relationships. It further functions significantly as: (1) a method of investigating our relationship construction, (2) a method of understanding and critiquing our subjectivities and identities, and (3) an ontological orientation towards our relationships.

We underscore these three elements using Levinas (1981), who describes dialogue as an encounter with the "other." Before we can even understand the self, we encounter the other. The self is generated as a response to the other in the moment of the "dialogic 'face-to-face' encounter" (Nealon 1997, 132). However, because in the very moment *prior to* the encounter my self is not-yet, I seemingly cannot respond to you. The ontological beauty comes from my very self functioning as my response to you. "'I' am never anything but that *response* to the other" (Nealon 1997, 132). Thus, we have Levinasian "responsibility." Indeed, "[o]ur very humanity rides on our ethical acts of ongoing [responsibility]" (Baxter & Akkoor 2008, 28). This process of self-as-response in the moment of the encounter embodies, for Levinas, dialogue.

Understood from the Levinasian view, dialogue is an intersubjective construction. Autoethnography is a productive method through which to engage the intersubjective self and other, as it interrogates the cultural locationality and social positionality of the self in order to provide social and self-critique. Autoethnographers make biographical, narrative, and self-reflexive turns for intercultural relationship studies, accentuating a "simultaneous treatment of the researcher self as interrogative instrument and [interrogative] site . . ." (Pensoneau-Conway & Toyosaki 2011, 386). Applied to intercultural relationships, autoethnography works as an ontological positioning wherein the processes of writing and living are perpetual processes of possibility.

3. Community Autoethnography

As a method drawing upon autoethnography, community autoethnography (CAE) (Toyosaki et al. 2009) accentuates both an experience in relationship-making and a simultaneous reflection on that making. The textual audiencing of self and other in the relational moment of CAE, allows participants to adopt both an in-the-moment and a distanced perspective. Engaging in CAE encompasses our commitment to the other as *cultural* other, and as additive to our *cultural* self. CAE embodies relationship by using autoethnographic texts in dialogue with one another. In challenging us to put our individual autoethnographic investigations into dialogical relations with each other, CAE equips us to embrace our intersubjectivity, our cultural complexity, and our intercultural relationship partners.

The community autoethnographic procedure is as follows. One of us starts by writing a short autoethnographic narrative about (a) cultural issue(s) in our relationship, then shares the narrative with the rest. Another who finds some theoretical, relational, and/or performative connection with that narrative responds with a thematically connected narrative, thus developing our collective autoethnographic dialogue. This process goes on. "There is no specific order by which the writing turns are organized except the connection we each bring to advance an understanding" (Toyosaki et al. 2009, 60) of our own intersubjective intercultural identity. Rather than identifying the specific themes prior to writing, Toyosaki et al. (2009) support letting the themes emerge from the experiential connections of the participants. Our CAE we engage in below simultaneously functions as research data, research methodology, nuanced theorization, and cultural criticism of our own intercultural relationships. While CAE is useful for interrogating any aspect of cultural identity or social phenomenon within intercultural relationships, our CAE below specifically focuses on the notions of race and ethnicity.

4. Community-Autoethnography: Doing Intercultural Relational Labor

4.1. Cultures Meet

Satoshi: This year marks Sandy's and my twelve-year best-friend anniversary. Through many ups and downs, she remains a precious presence in my life.

Sachiko: Encouraged by my friend, Farshad and I met in August 2005. Six months later, we married, and we now have a daughter. Farshad is my love and my life, someone with whom I would like to grow as a person, an educator, and a scholar.

Farshad: Since my young adulthood I have been enthusiastically interested in Japanese culture, and dreamed of my Japanese soul mate. Born and raised in Iran, I was exposed to Japanese classical cinema. My late brother Gholam used to tell me, "There is something about Japanese art and culture that is not expressible by words." In 2005, a friend saw me carrying Kurosawa's "Throne of Blood," and asked me to bring it over to watch it with her and her Japanese housemate. Since then I have cherished Sachiko's wonderful presence.

Sandy: Satoshi started simply as the "fashionable Japanese guy." He became my best friend, my research partner, and my housemate. He's now my daughter's "uncle." It hasn't always been easy, but we've had the wonderful opportunity to learn many unfamiliar ways of communicating with one another. The learning is the important part of the process.

4.2. Feeling Home

Sachiko: When Farshad visited my place for the third time, he brought with him Ozu's "Tokyo Story." He seemed to have a great amount of knowledge about my culture. Sitting strategically on the couch, carefully positioned so that my arm would not touch his without intention, I tried to hide the pounding of my heart. As soon as the film started, I felt so *home*. Most US-Americans I knew showed more of an Orientalist—rather than a genuine—interest in Japanese culture. They enjoyed sushi, chopsticks, or Zen philosophy.

As "Tokyo Story" moved toward the end, one of the main characters eventually passed away. Farshad and I sobbed with a deeper understanding and appreciation of the Japanese cultural concept, *mono no aware*—the transience of all earthy things. Farshad slowly covered my hand with his, comforting me as we continued to watch the sad unfolding of this story.

4.3. "On Becoming Japerican"

Farshad: Shortly after we met, Sachiko asked me if I would be interested in watching her perform her show, "On Becoming Japerican." I audienced her on the small living room stage, inspired by the performance and the way she elaborated on issues of gender, race, acculturation, and identity. Those were the issues that I was familiar with but never saw or felt through performance.

I became an active audience member, forced to think deeper about the issues she was exposing me to. I went home bombarded with ideas, thoughts, and feelings. I constantly juxtaposed the more familiar images of women in Japanese classical cinema against images of Sachiko's performance.

4.4. The Exotic Other

Sandy: I was born and raised amidst Illinois corn and Friday-night football. Satoshi was exotic—I had a cool Japanese friend. As our relationship grew analogous to our progression through graduate school and critical studies, our friendship became the subject of numerous scholarly conversations, particularly as I became more aware of my complicity in systemic (and relational) whiteness.

4.5. The Exotic Self

Satoshi: I felt cool having a white girl next to me hanging out, de-exoticizing me. I was born into Japan's (US-)American fever. I constructed my own Japanese identity around a lack of white skin, blonde hair, and blue eyes. After high school, I worked three part-time jobs to save money to come to the US in order to study "real" English—a mode of self-Westernization.

After my arrival, I spent much time de-exoticizing myself. Like many other Japanese, I thought that "social conformity is not a sign of weakness but of strong inner self-control" (Gannon 2001, 42). Often embarrassed by my Japanese identity, I "turn[ed my] own hostility inward" (Sue 1998, 208). For a long time, I stayed in this stage of self-depreciation (Atkinson, Morten, & Sue 1998, 35). I did not have any tools to question the effects of globalization and language politics on my own identity development. I met Sandy when I started my Ph.D. program. She felt cool—exoticized—having me around her, and I felt cool—de-exoticized—having her around me. Our relationship began before we even met in the ways we learned to idolize what the other represented.

4.6. Embodied Double-Bind

Sachiko: While growing up in Japan, the influence of the US, whiteness, and English had a large impact on my cultural identity. White bodies and English were *admirably embedded* in many of my daily practices. They would appear as the main characters in media such as picture books, TV programs, and films. Non-white bodies appeared, too, though only as an exotic, and often-barbaric or comedic Other. In school, we learned US-American, standard, white English, along with white perspectives and values toward cultural Others. I had a strong desire to be fluent in English and to learn the culture of the west—the land of opportunity and freedom.

Upon my arrival in the US to obtain my Ph.D., I started noticing nuances of the label "Asian," and the scrutinizing gazes of native US-Americans. I often told myself, "If I improve my English, eliminate my accent, and get accustomed to US-American ways of living, I will be fine." Yet, in the context of racial domination and anti-immigrant sentiments, I encountered the stereotype of the Japanese female non-native English speaker: "Speak English at all times, even with your friends from home—if you hope to be successful in the US!" "You are so innocent. You are so polite." "Can I help you?" "Don't worry about your renewal of a visa. You are not one of those crazy Middle Eastern guys." I started to understand these many well-intended, seemingly "inclusive" comments as patronizing, problematic, and double-binding (Shome 1999). The double-bind? "While the desired aim of such comments is to make me 'feel good,' they are nonetheless problematic and pernicious" (Shome 1999, 124). The compliments tend to encourage our becoming white.

Retrospectively, I believe that my attraction to Farshad and his complexity—an Iranian-born-and-raised and naturalized American—can be attributed in part to timing. After I established many relationships with US-Americans; after I experienced enough covert, mundane racism to recognize it; and after I finished my doctoral course work, I met Farshad.

4.7. A Cultural Revolution of the Self

Farshad: The first thirteen years of my life were strongly influenced by US-American culture. As kids, we idolized blue-eyed, blond actor, Lee Majors, the star of "The Six Million Dollar Man." We felt the US-Americans (and the West) were superior, and we Iranians (and the East) were inferior. Fanon (1952/2008) demonstrates the phenomenon of non-European audiences "plac[ing themselves] among the savages on the screen. . . The black man senses he cannot get away with being black" (131). Iran's revolution—with all its shortcomings and as another form of dictatorship—has positively taught millions of Iranians, including myself, the importance of critical examination of centuries-long political, economic, and cultural abuses of the West toward non-European nations. For me, this included my tendency to side with the white male and the way he tries to protect his "family" from the "savages."

When I came to the US, I was already practically aware of issues of race, power, and oppression. Sachiko brought me theoretical awareness. I asked her to provide me with readings on these issues, and she suggested I read Tatum's (1997) "Defining Racism: Can We Talk" and McIntosh's (1995) "White Privilege and Male Privilege. . . ." I read and re-read McIntosh's list of seemingly invisible privileges of being white and male.

4.8. Farshad and Sandy: Living in the Space of In-Between

Sandy: Farshad, I see in us a common theme of not necessarily wanting to be an "other," as Sachiko and Satoshi articulate through their processes of acculturation, but rather, an existential desire to be *with* an other. Your relationship with Sachiko helps you to be more *you*, and my relationship with Satoshi helps me to be more *me*.

This dialogue has challenged me to re-examine how my communicative performance of self is not always culturally additive! I don't always consider the ways my performance may be hurtful to my relational partners, and may reify cultural difference and domination. I am writing in a discourse system of intersecting privileges, and my attention to other systems of discourse is a choice, for better or for worse. When I fail to choose to situate micro-moments of communication within macro-systems of discourse, I reify that very system of domination and privilege that I purport to work against.

Farshad: I agree; we both have commonalities of not living in Japan. Even so, Sachiko and my sense of belonging is different from yours because you belong to here and we do not, although we live and work here. Our space is what I call an in-between space. A negative encounter with a clerk in a grocery store can take us into a long conversation about our positionality in this culture. This in-between-ness is there for us every day and every moment.

My learning about Japanese culture started long before meeting Sachiko. Deep cultural understanding of Japan permeates Iranian society. Through my history, my travels, my cultural knowledge, and my relationships, my sense of Japan is now tactile, one that I feel and sense deeply.

Sandy: The cultural privileges I have in the US come both because I was born here, but also because I am White, middle-class, and in the midst of the codes of the dominant culture. I appreciate the ways our dialogue calls me to become more aware of the mundane consequences of my privilege.

The in-between-ness you describe is poignant, as is the ways Japan has seemingly always been a part of who you are. This challenges our capacity to claim identification with a place, regardless of birth. Participating in your story encourages me to question the stability of cultural identity. Do you ever feel as though you are not just in-between Iranian and US-American culture, but in-between Iranian, US-American, and Japanese culture?

4.9. Sachiko and Satoshi: Japanese Identity in Intercultural Relationships

Satoshi: Looking back on my years in the US, I often concluded that my Japanese-ness hindered my ability to make friends with US-Americans. I said to myself, "This person does not have the ability to understand me." I accused my US-American friends of being "superficial"; I "understood" them through my own cultural logics.

I have often cognized my own subjectivity as a victim. However, my simplified coding of critical phenomena dichotomizes victimizers and victims. Whiteness and racism (or any sort of –ism) are complex and nuanced human phenomena. From the discourse of victimization and my own cultural logic, I claimed that I "understood" US-American others, though this was difficult to realize. I quickly served as a teacher, critic, and social scientist in my intercultural relationships. Others needed to learn my culture for them to be worthy of the term *friend*. I experimented on and hypothesized my friends' behaviors. Who wants to be friends with a constant teacher, critic, and social scientist?

The epistemological politics of "understood" negates collaboration, creativity, and dialogue—a praxis of understand*ing*. Sandy was patient with my place of underst*ood*. She tried to differently engage me and my tyrannical deployment of my own cultural logics that coded her as culturally insensitive. She offered her body for my cultural assault in maintaining our friendship, as though it was her ethical commitment to combat personal and systemic whiteness. However, I had come to really care about her body and soul, marked by my cultural assault and her own self-reflexive critiques. The caring functioned as the shift I needed to transform my way of thinking about my past intercultural relationships. My assumption of underst*ood* (as a fixed completion of knowing) shifted to a desire to engage understand*ing* (as a postmodern collaboration of knowing) Sandy. I hope my friends desire the same understand*ing* with me.

Sachiko: Similarly, I am grateful for what Farshad and I have become thus far. We continuously receive comments on our collective uniqueness—an Iranian-born-and-raised man married to a Japanese-born-and-raised woman, living in the US. This certainly expanded my understanding of identity, power/privilege, oppression, fluidity, and complexity.

When we met, I realized that the anti-Muslim, post-9/11 context heightened his mundane struggles and systematic oppression. I couldn't find a racial minority category that explained his oppression. I also sensed distance from white people, as he used "they" and not "we." He had a light complexion—but he cannot be white, I thought. My understanding of white male privilege clearly did not seem to apply to him. Or did I miss something?

"What is your race?" I asked Farshad when I started getting to know him (a potentially confusing and offensive question). "What?" he looked at me confusedly. "I study race and related issues. I feel extremely embarrassed, but I just don't know which racial category you claim." "I am white." He answered quickly. "What?" Now it was my turn to appear confused. What kind of category did I expect? Maybe I was hoping to learn an unknown racial category—something for Arabic and Persian descendants. What does it mean that he is a white male, yet certain privileges don't apply to him? His dark hair and moustache "appear" before his white skin. Where does the whiteness literature address the realities of ethnic white minorities from the Middle East in the US?

Much of my confusion stemmed from my limited cultural knowledge about Iran—and about Farshad. Power differences between us reflected in my ignorance about his culture compared to his vast knowledge about mine. Growing up in a rapidly developing phase of Japan, I didn't try to move beyond being a "cultural tourist" of non-Western cultures. However, many people in Iran have a good amount of knowledge about and genuine admiration toward Japan, Japanese culture, and Japanese people. When I visited twice, I was treated nicer than others—Iranians or otherwise—because I was Japanese. I saw a strong motivation among Iranian people to learn about Japanese culture, in strikingly similar ways as Japanese people are familiar with US-American culture. On the contrary, when Farshad and I go to Japan, people rarely acknowledge him as they did me in Iran. Instead, he is more often "someone who lives in the US."

Satoshi, you identified as problematic your avowal of "victim," and your claim that you "understood" US-American others from a minority standpoint. Earlier, both of us recalled our location in the "resistance and separatism" phase of identity development, avowing our minority status and rejecting "the values and norms associated with the dominant group" (Martin & Nakayama 2010, 176). I agree that we have to be careful not to oversimplify cultural phenomena and should be always mindful about our own and others' fluid and complex positionalities. Still, "members of other subordinate groups are likely to develop keen skills in interpreting members of dominant groups" (Wood 2004, 216).

My intercultural relationship with Farshad reminds me to reflect on my motivation and desire to "want to understand" his culture, contrasted to my motivation and desire to "want to understand" US-Americans and English. The question remains as to how much US-American friends in general—members of the dominant group—reciprocate with their "wanting to understand."

Satoshi: Your stories about trips to Iran and Japan are fascinating. They clearly highlight how our access to cultural representation influences our perceptions of cultural "others." What does this mean to us, intercultural communication scholars and intercultural relationship partners? Having information is not enough: We need to "want" to know our relationship partners and to examine the ways in which we come to know them in order to know more about them.

Yes, minority and dominant statuses influence our interpretations of self and other. We need those skills in order to survive in the dominant culture. Unfortunately, I cannot swallow relegating those skills to simply "survive" in our intercultural relationships. Is this what we want to call a "relationship"? Instead, I want "loving and caring skills."

Derridian deconstruction (Cavallaro 2001) helps us think about this relational love and caring: The self is always a fluid, changing text. I take myself apart, try to put the fragmented selves together, then repeat, then repeat. As an effect, our understanding of our relationship partners is always in such a flux, shifting the focus from "understood" to "understanding." The focus is not on being unders*tood*. Relational, dialogic love is the self-reflexive willingness to engage in understand*ing* between unstable selfhoods through self-reflexive deconstruction. Subjective instability is a foundation of dialogue—unity, relationship, and understanding.

5. Theorizing Intercultural Dialogue

Several important and related themes emerge that may contribute to understanding community autoethnography and intercultural relationships.

5.1. Problematizing Transactional Communication

A primary roadblock in understanding dialogue as transformative is the emphasis on a traditional, Western model of dialogue. This model—the foundation of our introductory communication courses—presumes dialogue to be two rather independent consciousnesses capable of decoding and encoding verbal and nonverbal communication. It further theorizes each communicator as a "whole of a single consciousness, absorbing other consciousness as objects into itself" (Bakhtin, cited in Baxter & Akkoor 2008, 24), thus rendering a relationship of mere exchange. Buber's distinction between I-Thou and I-it is helpful here (Johannesen 1996). Transactional communication does not promise dialogue; it promises I-it communication where one treats the other as an object of inquiry—each is "understood" (in the past tense), finished, fixed. The I-it relationship is monological and unethical in its objectification of the other.

We often end up engaging in I-it communication with our intercultural relationship partners—the politics of unders*tood* (in the past tense). This was most resonant at the beginning of our relationships. Sachiko engaged in communication with Farshad to appease her friend's desire for them to meet. Farshad engaged in communication with Sachiko since she embodied a culture about which he is genuinely interested and familiar. Sandy engaged in communication with Satoshi because he was an exotic "other." Satoshi engaged in communication with Sandy because he felt de-exoticized. When we function in the space of "understand" with our relationship partners, we fail to interrogate the origins of our understanding.

To some degree, Satoshi's victim status with Sandy, a status often employed in whiteness studies (as minority identities being victimized), protected "his" epistemological domination of his white relational partner. Likewise, as a result of her relationship with Farshad, Sachiko was able to cognize the ways her Japanese identity knew little about Farshad's Iranian identity, yet the converse was true.

5.2. Alleviating Epistemological Domination

We need to treat our intercultural relationship partners as "human," not as objects of inquiry ripe for epistemological domination—the assumption of one cultural logic as "better than" another. We cannot use others as tools to validate what we already know (what theories already say, and what we want to believe). Our intercultural relationships should transcend the "intercultural communication researcher." At the same time, our CAE valorizes our roles as always already *in* intercultural relationships, and our desires to build a home within those relationships, based on our mutual commitment to learn (about) one another as a mutually constitutive relational partner. Farshad opened himself up to understanding the role of a Japanese woman very differently once Sachiko invited him into the dialogue of her performance. Satoshi began to understand his epistemological domination as potentially destructive to both his and Sandy's identity, while Sandy began to engage in a reflexive engagement with her mundane performances of communicative oppression.

5.3. Engaging the In-Between

When we mutually engage in actively understand*ing* one another and build*ing* our relationships, we engage in two important shifts. The first is a linguistic shift from "understood" and "built" in the past tense, to "understanding" and "building" in the present-moving-toward tense. The second shift entails an ontological and communicative shift from a false sense of dialogue involving a monologic self and an objectified other, to a humane opportunity for relational, transformative dialogue. We detail the latter below.

Transformative dialogue conceptualizes selfhood as always already in-between. In this praxis of intersubjectivity, we engage communicative qualities of openness, vulnerability, engagement, love, and so on. Farshad poignantly narrates being *in* the US, yet not *belonging to* or *being from*—living *in-between*. With this in mind, we need to make the fundamental cognitive shift to postmodernizing the ways in which we understand both conception and performance of selfhood. Such a shift valorizes the polyvocality and incomplete ontology of the self—and by direct effect, valorizes the same of the other. The communicating self is unfinalizable; consequently, our linguistic acts, meanings, interpretations, and behaviors are unfinalizable. This unfinalizability is essential to the possibility of dialogue. The finalized self is a "spoken" subject, not a "speaking" subject, and negates the possibility of dialogue. As unfinalizable, our selves are already always intersubjective (Pensoneau-Conway & Toyosaki 2011; Schrag 2003). Indeed, "I" is impossible without "you." Thus, we author each other: we make us, us. As Sandy wrote to Farshad, being in the relationships theorized above contributed to both the individual senses of "I," and the collective senses of "us," one being impossible without the other. Each of us narrated the ways our relationships performed identity-in-process, and how we each discovered our self within the relationship—how we lived in-between *you* and *I*.

This intersubjective and dialogic nature is the essence of selfhood. Bakhtin (1990) offers his notion of "excess of seeing" (Baxter & Akkoor 2008; Holquist 1990) in explaining the decentered self. We all have our unique ways of coding and perceiving our lived experiences and our intercultural relationship partners. For Bakhtin, this uniqueness is the "excess of seeing," which "is defined by the ability I have to see things others do not" (Holquist 1990, xxv). Each person's excess of seeing is unique and irreplaceable. The person with whom I communicate has his or her excess of seeing, which is irreplaceable and unique from mine; thus, we co-author our existence, and fill in the lack created by the excess. Sachiko was able to see her lack of awareness of Farshad's cultural background, only through her relationship with Farshad. Sandy was able to understand belongingness of place only through her dialogue with Farshad. Satoshi was able to understand his potentially violent position as teacher, critic, and social scientist only through his relationship with Sandy. Thus, our selfhood is necessarily understood with our impossibility of seeing ourselves holistically and our reliance on others to become more whole, while we acknowledge, in our lives, we will not achieve full wholeness; our consciousness and selfhood are always already partial. You and I become more whole in the communicative space of intersubjectivity (Schrag 2003).

6. An Unfinalized Conclusion

In our community autoethnography, we take seriously Simpson's (2008) call for dialogue to be understood not as an event that succeeds or fails, but as an opportunity for transformation of thought. Simultaneously, we also take seriously McPhail's (2004) caution that "the symbolic resources of [cultural] essentialism . . . limit our collective capacity to ['engage each other dialogically and humanely']" (210). Our vision of intercultural relationships relies upon dialogical love built upon three axes. First, intercultural relationship partners ought to abandon the illusion of complete selfhood, as it hinders our capacity to love. Our selfhoods are always in flux, in-between, partial, and unfinalizable. Second, we ought to welcome each other's excess of seeing in order to become more whole *together*. There is no understood in love; there is only the process of understand*ing* on our way to become more whole. Third, we engage in understand*ing* because we love our intercultural relationship partners, devoting our attention to them, not for our own interest, but for them to become more whole. We "become" better people because we love each other.

This is difficult work. Engaging in community autoethnography is vulnerable, challenging work, particularly when our cultural identities are on the line. It requires trust, commitment, willingness to be uncomfortable, and understand*ing* that we each have different ways of processing our relationships. Most of all, it requires dialogic love. However, it is work in which we may not always want to engage. We can certainly discuss our commonalities; the difficult—but most important—conversations are those that involve differences. Is dialogic love the ideal towards which all intercultural relationships should strive? We do not claim to speak for *all* intercultural relationships. What we do claim is our hope for a more just, humane future where our relationships—on both a micro and a macro scale—embrace the unfinalized sense produced through dialogic love. We also claim to believe in the effect and not the intention, however difficult it is to live out that belief (and even in the times when we fail to live out that belief). Finally, we claim the complexity of our relationships, under-girding our journey of understand*ing* with a sense that the relationship is rarely—if ever—just as it seems in the moment. These are our claims as we move with and towards love.

References

Atkinson, D. R., Morten, G. M., & Sue, D. W. (1998). Within-group differences among racial/ethnic minorities. In D. R. Atkinson, G. M. Morten, & D. W. Sue (Eds.), *Counseling American minorities* (5th ed.) (pp. 21–50). Boston, MA: McGraw Hill.

Bakhtin, M. M. (1981). In M. Holquist (Ed.) *The dialogic imagination: Four essays by M. M. Bakhtin* (C. Emerson & M. Holquist, Trans.). Austin: University of Texas Press.

Bakhtin, M. M. (1990). In M. Holquist & V. Liapunov (Eds.), *Art and answerability: Early philosophical essays by M. M. Bakhtin* (K. Brostrom, Trans.). Austin: The University of Texas Press.

Baxter, L. A., & Akkoor, C. (2008). Aesthetic love and romantic love in close relationships. In K. G. Roberts & R. C. Arnett (Eds.), *Communication ethics: Between cosmopolitanism and provinciality* (pp. 23–46). New York, NY: Peter Lang.

Cavallaro, D. (2001). *Critical and cultural theory*. London: The Athlone Press.

Fanon, F. (2008). *Black skin, white masks*. (R. Philcox, Trans.). New York, NY: Grove Press. (Original work published 1952)

Gannon, M. J. (2001). Japanese garden. In M. J. Gannon (Ed.), *Understanding global cultures: Metaphorical journeys through 23 nations* (2nd ed.) (pp. 35–56). Thousand Oaks, CA: Sage.

Holquist, M. (1990). Introduction: The architectonics of answerability. In M. Holquist & V. Liapunov (Eds.), *Art and answerability: Early philosophical essays by M. M. Bakhtin* (K. Brostrom, Trans.) (pp. ix–xlvi). Austin: The University of Texas Press.

Johannesen, R. L. (1996). *Ethics in human communication* (4th ed). Prospect Heights, IL: Waveland.

Levinas, E. (1981). *Otherwise than being: Or beyond essence*. (L. Alphonso, Trans.). Dordrecht, The Netherlands: Kluwer.

Martin, J. N., & Nakayama, T. K. (2010). *Intercultural communication in contexts* (5th ed.). Boston, MA: McGraw Hill.

McIntosh, P. (1995). White privilege and male privilege: A personal account of coming to see correspondences through work in women's studies. In K. Rousmaniere (Ed.), *Readings in sociocultural studies in education* (2nd ed.) (pp. 189–195). New York: NY: McGraw-Hill.

McPhail, M. L. (2004). Race and the (im)possibility of dialogue. In R. Anderson, L. A. Baxter, & K. N. Cissna (Eds.), *Dialogue: Theorizing difference in communication studies* (pp. 209–224). Thousand Oaks, CA: Sage.

Nealon, J. T. (1997). The ethics of dialogue: Bakhtin and Levinas. *College English, 59*, 129–148.

Pensoneau-Conway, S. L., & Toyosaki, S. (2011). Automethodology: Tracing a home for praxis-oriented ethnography. *International Journal of Qualitative Methods, 10*, 378–399. Retrieved from http://ejournals.library.ualberta.ca/index.php/IJQM/article/view/10581/9361.

Schrag, C. O. (2003). *Communicative praxis and the space of subjectivity*. West Lafayette, IN: Purdue University Press.

Shome, R. (1999). Whiteness and the politics of location: Postcolonial reflections. In T. K. Nakayama & J. N. Martin (Eds.), *Whiteness: The communication of social identity* (pp. 107–128). Thousand Oaks, CA: Sage.

Simpson, J. L. (2008). The color-blind double bind: Whiteness and the (im)possibility of dialogue. *Communication Theory, 18*, 139–159. doi:1111/j.1468-2885.2007.00317.x.

Strine, M. S. (2004). When is communication intercultural? Bakhtin, staged performance, and civic dialogue. In R. Anderson, L. A. Baxter, & K. N. Cissna (Eds.), *Dialogue: Theorizing difference in communication studies* (pp. 225–242). Thousand Oaks, CA: Sage.

Sue, D. (1998). The interplay of sociocultural factors on the psychological development of Asians in America. In D. R. Atkinson, G. Morten, & D. W. Sue (Eds.), *Counseling American minorities* (5th ed.) (pp. 205–213). Boston, MA: McGraw Hill.

Tatum, B. D. (1997). Defining racism: Can we talk? In *Why are all the Black kids sitting together in the cafeteria?: And other conversations about race.* (pp. 3–17). New York: NY: Basic Books.

Toyosaki, S., Pensoneau-Conway, S. L., Wendt, N. A., Leathers, K. (2009). Community-autoethnography: Compiling the personal and resituating whiteness. *Cultural Studies ←→ Critical Methodologies, 9*, 56–83.

Wood, J. T. (2004). *Communication theories in action: An introduction.* (3rd ed.). Boston, MA: Wadsworth.

PART VI

Building Dialogue in Everyday Interactions

12

The Fusion of Language and Ethnic Identity: The Voices of Hispanic Emerging Adults in New Mexico and Oklahoma

David M. Duty

Key Words

- ► Hispanic
- ► Emerging adults
- ► Language
- ► Ethnic identity

1. Introduction

The rising US Hispanic population engenders a greater need to understand intercultural dialogue between this ethnic group and the dominant society. Hispanics are often viewed as a homogenous group (Umana-Taylor & Fine 2001); however, interactions of Hispanic groups with the dominant society will never be precisely the same because of diverse nationalities, immigration history, and familial generation status within the Hispanic culture. Comparing two different yet related Hispanic communities in New Mexico and Oklahoma provides a broader contextual understanding of the dialogue/relationship between Hispanics and the dominant society. Accordingly, investigating how these two groups of Hispanic emerging adults fuse their ethnic identity with their language practices will foster greater comprehension of the intricacies of intercultural dialogue, with specific reference to this group. This study demonstrates that groups—and individuals within them—utilize different approaches in their interactions with the dominant society. Not only are the language practices varied, but a wide-ranging ethnic identity orientation, from cultural fusion to individual ethnic identity achievement, is presented.

To illuminate the concepts of identity and language in this study, the theories of Communication Accommodation Theory (CAT) and Co-cultural Communication Theory provide a deeper and more precise perspective offering insights that help to shape intercultural dialogue. CAT, originally developed by Howard Giles in the early 1970s as speech accommodation theory (Gallois, Ogay, & Giles 2005), has become a seminal socio-psychological theory of language and social interaction that has been applied to various communication contexts. This theory explains the ways people modify or alter their communication as a strategy to gain approval of people from different ethnic and cultural groups.

According to CAT, there are two strategic forms of communication accommodation people use—convergence and divergence. Convergence is a strategy in which individuals adapt their communication behavior to become more similar to others. Conversely, divergence is a communication strategy in which individuals underscore the communication differences between themselves and others. Drawing upon social identity theory, CAT maintains that, via a strong positive affiliation with an in-group, individuals will communicate divergently. Just as intergroup communication dynamics is an important factor in CAT, it also constitutes a central focus in co-cultural theory.

Co-cultural theory (Orbe 1996, 1998; Orbe & Spellers 2005), adapted from the frameworks of muted group theory and standpoint theory, was developed to explain how co-cultural groups—disadvantaged or marginalized—communicate with people of the dominant group. Orbe (1998) explains, "co-cultural theory seeks to uncover the commonalities among co-cultural group members as they function in dominant society while substantiating the vast diversity of experiences between and among groups" (12). This theory structures co-cultural communication behavior as influenced by six components: field of experience, situational context, abilities, perceived costs and rewards, communication approach, and preferred outcome. According to this theory, co-cultural groups adopt various communication orientations intersected with three preferred outcomes (assimilation, accommodation, or separation) and three communication approaches (nonassertive, assertive, or aggressive). Moreover, to a greater or lesser degree, depending upon the aspects of the dialogic situation and other elements, individuals may adopt one or more of these outcomes or approaches. Co-cultural theory helps to elucidate the complex link between culture, power, and communication. Both CAT and co-cultural theory are practical theoretical perspectives to explore the relationship between language and identity and how those concepts manifest themselves in dialogue between Hispanics and the dominant society.

2. Language and Identity

According to the *2002 National Survey of Latinos* (Pew Hispanic Center/Kaiser Family Foundation), "One of the key traits that defines the Hispanic population and distinguishes it from other racial and ethnic groups in the United States is the large number of individuals who predominantly speak Spanish" (37). The quantity of Spanish speakers in the United States has grown over the years. Nearly a decade ago, more than 28 million US residents ages five and older spoke Spanish at home, which was approximately 10 million more than the entire people who collectively spoke all other languages, excluding English (National Research Council 2006). According to the U.S. Census Bureau (2009), the number of US residents ages five and older who spoke Spanish at home swelled 25% to 35 million—constituting 12% of US residents—illustrating the dynamism of the Spanish language within the United States.

Although the percentage of Hispanics ages five and older who speak Spanish at home is close to 80% (U.S. Census Bureau 2009), there also is a decline in the use of, preference for, and, as a result, fluency in Spanish within the second generation creating significant variation in the level of mastery of the language (National Research Council 2006). Nearly 100% of second and higher generations report they speak English very well (Hakimzadeh & Cohn 2007). Moreover, almost 80% of foreign-born Hispanics who arrived before age 11 and two-thirds of second-generation Hispanics disclosed being bilingual. Stavans (2001) contends that inhabiting the realm of bilingualism for Hispanics engenders the following: "To be or *ser*: that's the real question: Spanish and English, a native tongue and an adopted tongue, a foot here, another across the border and the Caribbean—a home at home and abroad" (153). Hence, for the Hispanic bilingual there is a fusion of language and identity.

According to Vásquez (2003), the bilingual individual offers a distinctive element to the relationship between language and identity. She states that bilinguals, within a monolingual-multilingual continuum have three identity options—they could form a strong ethnic identity, assume the identity of the dominant group, or develop a bifocal or multifocal view that "allows the self to flow in and out of two or more sets of norms and expectations" (33). Vásquez maintains these concepts of identity encompass both gain and loss; a gain from possessing an increased sense of belonging and solidarity, but also a loss owing to some aspect of sacrifice. Connected with ethnic identity is the role of language in culture. As Phinney et al. (2001) note, language significantly shapes ethnic identity. Consequently, the concept of the fusion of language and ethnic identity will be a focal point of this paper.

This study examines the melding of language and ethnic identity among Hispanic emerging adults in two distinct environments—the metropolitan areas of Albuquerque, New Mexico, and Oklahoma City, Oklahoma. These sites were selected because the former offers a unique history of Hispanic influence and the latter recently found its Hispanic population on the rise. As Anderson, Baxter, and Cissna (2004) assert, dialogue matters as an especially crucial model for effective communication (16). Thus, examining the voices of the Hispanic emerging adults who fuse their language and ethnic identity via the theoretical perspectives of Communication Accommodation Theory (CAT) and Co-cultural Theory can be utilized as a teaching/learning tool in promoting greater understanding of intercultural dialogue. *Emerging adult* is a term coined by Arnett (2000) to describe the development period from the late teens through the twenties, focusing on ages 18–25. It is a distinct period of life marked by five distinguishing features: identity exploration, instability, self-focus, feeling in-between, and possibilities (Arnett 2004; 2006). Previously, this transitional period of life was granted modest consideration by scholars (Arnett 2006). Comprehending how these emerging adults use language strategies to communicate can assist scholars in providing fundamental information that can facilitate future intercultural dialogue exchanges with emerging adults from the largest ethnic minority in the United States.

3. Hispanics in Oklahoma and New Mexico

The Hispanic population in the United States is predominately youthful (Passel, Cohn, & Lopez 2011). Accordingly, with emerging adulthood as a recent innovative area of research and given that population projections suggest Hispanics will comprise a larger and larger segment of the emerging adult populace, it is fitting to couple these two flourishing developments. Moreover, it is academically valuable to engage in a comparison/contrast of two distinct environmental settings because it allows for making inferences and drawing conclusions.

In Oklahoma, Hispanics are the fastest-growing ethnic group (Doucette 2002; Juozapavicius 2009; Murphy 2003). Unlike the numerous studies pertaining to Hispanics in New Mexico, there is a paucity of—yet assorted—research regarding Hispanics in Oklahoma (Gormley 2008; Lynch, Elledge, & Peters 2008; Garcia 2005). Owing to the scarcity of research regarding Hispanics in Oklahoma, the current study is intended to generate further knowledge of this growing segment of the state's population.

The Hispanic influence in New Mexico dates back to the sixteenth century when in July 1598 Spaniard Don Juan de Oñate founded the first permanent Spanish settlement. Hispanics are the largest racial and ethnic group in New Mexico (Guzmán 2001). Over several decades there has been a plethora of studies regarding the Hispanic culture in New Mexico (Carlson 1979; Gonzalez 1967; Nostrand 1992; Rinderle & Montoya 2008; Howard et al. 1983). Yet, it appears that only two studies have compared Hispanics in New Mexico with Hispanics in other states, notably southwestern states (Cantor et al. 2005; Smith, Mercy, & Warren 1985).

For this research seven participants in Oklahoma (three males and four females) and four participants (three males and one female) in New Mexico were interviewed. Both groups have a median age of 19 (New Mexico age range 18–23; Oklahoma age range 19–21). Emerging adults attending college were purposively selected because as students their current status affords them the opportunity to be articulate thinkers and more self-focused about their lives. Owing to this introspective nature, the participants, while few, were able to express themselves well providing a richer innate knowledge of their experiences. Pseudonyms have been used to protect the identity of the participants.

The Oklahoma City and Albuquerque participants were university and college students recruited by contacting their respective institution's Student Affairs office. The Oklahoma City focus group interviews were conducted in a large, empty classroom on campus, and the Albuquerque focus group interviews were conducted in a small conference room behind the main office of a department within Student Affairs. The study utilized semi-structured, open-ended questions. The open-ended and informal nature of the interviews, which lasted almost two hours, allowed the participants to answer questions in their own words and also provided them the flexibility to include information that was not directly inquired.

Following data collection, interviews were transcribed verbatim. Analysis involved repeated readings through the transcripts looking for recurring patterns and themes. In addition, the researcher, via member checking, verified the accuracy of observations and interpretations.

3.1. Oklahoma City Site Group

Of the seven participants interviewed six were of Mexican heritage and one of Colombian descent. Four were first generation (foreign born), two were second generation (no US-born parents), and one was 2.5 generation (one US-born parent and one foreign-born parent). The primary themes addressed in this section investigate the extent to which the English and Spanish languages are used in interactions with others and the role that ethnic identity plays in communication with others.

When asked how often they speak Spanish to their friends, the group stated they speak Spanglish in addition to a Spanish-English combination (one person speaks in Spanish and the other responds in English). For example, Elena, a 19-year-old second-generation Mexican, states:

> . . . because, like, my friends they can speak to me in Spanish, but I speak to them in English.

On the other hand, Gustavo, a 20-year-old 2.5 generation Mexican (born in Illinois, father born in Minnesota, mother born in Mexico), explained:

> I have to say depending on who I'm talking to 'cuz if it's somebody who only speaks Spanish, I'll only speak Spanish to them, somebody only speaks English, I'll speak English to them, you know, like . . . if I'm talking to Francisco *(another interview participant)* I would use Spanish words, English words, everything.

These two participants describe different language preferences. Elena's description of her comfortableness in using English relates to Orbe's (1998) co-cultural communicative practice of mirroring in which co-cultural group members adopt the behaviors of the dominant culture. Although her friends speak to her in Spanish, Elena expresses an assimilation communication style by speaking to them in English.

In regard to language use with family members the participants stated they either speak Spanish or English. Lela, a 21-year-old first generation Colombian, Francisco, a 19-year-old first generation Mexican, and Rosario, a 20-year-old first generation Mexican, all stated they only speak Spanish to their parents. Pilar, a 19-year-old second generation Mexican indicated she speaks Spanish and English with her parents. Asked if it were 50/50 between Spanish and English, Pilar specified it was more Spanish, but if she had a long conversation with her parents, it was more likely she would speak to them in English. Gustavo pointed out he usually talks to his father in English, but with his mother they speak Spanish. Moreover, Elena, stated she speaks English with her parents:

> . . . like, my mom, she speaks English to me. Most of the time it's English, but sometimes it can be Spanish. But my dad is always Spanish, but I always answer him in English.
>
> Researcher: Is that because you feel more comfortable with English or . . . ?
>
> Elena: Well, yeah. I feel that my Spanish is not the greatest.

The language the participants speak with their siblings is also mixed. Rosario related that she speaks "Spanglish—Spanish and English" with her brothers. Francisco stated he spoke Spanish and English with his siblings. However, Bernardo, a 19-year-old first generation Mexican, and Pilar said that they only spoke English with their siblings.

Because of varied answers regarding the use of Spanish or English toward family/friends, the following question was asked to which Lela gave a perceptive answer:

> Researcher: So with regard to speaking Spanish or English, it is just what you feel more comfortable with based on the person that you're talking to then?
>
> Lela: I would say the vocabulary. Like how you're going to express yourself.
>
> So, if you can express yourself using the same vocabulary in Spanish as you would in English, then it would be easier to do it in Spanish if that person spoke Spanish.

What Lela is describing is a strategic form of communication referred to as convergence in CAT. Speaker strategies, according to this theory, result from the manner in which a speaker yields to the needs or behaviors of another. Focusing on a partner's conversational needs thus can also lead to discourse management, a sharing of topic choice and development, in addition to shared conversational register. Although Lela's response could be considered convergence, another way to interpret her response is merely functional/semantic in nature or resembling linguistic relativity. "Linguistic relativity says that your language is the familiar room, the usual way of seeing the world and talking about it. Your language lays down habitual patterns of seeing and thinking and talking when you learn its grammar and vocabulary" (Agar 1994, 68). Lela's choice of language is a room she's comfortable with, that she knows how to move around in.

The Oklahoma City site group's use of more English and less Spanish is in accord with the linguistic trajectory or language shift that Veltman (2000) argues is occurring among the Spanish-speaking population in the United States. He states "native-born Hispanics in the late twentieth century adopt English in greater numbers than did Hispanics, 20, 30, or 40 years before" (63). Veltman goes on to state the adoption of English as a personal and professional language transpires extremely fast in immigrant groups and even more swiftly among children of immigrants.

The responses given by the Oklahoma City site group correspond with what Valdés (2000) maintains. She would consider the group to be circumstantial bilinguals because they acquired English in the realms of work, school, or neighborhood. Because there are a wide variety of bilinguals within the Mexican American communities, Valdés claims "that it is impossible to conjecture about language strengths and weaknesses based on generation, age, schooling, period of residence in the United States, or any other such criteria" (102).

Moreover, it appears from their comments that the Oklahoma City site group is not deliberately diglossic, meaning that English and Spanish have acquired particular purposes and are associated with definite areas of activity or subject matter (Valdés 2000). While English is considered the "high" language of prestige because it is the language of the larger society and because it is the language of several important areas, such as banking and the political process,

> Spanish, on the other hand, is the "low" language of intimacy, the language in which casual, unofficial interactions of the home and the in-group are conducted. In some communities, it is also the language of the church and of the surrounding neighborhood stores (Valdés 2000, 105).

A few participants indicated that when speaking to their parents and siblings they speak both Spanish and English, thus integrating both "high" and "low" language.

Moreover, it appears the participants misidentify code switching—alternating parts of speech between Spanish and English—for Spanglish—using "bastardised" Spanish words borrowed from the literal translations of English words. Valdés (2000) maintains that "a switch into Spanish, for example, by a Mexican American bilingual who is speaking English to another bilingual of the same background, may signal greater solidarity or a reference to values associated with the ethnic language (114). Yet, Morales (2002) suggests: "When we speak in Spanglish we are expressing not ambivalence, but a new region of discourse that has the possibility of redefining ourselves and the mainstream, as well as negating the conventional wisdom of assimilation and American-ness" (97). These viewpoints typify the gamut of the fusion of language and identity amongst Hispanics.

In summary, language use is mixed among the Oklahoma participants. Moreover, they engage in code switching/Spanglish which, according to scholars, can indicate greater ethnic identity and refute the notion of assimilation. Therefore, the fusion of language and ethnic identity for the bilingual Oklahoma participants is not predicated on which language is spoken.

3.2. New Mexico Site Group

The four participants interviewed were of either Spanish or Mexican descent. Rodrigo, 23 years old (2.5 or third generation), Beatriz, 19 years old (third or fourth generation), and Pedro, 18 years old (third generation) consider their culture of origin as Hispanic. Beatriz declared both sides of her mother's family came from Spain; her father was born in Colorado and her mother was born in New Mexico. Pedro's paternal great-grandparents originated from Spain, and his maternal grandmother from Mexico and his maternal grandfather from Spain; both his parents were born in New Mexico.

Nineteen-year-old Eliazar, born in Española, New Mexico, views his culture of origin as Spanish. His mother was born in Santa Fe and his father was born in Colorado. His maternal grandmother was born in Santa Fe and a grandfather was born in a town between Española and Santa Fe called Cuyamungue. I queried Eliazar if his great-grandparents came over from Spain and he explained that he did not know, but his family had been in New Mexico for hundreds of years. As with the previous section, the principal foci in this section examine the degree of Spanish and English spoken among interlocutors and how ethnic identity is linked to language use.

When I asked them how often they spoke Spanish with their friends they professed they did not actually know Spanish; though, their family members spoke Spanish. Pedro stated his grandparents and parents are fluent in Spanish and converse in English. He related his grandparents and parents speak Spanish to each other, but not to him. I asked Pedro how it was that he did not speak Spanish and he replied, "They never taught me, I guess. Just didn't pick it up, I guess." Regarding his siblings, Pedro explained only one spoke Spanish fluently because "she's married to a Mexican in New Mexico."

Rodrigo declared his grandparents and his mother communicate in Spanish, but he, his brothers and sisters do not. He explained: "Like, to us, they talk to us in English, but among themselves they would talk in Spanish, but when we would walk in the door, English." I also questioned Beatriz whether it was the same in her household wherein her parents or grandparents spoke Spanish. She replied that it was "kind of Spanglish." In addition, I asked her whether her brothers and sisters converse in Spanish. Beatriz replied, "Oh, no. We don't speak Spanish. But because I hear it I can understand what they're saying; I just can't communicate that much in Spanish."

Eliazar mentioned he does not know Spanish, but states "my grandparents they speak Spanglish—what they call English and Spanish together." He continued: "I mean I should know Spanish. I really should. I think we all should. Everybody in New Mexico should know Spanish, but umm....I don't think we really meet people who are always speaking Spanish."

I also asked him if there was a reason why he had not learned Spanish and he replied:

> The reason was because, what, like, my grandpa grew up and he only knew Spanish and then when he went to school...they couldn't speak Spanish. They'd get hit if they spoke Spanish. So they were Americanized...and, like, it was installed [sic]

in him that speaking Spanish was bad, I guess, like, so they weren't teaching to my mom and she didn't teach it to me.

I asked Pedro the same question and he replied he did not know why he does not speak Spanish. He stated, "My grandparents taught my dad and his brothers and sisters, but I don't really know why my parents never taught us."

The New Mexican participants' inability to speak Spanish is a notable occurrence. In general, it appears the teaching of Spanish stopped with this generation. Possibly through encounters with dominant group members the participants' parents led to them not teaching their children Spanish in order for their children to integrate with the dominant culture. As a consequence, the communication strategies of emphasizing commonalities, mirroring, and dispelling stereotypes (Orbe 1998) becomes either the purposeful or inadvertent approach these parents desired for their children to communicate with dominant group members. Through emphasizing commonalities—such as speaking English—the participants down-play co-cultural differences, and through mirroring the participants make their co-cultural identities less visible. In addition, the participants' usage of English instead of Spanish dispels the stereotype that Hispanics only speak Spanish and lack the skills to speak "good" English, which could convey a positive example to dominant group members.

Even though "being Hispanic and being a Spanish speaker are not synonymous" (Ardila 2005, 62), nevertheless, it is surprising none of the participants converse in Spanish until one considers this situation from an historical standpoint. Marger (2000) discusses that the aspects of internal colonialism: (a) forced entry of the dominant group; (b) alteration of the indigenous culture; (c) administration by the dominant group; and (d) the application of a racist ideology all occurred within the Southwest following the US conquest.

Therefore, when Eliazar explains his grandfather grew up in New Mexico knowing only Spanish, but could not speak it after starting school because "they'd get hit if they spoke Spanish," Eliazar is describing a characteristic of internal colonialism. As a consequence, this perception of speaking Spanish as "bad" was subsequently passed on to other generations, thus perpetuating internal colonialism. Nevertheless, Portes and Rumbaut (2001) contend that the United States tends toward linguistic assimilation because the use of American English is a binding tie across the nation since the country has few grounded elements of national identity (114).

On the other hand, some would argue the New Mexico participants are acculturated (Gordon 1964) or are culturally and structurally assimilated (Marger 2000) into the larger society having fully blended behaviors, values, and beliefs—their cultural traits. Yet, in Eliazar's case he is not necessarily acculturated/assimilated. Although he does not know Spanish and only speaks English, Eliazar does not consider himself "American," he regards himself as "New Mexican." Moreover, he acknowledges that he should learn Spanish. However, for the other participants their perspective on learning Spanish is negligible. Even though the participants took Spanish classes either in middle school or in high school, when asked if they were thinking about taking Spanish classes, the responses were unenthusiastic.

The participants' nonchalant attitude toward learning Spanish does not render an indifferent disposition regarding their ethnicity. Some scholars, such as Anzaldúa (1987) argue there is a fusion of language and identity: "Ethnic identity is twin skin to linguistic identity—I am my language. Until I can take pride in my language, I cannot take pride in myself" (59). In addition, others contend that "losing a language is also losing part of one's self that is linked to one's identity and cultural heritage" (Portes & Rumbaut 2001, 144). Yet, the ethnic pride the New Mexico site group participants have is not at all connected to their linguistic identity. The English monolingualism of the New Mexico site group is not a deterrent to the pride they exhibit for their culture or the pride they exhibit for themselves. As Phinney (2006) writes, "in their 20s, young people become capable of seeing ethnicity in a wider context. They can take the perspectives of other ethnic or racial minority groups and of the dominant ethnic group" (121).

The losses of culture, of self, and of pride that supposedly occur from not knowing Spanish may be absent from the purview of the New Mexico participants because of their emerging adulthood. As emerging adults, they are in a stage of life where optimism flourishes and hopes abound and the sensation of loss is nonexistent. The New Mexico emerging adults appear to be constructing their own unique ethnic identity. Moreover, the environment of New Mexico itself may figure in the construction of their ethnic pride. Research has shown ethnic identity may have varying salience and meaning for the same ethnic group members in different geographical contexts (Phinney 2006; Umaña-Taylor & Shin 2007).

In summary, although the New Mexico participants are English monolinguals, there are no indications that speaking only English fosters the loss of culture, self, or ethnic pride as previous scholarship suggests. Therefore, the fusion of language and ethnic identity for the New Mexican participants is not reliant solely on Spanish proficiency.

4. Conclusion

With Hispanic emerging adults likely taking more active roles as leaders and workers (Hernández, Siles, & Rochín 2000), the opportunities for dialogue between Hispanics and the dominant society will exponentially grow. Dialogue enables people "to connect within and across cultures, forming and sustaining communities through intersubjectivity and cultural creativity" (Jenlink & Banathy 2005, 3). Comprehending the various cultural experiences in the lives of Hispanic emerging adults aids the praxis of intercultural dialogue.

Understanding how Hispanic emerging adults—in their own words—fuse language and ethnic identity provides valuable insights into this demographic group vis á vis intercultural dialogue because as Wood (2004) describes, "Each communicator is implicated in a particular historical-social-political discursive context, which frames and, in turn, is framed by communicators and what happens between them" (xvi). Accordingly, as this segment of the population expands and its attendant discursive interactions broaden, the intercultural discourse of the United States will be transformed through a myriad of social, political, economic, and religious issues.

There is diversity within the Hispanic population, from differences in languages spoken, differences in immigration history, to differences in nationalities. As the data suggest, there are also differences in and where, how and why either English or Spanish is spoken. Owing to their explanatory features, CAT and co-cultural theory are constructive theoretical frameworks for exploring the intersection of language and identity. These theories have great utility for exploring the probable motivations concerning how and why either English or Spanish is spoken by Hispanic emerging adults.

The motivations for language use by the Oklahoma participants can be examined from the type of co-cultural communication orientation applied. For instance, the communication practice of mirroring that Elena utilizes could be considered an aggressive assimilation orientation based on an effort to fit in with or to be seen as one of the dominant group. Gustavo's communication tactic of emphasizing commonalities could be perceived as a nonassertive assimilation orientation that provides him an opportunity to blend into the dominant society. Moreover, Lela's communication approach of interacting with dominant group members in a genuine manner (communicating self) might be recognized as proclivity toward assertive accommodation in order to work with others to alter current dominant structures (Orbe & Spellers 2005). Likewise, CAT is a useful theory to explore the reasons why English or Spanish is used by Hispanic emerging adults as it takes into account both the interpersonal and the intergroup accommodation aspects of intercultural dialogue. For instance, Lela's accommodation strategy may be driven by interpersonal reasons (e.g., to develop a stronger self-concept) or by intergroup motives (e.g., to encourage ethnic group strength).

Even though some scholarship identifies the notion of both loss and gain regarding identity for the bilingual individual (Vásquez 2003), this perception did not transpire from my interview with the Oklahoma participants. Even though Vásquez contends "the attempt to participate in more than one disparate cultural system can leave the bilingual in a continuous state of psychological tension" (33), this does not appear to be the case for these participants. In general, the participants were focused on accommodating their communication toward others. By implementing a convergence speaker strategy it does not appear that the bilingual participants are in a constant state of psychological strain.

Furthermore, the rationale for the New Mexico participants speaking only English could be related to co-cultural theory's notions of assimilation and accommodation, and CAT's assumption that intergroup encounters occur in a sociohistorical context. The bilingual parents of these emerging adults may believe that to participate effectively in the dominant society their children must conform to its norms. As Gallois, Ogay, and Giles (2005) explain: "Intercultural encounters take place in the context of an intergroup as well as interpersonal history, and in the context of different (and sometimes contradictory) social norms" (143). As a result, the communication practices outlined by co-cultural theory, such as emphasizing commonalties, mirroring, and dispelling stereotypes, are fitting concepts to explore in examining the fusion of language and ethnic identity.

Nevertheless, the assimilationist orientations of these emerging adults do not, by themselves, negate their ethnic or co-cultural identity. The ethnic pride these individuals feel may well present itself in the form of accommodation and separation orientations in intercultural dialogue exhibited through the communication practices of intragroup networking, educating others, and exemplifying strength. Thus, as the data indicate, the fusion of language and identity does not produce a trajectory that is solidly assimilative, accommodative, or separate.

Interactions with others and the surrounding environment have profound effects, both psychologically and socially, as individuals are the end results of various socio-cultural circumstances (Eccles et al. 2003; Garza & Gallegos 1985). The challenges and opportunities that accompany intercultural dialogue do not operate in a vacuum, but revolve around contextual factors. It is worthy to examine the similarities and differences between areas that historically have had a Hispanic presence and areas that are newly experiencing dramatic increases in their Hispanic populations to understand the extent to which the links between language, context, and identity affect the dialogue/relationship between Hispanics and the dominant society. Hence, the results of the present study should not only provide fundamental dialogical information regarding emerging adults from the largest ethnic minority in the United States, but also—through the theoretical lenses of CAT and co-cultural theory—advance greater knowledge regarding the fusion of language and ethnic identity among Hispanic emerging adults and how those concepts coalesce in dialogue between Hispanics and the larger society.

References

Agar, M. (1994). *Language shock: Understanding the culture of conversation.* New York, NY: HarperCollins.

Anderson, R., Baxter, L. A., & Cissna, K. N. (Eds.) (2004). *Dialogue: Theorizing differences in communication studies.* Thousand Oaks, CA: Sage.

Anzaldúa, G. (1987). *Borderlands/La frontera: The new mestiza.* San Francisco, CA: Spinsters/Aunt Lute.

Ardila, A. (2005). Spanglish: An anglicized Spanish dialect. *Hispanic Journal of Behavioral Sciences, 27*(1), 60–81.

Arnett, J. J. (2000). Emerging adulthood: A theory of development from the late teens through the twenties. *American Psychologist, 55,* 469–480.

Arnett, J. J. (2004). *Emerging adulthood: The winding road from the late teens through the twenties.* New York, NY: Oxford University Press.

Arnett, J. J. (2006). Emerging adulthood: Understanding the new way of coming of age. In J. J. Arnett & J. L. Tanner (Eds.), *Emerging adults in America: Coming of age in the 21st century* (pp. 3–19). Washington, DC: American Psychological Association.

Cantor, S. B., Byrd, T. L., Groff, J. Y., Reyes, Y., Tortolero-Luna, G., & Mullen, P. D. (2005). The language translation process in survey research: A cost analysis. *Hispanic Journal of Behavioral Sciences, 27*(3), 364–370.

Carlson, A. W. (1979). Corrales, New Mexico: Transition in a Spanish-American community. *Red River Valley Historical Review, 4,* 88–99.

Doucette, B. (2002, April 28). Suburbs among state's fastest-growing cities. *The Oklahoman.* Retrieved from http://www.newsok.com

Eccles, J., Templeton, J., Barber, B., & Stone, M. (2003). Adolescence and emerging adulthood: The critical passage ways to adulthood. In M. H. Bornstein, L. Davidson, C. L. M. Keyes, & K. A. Moore (Eds.), *Well-being: Positive development across the life course* (pp. 383–406). Mahwah, NJ: Erlbaum.

Gallois, C., Ogay, T., & Giles, H. (2005). Communication accommodation theory: A look back and a look ahead. In W. B. Gudykunst (Ed.), *Theorizing about intercultural communication* (pp. 121–148). Thousand Oaks, CA: Sage

Garcia, C. (2005). Buscando trabajo: Social networking among immigrants from Mexico to the United States. *Hispanic Journal of Behavioral Sciences, 27*(1), 3–22.

Garza, R. T., & Gallegos, P. I. (1985). Environmental influences and personal choice: A humanistic perspective on acculturation. *Hispanic Journal of Behavioral Sciences, 7*(4), 365–379.

Gonzales, N. L. (1967). *The Spanish-Americans of New Mexico: A heritage of pride.* Albuquerque: University of New Mexico Press.

Gordon, M. M. (1964). *Assimilation in American life: The role of race, religion, and national origins.* New York: Oxford University Press.

Gormley, Jr., W. T. (2008). The effects of Oklahoma's pre-K program on Hispanic children. *Social Science Quarterly, 89*(4), 916–937.

Guzmán, B. (2001, May). The Hispanic population (Census 2000 Brief No. C2KBR/01-3). Washington, DC: U.S. Census Bureau.

Hakimzadeh, S., & Cohn, D. (2007, November). *English usage among Hispanics in the United States*. Washington, DC: Pew Hispanic Center.

Hernández, R., Siles, M., & Rochín, R. I. (2000). Latino youth: Converting challenges to opportunities. In M. Montero-Sieburth & F. A. Villarruel (Eds.), *Making invisible Latino adolescents visible: A critical approach to Latino diversity* (pp. 1–28). New York: Falmer Press.

Howard, C. A., Samet, J. M., Buechley, R. W., Schrag, S. D., & Key, C. R. (1983). Survey research in New Mexico Hispanics: Some methodological issues. *Journal of Epidemiology, 117*, 27–34.

Jenlink, P. M., & Banathy, B. H. (2005). Dialogue: Conversation as culture building and consciousness evolving. In Banathy, B. H., & Jenlink, P. M. (Eds.), *Dialogue as a means of collective communication* (pp. 3–14). New York: Kluwer Academic/Plenum Publishers.

Juozapavicius, J. (2009, May 14). State sees 55% increase in Hispanic population. *The Oklahoman*, 10A.

Lynch, R., Elledge, B., & Peters, C. (2008). An assessment of lead leachability from lead-glazed ceramic cooking vessels. *Journal of Environmental Health, 70*(9), 36–40.

Marger, M. N. (2000). *Race and ethnic relations: American and global perspectives* (5th ed.). Belmont, CA: Wadsworth.

Mead, G. H. (1934). *Mind, self, and society*. Chicago, IL: University of Chicago.

Morales, E. (2002). *Living in Spanglish: The search for Latino identity in America*. New York, NY: St. Martin's Press.

Murphy, S. (2003, June 17). Hispanics are the fastest growing ethnic group in Oklahoma. *The Norman Transcript*. Retrieved from http://normantrancript.com

National Research Council (2006). *Multiple origins, uncertain destinies: Hispanics and the American future*. Panel on Hispanics in the United States. M. Tienda and F. Mitchell, (Eds.), Committee on Population, Division of Behavioral and Social Sciences and Education. Washington, DC: The National Academics Press.

Nostrand, R. L. (1992). *The Hispano homeland*. Norman: University of Oklahoma Press.

Orbe, M. P. (1996). Laying the foundation for co-cultural communication theory: An inductive approach to studying "non-dominant" communication strategies and the factors that influence them. *Communication Studies, 47,* 157–176.

Orbe, M. P. (1998). *Constructing co-cultural theory: An explication of culture, power, and communication*. Thousand Oaks, CA: Sage.

Orbe, M. P., & Spellers, R. E. (2005). From the margin to the center: Utilizing co-cultural theory in diverse contexts. In. W. B. Gudykunst (Ed.), *Theorizing about intercultural communication* (pp. 173–191). Thousand Oaks, CA: Sage

Passel, J. S., Cohn, D., & Lopez, M. H. (2011). *Census 2010: 50 million Latinos. Hispanics account for more than half of the nation's growth in the past decade*. Washington DC: Pew Hispanic Center.

Pew Hispanic Center/Kaiser Family Foundation (2002). *2002 national survey of Latinos: Summary of findings.* Menlo Park, CA/Washington DC: Author.

Phinney, J. S. (2006). Ethnic identity exploration in emerging adulthood. In J. J. Arnett & J. L. Tanner (Eds.), *Emerging adults in America: Coming of age in the 21st century* (pp. 117–134). Washington DC: American Psychological Association.

Phinney, J. S., Romero, I., Nava, M., & Huang, D. (2001). The role of language, parents, and peers in ethnic identity among adolescents in immigrant families. *Journal of Youth and Adolescence, 30* (2), 135–153.

Portes, A., & Rumbaut, R. G. (2001). *Legacies: The story of the immigrant second generation.* Berkeley, CA: University of California Press.

Rinderle, S., & Montoya, D. (2008). Hispanic/Latino identity labels: An examination of cultural values and personal experiences. *Howard Journal of Communications, 19*, 144–164.

Smith, J. C., Mercy, J. A., Warren, C. W. (1985). Comparison of suicides among Anglos and Hispanics in five southwestern states. *Suicide and Life-threatening Behavior, 15*(1), 14–26.

Stavans, I. (2001). *The Hispanic condition: The power of a people* (2nd ed.). New York: HarperCollins.

Umaña-Taylor, A. J., & Fine, M. A. (2001). Methodological implications of grouping Latino adolescents into one collective ethnic group. *Hispanic Journal of Behavioral Sciences, 23*(4), 347–362.

Umaña-Taylor, A. J., & Shin, N. (2007). An examination of ethnic identity and self-esteem with diverse populations: Exploring variation by ethnicity and geography. *Cultural Diversity and Ethnic Minority Psychology, 13*(2), 178–186.

U.S. Census Bureau (2009, September 14). *Facts for features: Hispanic heritage month 2009: Sept. 15–Oct. 15.* Retrieved from http://www.census.gov/Press-Release/www/releases/archives/facts_for_features_special_editions/013984.html

Valdés, G. (2000). Bilingualism and language use among Mexican Americans. In S. L. McKay & S. C. Wong (Eds.), *New immigrants in the United States: Readings for second language educators* (pp. 58–94). Cambridge, UK: Cambridge University Press.

Vásquez, O. A (2003). *La clase mágica: Imagining optimal possibilities in a bilingual community of learners.* Mahwah, NJ: Erlbaum.

Veltman, C. (2000). The American linguistic mosaic: Understanding language shift in the United States. In S. L. McKay & S. C. Wong (Eds.). *New immigrants in the United States: Background for second language educators* (pp. 58–94). Cambridge, UK: Cambridge University Press.

Wood, J. (2004). Foreword: Entering into dialogue. In R. Anderson, L. A. Baxter, & K. N. Cissna (Eds.), *Dialogue: Theorizing difference in communication studies* (pp. xv–xxiii). Thousand Oaks, CA: Sage.

PART VII

Building Dialogue at the Institutional/
Organizational Level

13

"Why Did it All Go So Horribly Wrong?" Intercultural Conflict in an NGO in New Zealand

Prue Holmes

Key Words

- ► Workplace communication
- ► Chinese communication
- ► Intercultural competence
- ► Intercultural conflict
- ► Non-governmental organisation
- ► Migrant and refugee employment

1. Introduction

This case study examines problematic intercultural communication in a non-governmental, not-for-profit small organization in an attempt to make sense of how and why the communication failed. Such organizations tend to employ people who have empathy for the trans-cultural and transnational flows of people, such as economic migrants and refugees, or those very people who have undergone such an experience themselves. Thus, they are often characterized by fairly flat organizational structures, and populated by management and employees who are socialized toward and knowledgeable about migrant intercultural communication and adaptation issues, either because employees are migrants themselves, or in the case of non-migrants, they have experience of volunteering and community work to aid settlement of mobile people. In other words, the people employed within these organizations, and their end-users, are typically intercultural and multilingual.

The context of this case study is no exception. Within New Zealand there are many small, not-for-profit community organizations—culture-specific and multicultural—which rely on both paid and voluntary labor, and which are established to aid immigration and settlement of migrants and refugees. In one sense, then, the context is ripe for successful intercultural dialogue; yet like most workplaces, misunderstandings, culturally informed rules for communication, and organizational processes challenge possibilities for successful dialogue. I draw on these aspects in this case to illustrate how communicative practices may both enable and constrain intercultural dialogue.

Taking the European White Paper's definition of intercultural dialogue as "a process that comprises an open and respectful exchange or interaction between individuals, groups and organizations with different cultural backgrounds or world views" (Council of Europe 2008, 10), I aim to demonstrate how this process is critical in emphasizing consensus and collaboration as an outcome, and its potential for managing unresolved conflict. However, to realize that potential requires that communicators display (aspects of) intercultural competence, and in particular, critical cultural awareness, embodied in the notion of the intercultural speaker (Byram 2008), the person who can mediate, in real time, intercultural dialogic processes with someone from another culture, and who is capable of taking the perspective of the other. It also includes the need to make salient the intertwined and cyclical processes that underpin intercultural experience and encounters (Holmes & O'Neill 2012). These include the preparation individuals undertake leading up to the encounter, the engagement itself, the evaluation of the encounter, and reflection on the experience. As this case illustrates, the ability for individuals to manage these processes that underpin intercultural competence is difficult, especially where there are unrecognized culturally informed organizational communicative practices and competing interests.

Aside from enabling any organization to achieve its goals, successful workplace communication is important for several reasons. In the New Zealand context, a number of studies attribute intercultural communication problems in the workplace to language issues which further impact workplace integration (e.g., *Connecting Diverse Communities 2008;* Henderson, Trlin, & Watts 2006). Immigration New Zealand's IMSED Report (2010) reveals that almost two-thirds of migrants make new friends at work rather than via neighbors who are often seen to be indifferent to migrants or in the community more generally. Further, North (2007) asserts that many New Zealand employers think favorably of migrants, characterizing them as diligent, committed, hardworking, dedicated, and loyal. The pluricultural/plurilingual workplace, where the national culture is not dominant, and where speakers use multiple languages and intermingle them according to which language is salient in the communication, is therefore an important location for building integrated communities in the face of transcultural flows of languages and cultures (Risager 2006). While these studies point to the importance of intercultural communication in the workplace, they do not account for understandings of how individuals come to socially construct their knowledge of and rules for workplace communication, or the values and attitudes learned through socialization—in the family, school, and workplace—in the first culture (Berger & Luckmann 1966), or how they experience and negotiate intercultural conflict. This case study explores these processes of intercultural communication in an attempt to unravel and make sense of the differing perspectives of those involved.

2. Constructing the Case: Background and Methodology

The case is a narrative reconstruction (Van Maanen 1988), based on my research, consultancy and service in the migrant/refugee community. The case is illustrative of many of these New Zealand NGOs serving the adaptation/adjustment needs of migrants and refugees, from East and South East Asia, East Africa, and the Middle East, who have been settling in many New Zealand cities in recent years. The activities of these organizations include providing these new settlers with further information and support in language, health, welfare, social support, and New Zealand society more generally. The case describes three critical incidents concerning the lived experience of migrants working in a medium-sized community centre (MCC) as they communicate with their local New Zealand colleagues. The narrative represents a construction of multiple examples of intercultural communication that I have encountered in these organizations, and therefore, is not located in any specific context or organization. The narrative is exemplified through the perspectives of two protagonists: a white New Zealand manager (Ian), and his Chinese colleague (Felix), a migrant employed there. A limitation to this narrative is my inability to fully explain Felix's perspective. As a white female, although having researched aspects of Chinese communication extensively, I cannot claim to understand the motivations and rationale for Chinese communication. Further, my work in these organizations did not always enable me to gain access to employees' inner thoughts and feelings.

Ian, in his early thirties, came to MCC having spent a couple of years in social work with migrants and refugees. This experience included managing small community grants in the not-for-profit sector. His appointment to manager at MCC represented a significant step up for him in his organizational leadership and management career. However, his previous successes in the sector, his testimonials, and his academic achievements all vouched for his ability to assume the role of managing the twelve or so employees who worked on various community contracts associated with MCC.

Felix's job, funded by the local health authority, consisted of providing health counseling and advice to migrants from the ethnic Chinese community. As a certified doctor, with a medical degree from a prestigious university in Beijing and several years of experience in a large hospital there, Felix brought considerable skills to the role, including reasonable English language skills, although much of his communication with his Chinese migrant clients was in

Mandarin. Having resided in New Zealand for only three years, and as yet unable to have his medical qualifications recognized, Felix was, in a sense, under-employed.

However, it was not in the workplace that Ian and Felix first met. They came to know each other during Saturday morning school football matches as their daughters both played on the same school team. They also had other prior associations. They shared their keen interest in football by attending matches together at the local stadium. These commonalities had brought them together into what Ian described as a friendship, especially since Felix often asked Ian for advice on matters of schooling, occasional proofreading of written work-related documents, and other issues about life in New Zealand generally.

Prior to Felix becoming employed full-time at MCC, he and Ian had been working on community contracts together. Felix had already been contracted on a part-time basis for two years by the health authority and engaged in negotiations, trying to make sense of the vagaries of public funding to community organizations. Ian watched Felix taking notes during the meeting and was impressed at how Felix seemed to make sense of all the often complex and confusing financial and technical aspects of these publicly-funded employment contracts. He came to know Ian during this time as Ian was also involved in obtaining public health funding for East African refugees. So when it was time for Felix to renegotiate his annual contract with the health authority, and this time, from part-time to full-time, he decided to ask Ian to be a support person at the meeting. The health authority decided to transfer the new full-time contract from its own regional governance to MCC, and thus, Felix would now be managed by Ian and need to report to him, although much of his day-to-day work would be outside of Ian's expertise and oversight.

It was under these circumstances that Felix and Ian begin working together at MCC, with Felix's office located adjacent to Ian's and their sharing a connecting door.

2.1. First Incident: Direct versus Indirect Communication—Owning the Fault (through a performance appraisal), or Using a Third Party to Save Face?

Ian's first months at MCC provided a steep learning curve requiring him to set up processes and practices around MCC's expansion, and incorporating new employment contracts, like that of Felix's, into MCC's structure. This meant checking important documents signed off by employees to make sure that MCC was meeting its contractual obligations. Ian had a high opinion of Felix's professional abilities in his health counseling role. However, Felix was less meticulous over paperwork, and Ian had already had to correct Felix's errors too numerously; Ian decided that he needed to clarify this shortcoming with Felix. Ian thought about how he would approach Felix on this matter. After all, this was new territory in their relationship as "friend"; now "support person" roles were replaced by that of "boss." Ian thought about the strategy he would adopt to deal with the latest shortcoming—failing to keep detailed records about how he spent his time during the day. Perhaps Felix didn't realize the health authority would need these details when he would need to renegotiate his contract. Ian called a meeting with Felix in his office and approached the matter directly.

"Felix, these forms need to be filled out in more detail."

"Oh well, we never do (sic) that before. Cynthia [previous administrator at MCC and now departed] always took care of that," was Felix's casual response.

"But we need to take care of that ourselves. Here's what we need to do. Here's the reporting template." And so Ian explained exactly what he wanted Felix to do and how to do it. Ian noticed two things concerning his own communication from this interaction. First was his use of language. Perhaps in past exchanges, not just with Felix, but with other colleagues who had English as an additional language, Ian's communication was too complex. Perhaps he had been careless in running sentences together and confusing issues instead of specifically pointing out things on a step-by-step basis. He needed to use shorter sentences, and not embedded phrases that included conditional phrases added onto them. He made a mental note to adopt this more direct use of language in future communication.

Second, he had noticed how Felix had often referred to Cynthia in past exchanges when things had not been quite right, and that Cynthia had not expected them to do this or that. Using Cynthia as the scapegoat, the third person, or perhaps cultural broker, started to become a useful practice that Ian, too, found himself imitating. Even in meetings with others, he found himself saying, "This hasn't happened because Cynthia didn't do this, but now we need to change...."

However, things didn't change that much. From Ian's perspective, Felix was still underperforming and these issues had not been addressed. Felix's performance appraisal was coming up so Ian decided to address the underperformance though this forum; he decided to take what he considered to be an upbeat approach in discussing performance issues and expected outcomes:

"Felix, these are the issues we need to work on. This is what you have to do in the next six months. This is how we are going to do them. I'll review them in six months' time and I'm looking forward to it being a very positive performance appraisal. This new appraisal will be sitting on your file, along with a description of the way that you have worked through the issues."

Ian began to wonder if he had dealt with the appraisal situation appropriately, especially in being so explicit. He was unsure if such things existed in Chinese culture, and how underperformance was dealt with in Chinese organizations. Perhaps he had caused Felix to lose face by implicitly criticizing his performance and offering a path to improvement. After all, having the third party to blame had enabled Ian, too, to maintain harmony in the relationship and to keep things on a much more even keel in the office. Ian felt that Felix appeared consoled by the prospect that he (Felix) had the opportunity to improve his performance. Not only would he be able to show Ian that he was good at his job, but he would also be able to regain face.

2.2. Second incident: Relationality—Breach of confidentiality, or breach of friendship?

Things went along smoothly for the first few weeks after this meeting. However, one morning Ian received notification of the termination of a funding agreement, a small health-related project funded by a local agency. Unfortunately, the employee, another Chinese health worker, would have to have her contract terminated. The uncertainty of such contracts in the sector was not unusual, but the consequences, inevitably having to tell good employees that their services were no longer required, was common enough, and a situation that Ian always found uncomfortable vis-à-vis these loyal and committed workers. Discussions with the Chinese employee, Yu Xie, and then her manager, Phyllis, ensued. It was during this latter discussion that proceedings were suddenly interrupted as Felix burst through the door into Ian's office:

"I need to see you now!" exclaimed Felix forcefully.

"Well, I'm in the middle of discussion right now, Felix. Can it wait?" Ian replied calmly.

"No! No! I need to see you now. It's VERY important. It's very, it's URGENT!" Felix almost shouted.

Ian continued calmly, although somewhat perturbed. "It can't be that urgent. Can it wait 20 minutes! I'm in the middle of an important discussion."

"No! I need to see you now!" continued Felix unrelentingly.

At that point Ian asked Phyllis to wait a moment while he went into Felix's office to speak to him in private. Once Ian had closed the door, Felix said, "You can't do this! You don't know enough about MCC and Yu-xie's work to do (sic) this decision."

Ian, reminding himself to breathe deeply, continued calmly to try to control the situation. He informed Felix that he was unable to discuss this matter now, left Felix's office, and then took the discussion with Phyllis to another room in the building.

Ian had not taken the matter of Felix listening into the conversation through the closed door lightly. As his first conflict with Felix, he was unsure of how to make sense of it. He thought about it a lot for a few days. Keeping the matter "in-house," he also discussed it with the Chairperson of MCC's governance board. He knew he had to address this serious breach of confidentiality and process with Felix, and also move Felix's office away from his own in order to avoid such breaches in the future. Ian arranged a meeting with Felix.

However, what Ian imagined would be a careful and reasoned exchange of positions and motivations for the communication, in fact, did not happen. As Ian explained his need for confidentiality in discussions with staff at MCC and therefore the need for Felix to move his office, Felix became very upset.

"But Cynthia [the previous manager of MCC] talk (sic) to me all the time about these things. I tell her why Chinese people behave like that, and she listen to me. I don't think you know what you do here."

Ian, confused by this response, continued phlegmatically and categorically that he was responsible for managing staff in MCC, he had to act in a way that was best for everyone, and this meant not involving Felix in discussions over the contracts of other staff, and further, that Felix would need to move his office away from Ian's. On hearing these two outcomes, Felix became visibly offended. The meeting ended abruptly and Felix left Ian's office with an ill humor. Ian knew the matter had not been resolved, but felt he was moving toward resolving the situation, first, by discussing the matter with Felix and allowing him to respond, and then by asking Felix to move offices, thus avoiding the incident happening again.

Ian was also concerned about how much the previous manager had used Felix as a cultural broker. Felix and Cynthia had worked together for a couple of years prior to Ian's arrival, so Cynthia may have shared interpersonal management issues within MCC informally with Felix in an attempt to deconstruct and understand for herself the communication among staff, especially where Chinese staff were concerned. He decided to check out these suppositions and went back to Cynthia. Cynthia denied sharing personal information of such a nature. Then Ian wondered if perhaps Felix had misinterpreted exactly the level of Cynthia's divulgence, imagining the relationship to be more open than it in fact was. Ian also wondered if Felix thought he (Ian) was guarding information by refusing to discuss Yu Xie's case and then forcing him to move offices.

Ian was also aware of his own communication style: that he presented and represented situations in a clear-cut and open manner, a management style he'd been praised for by his New Zealand colleagues. He began to mull over these issues in his mind, wondering where he was going wrong and why Felix was misrepresenting his intentions, which in Ian's mind, were all about managing people and processes efficiently and effectively.

2.3. Third incident: Power relations—Building collegiality, or demarcating boundaries?

Ian informed Felix that Felix would need to move offices, and since there were no more single offices, he would need to share with two other employees. In Ian's eyes, this would be a good thing. He assured Felix that a shared office—with a Korean and a New Zealander—would be beneficial. Felix would be able to discuss work issues with these colleagues, have the opportunity to build on his intercultural and language skills, and learn more about the working environment in New Zealand. Ian thought this was a win-win solution.

Felix, however, felt differently. He did not want to move offices. He had got used to having an office to himself. It gave him status among his co-workers, and also his clients. What would these people think of him now that he would have to share with others! Besides, they were younger than he, less experienced, and with limited qualifications!

This third incident both confirmed and cemented a shift in the relationship between Ian and Felix. Ian's new role as manager of MCC meant that his relationship with Felix, at least in the work context, had changed—from "friend" to "employer." Once, they had been able to discuss work relationships and complicated matters similar to the incidents each was experiencing now. But now it seemed that such discussions were no longer possible. Ian conjectured that maybe Felix assumed that, even though Ian was now manager, he would still share this information. After all, Ian recalled how happy and excited Felix was that Ian had been appointed manager. Perhaps Felix imagined that the friendship would mean that Ian, in his new role, would continue to confer with and confide in him, as friends did, and they would work things out together, side by side with the equal status that such a relationship implied. Clearly, Ian's behavior towards Felix was demarcating their relationship. Even though Ian worked to create a non-hierarchical environment in MCC, encouraging collaboration and shared problem solving through shared offices and weekly meetings, in the workplace they were colleagues with roles to play, which may mean safeguarding confidences. Perhaps Felix didn't understand this difference, Ian wondered. Perhaps Felix felt picked on! Perhaps he felt his job, and his position at MCC, was under threat! Ian felt overwhelmed by all the complexities and consequences of the incident of breach of confidentiality and Felix's affront at being asked to move offices.

2.4.   Climax: Working out Another Temporary Contract or Withdrawing!

Not only were things going badly for Ian and Felix in the office, but to top it all off, the health authority contacted Ian to notify him that the contract under which Felix was employed was to terminate. They wanted to meet with Ian and Felix to discuss this termination, and the possibility of establishing a new contract, but with quite a different direction. Ian and Felix duly attended several meetings with the health authority to iron out problems and issues in the past contract, and to discuss the brief for the next one. Felix listened with enthusiasm, took notes, and contributed to the discussions. Again, Ian noted how competently Felix seemed to manage these sessions, although there were times when Felix clearly had not understood the subtleties of and intentions behind the brief that was emerging. In fact, as discussions advanced, Ian became suspicious of the health authority's motives, and wondered if there would be a contract at all. It was at that point that Ian began to doubt that Felix was understanding the full implications of the situation. Even Ian admitted to himself that he had needed to read between the lines. The discussions with the health authority were anything but clear. He recalled from past conversations, when he and Felix had deconstructed these meetings, that Felix had often not understood everything.

Thus, when the letter from the health authority arrived, stating the contract under which Felix was employed would be terminated, Ian was not surprised. With only two months left for Felix to work it out, Ian knew he had to notify Felix and went into action immediately. Within twenty minutes, Ian had requested Felix to come to his office.

"The Health Authority has decided not to renew your contract when it ends in eight weeks. I'm really sorry that all of our negotiations and discussions together and with the funding body have come to nothing. So we're going to have to discuss how you work out your remaining time here. You've still got four weeks of leave remaining, and you're going to have to take some of this before you leave. We need to make a plan of what days you could take off. We also need to finalize the projects you are working on and finish them off. So we need to develop a plan to work through over the next few weeks."

Felix became distressed at the prospect of termination of his employment. His only response was to ask Ian not to tell anyone that his job was finishing. Felix then ceased to attend staff meetings, and although partially civil to Ian, for the most part avoided discussions with him. Ian did hold a couple of meetings with Felix as there were practical details around Felix completing his employment at MCC that needed to be discussed. However, these discussions resulted in Felix shouting at Ian, and blaming him for not getting the contract renewed. It was at that point that Ian suggested mediation.

Felix did not understand what this term meant, so Ian explained. Felix also asked several of his colleagues and other New Zealand people he knew to explain the concept. New Zealand law offers legal support to employees in contractual and employment disputes; Felix decided to take up this route, believing it would allow him to redeem his position and loss of face. After all, he was sure that Ian had somehow conspired against him, causing the contract to end and thereby forcing his unemployment. He also felt that Ian had lied that the health authority were terminating it, and instead, wanted Felix out. Mediation meetings proved unsuccessful, with Felix shouting across the table at Ian and Ian feeling powerless in the face of these hostilities.

Thus ended Felix' employment at MCC, along with his friendship with Ian. Later, Ian heard from a Chinese colleague that Felix had found another part-time contract in another NGO, working with new Chinese migrants in the health sector. Ian felt saddened that his relationship with Felix had broken down. Why had it all gone so horribly wrong!

3. Analysis of Intercultural Dialogue in the Critical Incidents

The three critical incidents above can be interpreted according to the following intercultural communication concepts, all of which impact processes of intercultural dialogue. These are culturally-appropriate communication in conflict situations; cultural communication styles, with particular reference to Chinese communication; relationality; and identity challenges.

3.1. Culturally-Appropriate Communication in Conflict Situations

The intercultural conflict taking place in this case study is anathema to processes of intercultural dialogue—open and respectful exchange.

For example, Ian adopted an integrative style of communication, highly valued in the New Zealand context for resulting in win-win outcomes, a style described as reflecting "a need for solution closure in conflict and involv[ing] both parties working together to substantively resolve the issue" (Ting-Toomey & Oetzel 2003, 131). Ian expected to negotiate the conflict by showing a willingness to listen to Felix's point of view, a respect for his feelings, and a desire to share each other's personal viewpoints in a face-sensitive manner. He had also expected that mediation would lead to a similar outcome and was somewhat surprised when it failed.

Western views of Chinese conflict management are often simplistically and stereotypically analyzed in terms of obliging or avoiding styles, perceived from a Western standpoint as being negatively engaged, that is, "placating" or "flight" (Ting-Toomey & Oetzel 2003, 143). Instead, Ting-Toomey and Oetzel suggest that Chinese people adopt a dominating approach and emotional expression in situations of intercultural conflict, especially when they have high self-face concern and an independent self, which may explain Felix's confrontational communication approach towards Ian.

Further, Felix exhibited elements of what Hwang (1997, cited in Oetzel et al. 2003) described as confrontational conflict with an outgroup or with strangers. Hwang notes that people use this conflict style to fight for principles, in Felix's case—loss of status through under-employment and having to share offices, loss of friendship with Ian as Ian asserted what Felix perceived to be a hierarchical management style over him which also negated his status as a qualified doctor (albeit in China). Rarely does Felix use *huibi*, an evading style and the preferred Chinese approach in managing conflict (Hwang). This could be because Felix had ceased to include Ian in his in-group (as Ian had perhaps mistakenly believed), evidenced in Felix's break with Ian in their interpersonal relationship outside of the MCC work context.

To some extent, direct and indirect communication styles also underpin how Ian and Felix approached the conflict. Ian adopted a direct communication style, focusing on reasoned and open discussion and outcomes, as he clearly set out the issues and steps required to resolve problems. In being "open," Ian caused Felix to lose face, and threatened Felix's understanding of their harmonious relationship. By contrast, Felix adopted an indirect style, as indicated by the use of Cynthia as a scapegoat in the first incident. This style would enable Felix to maintain harmonious relations with Ian, and thus indirectly shift responsibility for what Ian was labelling as a poor performance away from himself to include a third person (Cynthia).

3.2.   Chinese Communication Styles

Harmony and relationality are generalized as being central to Chinese communication (Miike 2003), and the preferred communication style in guarding and maintaining relationships both with in-groups and outgroups. To achieve this harmony, human relations are characterized by *gan qing*, or warm human feelings resulting from empathy, friendship, and support; and reciprocity, by showing gratitude and indebtedness (Chen 2002; Gao & Ting-Toomey 1998). Chinese also seek to establish *guanxi* with others which includes the saving of the other's face. These communication styles often give rise to indirect communication patterns, and the use of an intermediary in case of conflict (Chen & Starosta 1997), as in the deference to Cynthia in the early stages. Harmony can be achieved in interpersonal relationships through self-restraint/self-discipline, saving/giving face, indirect expression of disapproval, reciprocity, and emphasis on particularist relationships (Chen 2002). Evidence of Ian abandoning some of these behaviors in the early stages of his management role at MCC may have destroyed any feelings Felix may have had about their sharing a harmonious relationship. For example, Ian asking Felix to move offices and not sharing confidential issues over another Chinese employee (Yu Xie) breached notions of reciprocity and Felix's "particularist" relationship with Ian.

Miike (2003) notes that Chinese society functions as a result of the complex webs of relationships that Chinese people build through their lives to enable them to gain employment, accomplish tasks, and manage necessities in their daily lives. Maintaining harmony in a relationship is thus a way to both strengthen and safeguard it. To some extent, in Felix's view, his relationship with Ian embodied this web, yet the intercultural communication conflict exhibited in these incidents denied that relationship. Felix felt betrayed!

Intercultural dialogue, valuing open and respectful exchange, highlights the importance of successful face work. For Chinese people, face, *mianzi,* concerns the image, or integrity and moral character of an individual (Gao & Ting-Toomey 1998; Oetzel et al. 2003). Losing face invariably brings shame and disgrace to the individual and his/her family and relational network. Face also concerns the public image one projects, represented in social position and prestige gained from performing certain social roles. Jia (cited in Oetzel et al., 556) states that *mianzi* includes the following four major characteristics: "relational (connoting harmony, interdependence, and trust), moral (primary carrier of moral codes and reputation), communal/social (public censure for any deviation from the community norms), and hierarchical (emphasizing the relational hierarchy by age, power, and blood ties, etc.)."

Much of Felix's communication choices and strategies can be understood in terms of these culturally learned communication styles, at least in the earlier stages where he seeks to maintain and strengthen his relationship with Ian, and thereby maintain harmony. Felix exemplified some of these behaviors in two ways: first, by placing responsibility for his poor reporting practice on the fact that the former manager, Cynthia, did not require him to do it, thus playing up the relational interdependence he held with his former boss; and second, in defending his Chinese colleague, Yi-Xie, as she was about to lose her job. His communication demonstrated his communal social support for a colleague in the organization, and his understanding of a hierarchical equivalence based on what had been a supportive and friendly relationship with Ian in former times, and on his close interpersonal relationship with his former boss, Cynthia.

3.3. Relationality

A further aspect of maintaining harmonious relations and thus accomplishing relational goals (Gao & Ting-Toomey 1998) is manifested in acknowledging the inter-relational self (Yang 1981). Ma (2002) noted that Chinese communicators achieve this by valuing and maintaining interpersonal and hierarchical relationships, preserving and saving face, controlling emotion, and expressing feelings indirectly. This "other" orientation results in social conformity, concern about external opinions, and adopting a non-offensive communication strategy for the purposes of harmony maintenance (Yang). It also includes the recognition of the inter-relationship between two parties, or *guanxi.* (Chen 2002; Gao & Ting-Toomey). Further, "other" orientation acknowledges recognition of and respect for hierarchy and role differentiation.

However, as exemplified in the above discussion, the breaking down of relational ties between Felix and Ian and the termination of Felix's contract marked a shift in Felix's mind to "out-group" status, thus resulting in his confrontational strategy.

3.4. Identity

Much of Felix's earlier communication points to his identity arising from his Chinese experience as a doctor, and the associated high social position that this identity affords in Chinese society. As a migrant in a much less hierarchical society, Felix may have been unable to reconstruct and renegotiate his identity and role in the workplace. In other words, his avowed identity is inconsistent with the identity ascribed to him by Ian (Collier 2005). Similarly, while Ian acknowledges that they had shared an equal friendship, he sees a demarcation between their personal and professional life. As manager of MCC he is required to draw lines between professional and social life which Felix does not appear to either accept or understand. Their differing conceptions of their identities, and the professional and social roles they enacted through these identities, resulted in conflicting understandings of power relations and positions as they each sought to negotiate a face-saving position.

4. Conclusion

On a theoretical level, the case study affords the possibility of a nuanced understanding of intercultural conflict, communication, and negotiation that goes beyond simplistic East/West and Chinese/Anglo representations as Ian and Felix display their own individual cultural identity trajectories. The outcomes of this case suggest unproductive communication and spiraling conflict that left both protagonists feeling perplexed and frustrated. In the face of Ian's direct communication style and unawareness of aspects of Chinese communication, Felix, placed in the position of outsider, adopted a confrontational strategy. In failing to comprehend Ian's signals to separate work and non-work relations, Felix felt disavowed and devalued. Attempts at intercultural dialogue, that is, open and respectful exchange of positions, appeared to have broken down as the complex social and professional relationships shared by Ian and Felix went to some extent unrecognized and negotiated.

Referring again to the Council of Europe's White Paper (2008, 10), intercultural dialogue aims to "develop a deeper understanding of diverse perspectives and practices; to increase participation and the freedom and ability to make choices; to foster equality; and to enhance creative processes." Implicit in this definition is that dialogue should not be restricted to practices involving consensus, but to also include collaboration and contradiction (Ganesh & Holmes 2011, practices that entail a tolerance for conflict in communication. As this case demonstrates, contradiction underpins the communicative processes between these two protagonists. What is missing is an understanding of the origins and meaning of these contradictions to bring about collaboration, and the competence to be able to manage it; a starting point for dialogue might well be communication about and tolerance for difference. But successful intercultural dialogue is more than that: it is also contingent on intercultural competence, the ability to be an intercultural speaker, and skills in managing intercultural encounters; it also requires tolerance for ambiguous and contradictory positions, and creative communication processes to expose and negotiate these positions. In Ian and Felix's communication, these aspects of intercultural dialogue appear to be undeveloped.

References

Berger, P., & Luckmann, P. (1966). *The social construction of reality*. Penguin: Harmondsworth.

Byram, M. (2008). *From foreign language education to education for intercultural citizenship*. Clevedon: Multilingual Matters.

Chen, G.-M. (2002). The impact of harmony of Chinese conflict management. In G.-M. Chen & R. Ma (Eds.), *Chinese conflict management and resolution* (pp. 3–17). Westport, CT: Ablex.

Chen, G.-M. & Starosta, W. (1997). Chinese conflict management and resolution: Overview and implications. *Intercultural Communication Studies, 7*, 1–16.

Collier, M.-J. (2005). Theorizing cultural identification: Critical updates and continuing evolution. In W. B. Gudykunst (Ed.), *Theorizing about intercultural communication* (pp. 235–256). Thousand Oaks, CA: Sage.

Connecting Diverse Communities (2008). *Report on 2007/2008 public engagement*. Ministry of Social Development & Office of Ethnic Affairs, Wellington, New Zealand. Retrieved from http://www.msd.govt.nz/documents/about-msd-and-our-work/publications-resources/research/connecting-diverse-communities/cdc-public-engagement-2007.pdf

Council of Europe. (2008). *White paper on intercultural dialogue "Living together as equals in dignity"*. Retrieved from http://www.coe.int/t/dg4/intercultural/Source/Pub_White_Paper/White%20Paper_final_revised_en.pdf

Ganesh, S., & Holmes, P. (2011). Positioning intercultural dialogue—Theories, pragmatics, and an agenda. *Special issue on intercultural dialogue. Journal of International and Intercultural Communication, 4*(2), 81–86.

Gao, G. & Ting-Toomey, S. (1998). *Communicating effectively with the Chinese*. Thousand Oaks, CA: Sage.

Henderson, A., Trlin, A., & Watts, N. (2006). *English language proficiency and the recruitment and employment of professional immigrants in New Zealand*. Occasional Publication No. 11, New Settlers Programme, Massey University, Palmerston North, New Zealand.

Holmes, P., & O'Neill, G. (2012). Developing and evaluating intercultural competence: Ethnographies of intercultural encounters. *International Journal of Intercultural Relations, 36*(5), 707–718.

IMSED Research Work Programme (2010). Department of Labour, Wellington, New Zealand. Retrieved from http://dol.govt.nz/publications/research/imsed0809/imsed0809.pdf

Ma, R. (2002). Negotiation within Chinese Culture: The PRC vs. Taiwan. In G.-M. Chen & R. Ma (Eds.), *Chinese conflict management and resolution* (pp. 277–287). Westport, CT: Ablex.

Miike, Y. (2003). Beyond Eurocentrism in the intercultural field: Searching for an Asiacentric paradigm. In W. Starosta & G.-M. Chen (Eds.), *Ferment in the intercultural field: Axiology/value/praxis* (pp. 243–276). Thousand Oaks, CA: Sage.

North, N. (2007). *The employment of immigrants in New Zealand: The attitudes, policies, practices and experiences of employers*. Occasional Publication No. 18, New Settlers Programme, Massey University, Palmerston North, New Zealand.

Oetzel, J., Arcos, B., Mabizela, P., Weinman, A., & Zhang, Q. (2003). Historical, political, and spiritual factors of conflict. In J. Oetzel and S. Ting-Toomey (Eds.), *The Sage handbook of conflict communication: Integrating theory, research, and practice* (pp. 549–574). Thousand Oaks, CA: Sage.

Risager, K. (2006). *Language and culture: Global flows and local complexity. Clevedon: Multilingual Matters.*

Ting-Toomey, S., & Oetzel, J. (2003). Cross-cultural face concerns and conflict styles: Current status and future directions. In W. B. Gudykunst (Ed.), *Cross-cultural and intercultural communication* (pp. 127–147). Thousand Oaks, CA: Sage.

Van Maanen, J. (1988). Tales in the field. Chicago, IL: University of Chicago Press.

Yang, K. S. (1981). Social orientation and individual modernity among Chinese students in Taiwan. *Journal of Social Psychology, 113,* 159–170.

14

Leadership in Intercultural Dialogue: A Discursive Approach

Jolanta Aritz and Robyn Walker

Key Words

- ▶ Discourse analysis
- ▶ Intercultural communication
- ▶ Discursive leadership

1. Introduction

The emerging scholarship on intercultural dialogue has adopted a working definition of the term as promoting "an open and respectful exchange or interaction between individuals, groups, and organizations" (Ganesh & Holmes 2011, 81). The goal of such exchange is to develop a deeper understanding of diverse practices and to increase participation in making choices and decisions. This chapter contributes to the concept of intercultural dialogue by examining the construct of leadership as central in accomplishing the goal of fostering mutual respect, advancing dialogue, including different perspectives, and avoiding unilateral decision-making. In our case study, we examine leadership as a dialogic, skill-based phenomenon grounded in intercultural competence. More specifically, we analyze leadership from the perspective of how it may resolve some of the problems associated with working in intercultural groups in diverse organizational settings (Earley & Gibson 2002; Jehn, Northcraft, & Neale 1999; Earley & Mosakoski 2000; Ravlin, Thomas, & Ilsev, 2000).

The study of leadership has traditionally been undertaken by management studies, whose upsurge has been attributed to the political, technological, and economic superiority of the US in the post-war years (Foster 1962; Hofstede 1980; Collard 2007). As a result, it is laden with theories, practices, and modes of operation that reflect US cultural assumptions characterized by consumerism, individualism and self-sufficiency, competitiveness, toughness, and rationality, while being exemplified in some non-Western countries as new, modern, scientific, and results-oriented (Bellah et al. 1985; Lam et al. 1999; Pilkington & Johnson 2003). Therefore, intercultural leadership studies often take an etic approach, when a theory or a measure developed within one social group is validated in another. Moreover, when validating their theories on other groups or in other countries, management scholars have been primarily interested, not in understanding how the theories worked but only in seeing that they worked. Leadership researchers rarely have done cross-cultural studies to learn the limitations of their theories (Ayman & Korabik 2010).

In contrast to the traditional approach to leadership, we use an inductive approach to analyze leadership as a dialogic skill (Bakhtin 1981) and apply discourse-analysis techniques to identify how leadership emerges in dialogue in intercultural teams composed of participants from the United States and East Asian countries. Our research is grounded in a social constructionist perspective that examines leadership by looking at language and approaches the phenomenon as an act of social constructionism (Alversson & Karreman 2000; Fairhurst 2008; Fairhurst & Cooren 2004). From the social constructionist perspective, leadership is viewed in the context of what leaders do and is thus discursive in nature. In other words, leadership emerges and is co-constructed through linguistic interaction. Whereas a discursive leadership perspective has provided us with an insight into the language of leadership in the Western context (Fairhurst 2010; Wodak et al. 2011; Marra et al. 2008), few studies have examined discursive leadership across cultures and addressed ways in which such insights might advance intercultural dialogue and facilitate progress and joint decision-making in intercultural settings. The objective of this chapter is to examine how leadership emerges and is constructed in talk in intercultural settings that involve participants of American and Asian origin. We are particularly interested in how the different leadership styles that emerge in these interactions affect participants from different cultures.

Bargiela-Chiappini (2004) identifies contrasting cultural discourses and the "cultural other" as the future research agenda in the field of organizational discourse. The goal of such inquiry is to recognize the existing differences and find ways to effectively manage them and at the same time facilitate the process of intercultural dialogue. Oftentimes the "Other" is defined in negative terms and is viewed as inferior, especially in cases where the Western paradigm is pervasive, such as in the socialization process of managers modeled after US-centered MBA programs (Westwood 2001). In order for Western leaders to interact successfully and effectively on a global scale, it is imperative to learn more about cultural

"Others" and to include this knowledge in their intercultural interactions in order to move forward to more equal and collaborative partnerships.

In this chapter, we use descriptive and interpretive modes (Carbaugh 2007) to address the question of how specific discursive strategies contribute to organizational functioning of multicultural teams, and whether knowledge can be drawn from an examination of natural interaction and close text analysis that would help us better understand the dynamics of intercultural teams and the emergence of leadership in an intercultural context.

2. Methodology

Our study uses a situational and interactive model developed by Gumperz (1996) that underscores the importance of cultural norms and socio-cultural knowledge. Individuals from different cultures often learn the other's language but apply their own discourse conventions when using it. More specifically, we use a model of turn-taking developed by Sacks (Sacks et al. 1974) and expanded by Coates (1993) to analyze conversational interaction and to examine different leadership styles and team dynamics. Studies in conversation analysis showed that turn-taking serves as the mechanism for decision-making that involves organized sequences of interaction exchange; however, the analysis of turn-taking alone is not sufficient to explain decision-making as interaction since it is based on cultural presuppositions (Baraldi 2013). We draw on Carbaugh's invitation (2007) to produce interpretive analyses of cultural discourses by applying turn-taking (micro) analysis and to provide cultural interpretation of such interactions (macro analysis).

Three excerpts from three decision-making meetings are used to analyze the emergence of leadership in intercultural teams and to identify different leadership styles. We are interested in how leadership emerges in an intercultural context and whether different leadership styles affect interaction in mixed teams consisting of members from collectivist and individualist cultures. Our methods of analysis include (1) one applied in our previous research (Aritz & Walker 2009, 2010), an extension of Tannen's (1990) high considerateness and high involvement style into the realm of culture and (2) a model developed by Coates (1993), which is used to analyze different conversational styles that vary in their turn-taking strategies and their degree of involvement and dominance in conversation.

According to Tannen (1990), speakers who put the signaling load on involvement are described as having a high involvement style, while speakers who use strategies to express the need not to impose are characterized as having a high considerateness style. A high involvement style is characterized by fast talk and overlapping of others' speech while those who prefer high considerateness style may find this style makes it difficult for them to participate; they may feel "crowded" out of the conversation. Tannen notes that a key issue for many high considerateness style speakers is that of pace. They prefer a slower pace of interaction. We extended Tannen's high involvement and high considerateness style to characterize Western and Asian preferences for different types of interaction, with Western speakers exhibiting preferences for high involvement style and Asian speakers showing a preference for high considerateness conversation style (Aritz & Walker 2009, 2010).

Coates' model focuses on the following areas: (1) the meaning of questions, (2) links between speaker turns, (3) topic shifts, (4) listening, and (5) simultaneous speech.

Meaning of questions: Questions are speech acts that require a subsequent speech act and thus, ensure that conversation continues. Questions may have different meanings; they can facilitate the conversation and not necessarily expect information in response; whereas other questions can be taken at face value. This difference between direct and indirect modes often results in miscommunication.

Links between speaker turns: When the speaker takes a turn, he or she can acknowledge the contribution of the previous speaker or talk on the topic directly without acknowledging the contribution of the previous speaker.

Topic shifts: Shifts between topics can be abrupt or participants may build upon each other's contributions.

Listening: Listening involves the analysis of minimal responses, or backchanneling, and their different functions. Backchanneling gives the speaker an indication that the hearer is still listening. It is intended to keep the communication going by confirming or reacting to a preceding statement (Clyne 1994). Some researchers regard back-channeling as positive interruptions. Backchannels consist of such vocalizations as "yes," "uh huh," and "I see."

Simultaneous speech: Simultaneous speech involves the analysis of overlaps. Conversational overlaps are defined as periods when both speakers talk at the same time and the conversational contribution of one speaker overlaps with that of another. In the case of cooperative overlaps, speakers do not change topic but elaborate upon the current one. Interruptions, on the other hand, are defined as periods when both speakers talk at the same time, but the contribution of the second speaker contradicts or disrupts that of the first speaker. Interruptions are also generally considered to be evidence of a high involvement discourse style and can be perceived as dominating and inconsiderate (Tannen 1990).

This close text analysis is then used to analyze how the combination of these strategies affects distribution of talk in culturally diverse teams.

3. Data

The selected data set consists of three transcripts of videotaped recordings of three small group decision-making meetings. Seventeen business professionals, who were native speakers of English and native speakers of East Asian languages enrolled in an MBA program at a private university in Southern California, were chosen to participate in the simulation. The study used graduate students, who had all worked in the professional workplace for at least two years. Each of the three groups consisted of five to six members, totaling eight native speakers of English and nine native speakers of East Asian languages. East Asian participants were primarily from Japan, China, and Korea. Each group consisted of both female and male participants, with a total of nine males and eight females.

The simulation used in the study, Subarctic Survival, asked each five- or six-member group to take up the role of airplane crash survivors. Groups were then asked to discuss and ultimately agree upon the ranking of the items that were salvaged from the aircraft in terms of their critical function for survival. The meetings were twenty minutes in length and were held and videotaped in an experiential learning laboratory equipped with professional facilities and technicians. The meetings were held in English, and the videotapes were then transcribed. The transcripts were then analyzed using Coates' method and applying the interpretive mode of cultural discourse analysis (Carbaugh 2007).

4. Analysis

This section analyzes two decision-making meetings looking at the emergence of leadership within each group. It then looks at a third meeting to analyze an unsuccessful attempt at leadership.

Excerpt #1

Excerpt #1 analyzes the talk of an American male participant (Speaker 1) who uses a directive leadership style to assert his preference over those of the group by using discursive tactics characteristic of the Western model of leadership to which produce an aggressive, decisive, and domineering style. The group in Excerpt 1 consists of five members, three Asian participants (two males and one female) and two American participants (one male and one female).

Analysis of questions: In lines 1–35, Speaker 1 (S1) emerges as a group leader. In line 1, S1 is the first to announce his choice of the most vital item for survival—matches: "I figure you can use fire, otherwise you're screwed." In what follows, S1 uses questions in a competitive way to defend his decision. When his choice of the most important item for survival gets questioned in line 3, he interrupts S4 in line 6 and uses a tag question to challenge S4 and any alternative choice suggested, "[well] at least you can start a fire though, don't you think?"

1. S1: I figure you can use fire, otherwise you're screwed.
2. S4: Okay, so let's
3. S3: z but if you, but if you just have matches what are you going to do with
4.   [them?]
5. S4: [Yea] at least with the [xxxx][1]
6. S1: [well] at least you can start a fire though, don't you think? . . . I mean it could be one or two, it doesn't matter

In line 22, S1 uses an indirect question to reassert his point, "You know what I am saying?" In line 31, S1 asserts himself again and has his choice for matches being item #1 recorded as the group decision. Speaker 1 does not use a question once to facilitate a conversation or solicit information from other team members.

What is interesting to note is that the only team members questioning S1's choice are other native speakers of English. For example, S3 in line 3 makes an attempt to question the choice of "matches" as the number 1 item: "but if you, but if you just have matches what are you going to do with them?" When S4 offers an alternative ranking in line 16, "Okay, so, are we doing sleeping bag first and the matches second?" They are not successful at introducing an alternative ranking as S1 ignores these suggestions and takes the group back to his number one choice in line 17 by saying, "um . . . I think that just not having fire is like . . ."

Analysis of links between speaker turns: In Excerpt #1, Speaker 1 does not make a link with the previous speaker's contribution but rather concentrates on making his own point as demonstrated by his turns in lines 9, 24, and 31. The only acknowledgments Speaker 1 makes is when the previous speaker supports S1's point, as illustrated in line 6 above and line 23:

21. S3: [That's true because] it's light and
22.   [it's heat]
23. S1: [it's suicide] z Yea, it's light and its heat and 'cuz either way if you start a fire and all of a sudden no matter better than any sleeping bag. You know what I'm saying?

Analysis of topic shifts: Speaker 1 does not show an attempt to create smooth transitions between topics. In line 16, S4 asks a question that invites a discussion; however, in line 17 S1 shifts the topic back to his agenda and forgoes the possibility to open the discussion and include additional items, "um . . . XXX I think that just not having fire is like…"

16 S4: Okay, so, are we doing sleeping bag first and the matches second? Or the other way around?
17 S1: um...XXX I think that just not having fire is like [xxxx]

There is little elaboration and continuity of the topics introduced into the conversation; instead, Speaker 1 shifts abruptly to his agenda, to record matches as the most important item for the group's survival.

Analysis of listening: In Excerpt #1, Speaker 1 does not use minimal responses in the form of *yeah* and *mhm* to signal listening. The only minimal response by Speaker 1 is offered in line 33, *yeah,* where in fact it does mean agreement with Speaker 4, who endorses S1's idea of putting matches as the most important item on the survival list.

Analysis of simultaneous speech: Speaker 1 uses overlaps that interrupt the previous speaker rather than cooperative overlaps that support the previous speaker's contribution numerous times, as seen in lines 6 (above), 21, 23, and 26. In addition, Speaker 1 responds to interruptions by continuing to speak and keeping the floor, as shown in line 21:

```
21  S1:  [it's suicide] z Yea, it's light and its heat and 'cuz either way if you start a fire and
         all of a sudden no matter-better than any sleeping bag. You know what I'm saying?
22  S3:  Th[at's true, that's true.]
23  S1:  [you can also xxxxxx]
24  S2:  [xxx]
25  S4:  [es]pecialy if you find shelter          and it's going to rain
26  S1:  and if                                    z and you [and] you're wet  [you know]
```

The cumulative effect of such competitive, authoritative discourse style has an interesting effect on Asian speakers who come from collectivist cultures and share different conversational norms characterized by a high considerateness style that expresses the need not to impose (Tannen 1990). Interestingly enough, two male Asian team members are not taking part in the struggle for dominance and do not try to grab the floor. Speaker 2, an Asian speaker, uses latching, instances where a second speaker begins speaking without any perceptible pause but without overlapping with a previous speaker (Tannen 1990), once in line 8 validating S1 by saying "Okay."

```
7  S1:  [well] at least you can start a fire though, don't you think? . . . I mean it could be
        one or two, it doesn't matter
8  S2   z Okay
9  S1:  z I mean I figured the two most   [important]
```

Latching serves the function of active listenership and co-participation rather than interrupting, which denies the previous speaker the ability to complete his or her turn. Previous studies noted that latching can be perceived as intrusive by high considerateness style speakers (Asian group members, in this case), but high involvement speakers usually do not show evidence of discomfort or annoyance. In line 18 and again in line 25, S2 tries to take the floor but is not successful. The Asian speaker is going outside of his comfort zone here potentially to take the floor, but because latching is not an aggressive move, it is ignored by the American speaker and S2 does not succeed in entering the conversation and keeping the floor.

```
17  S1:  um...XXX I think that just not having fire is like [XXXX]
18  S2:                                                     [XXXX]
19  S3:                                                     [That's true because] it's light and
                                                            [it's heat]
```

TABLE 1 Contribution to decision-making meetings by cultural group, Excerpt #1

Cultural group	Average number of turns	Average number of words	Average words per turn
Asian speakers	39	127.5	3.2
American speakers	151	1170	7.7

Both speakers are relatively silent compared to native speakers of English. In fact, as Table 1 indicates, the competitive leadership style exhibited by Speaker 1 resulted in a greater imbalance in member contribution by cultural group.

Excerpt #2

The group in Excerpt 2 consists of six group members, four Asian participants (two males and two females) and two American participants (one male and one female). Excerpt #2 analyzes the talk of an American female participant who exhibits a leadership style organized more cooperatively. Her cooperative leadership style produces a more inclusive style of group communication characterized by a more balanced contribution in a group whose team members are from both individualist and collectivist cultures.

Analysis of questions: Lines 1–73 show a parallel process of an emerging leader in our second intercultural group. However, Speaker 1, a female native speaker of English, emerges as a leader in a very different way. Her use of questions is very different from the male Speaker 1 in Excerpt 1 and positions her as a different kind of leader in a group. At the beginning of the meeting, it appears that Speaker 6, an older Asian speaker, may take the leadership role. In line 2 he opens the discussion by asking, "Okay, which of you chose, the uh, most important one?" S6 then is quite active in the beginning of discussion by taking three significant turns in lines 8, 18, and 22.

```
 7   S1:   Did everybody [choo]se the compass?
 8   S6:   [why?]

17.  S3:                              [ohh]
18   S6:                              z I know, but here it says like you
         pretty much know where you're at from the map so
19   S3:                              z xx use com[pass]

21   S3:                              z xx use  com[pass]
22   S6:   [if you] if you like start off by okay I'm going to go that direction then you don't
         need the compass anyway
```

It is through the use of her questions that Speaker 1 emerges as a group leader a couple of minutes into the discussion. Instead of using questions to assert herself or challenge others, in line 7, Speaker 1 asks yes/no and open-ended questions soliciting information about other group members' choices, "Did everyone choose the compass?" In line 36, she directs the question to the group members (two Asian females) who have not yet spoken, giving them a chance to join the group, "What did you guys put as the number one?" In lines 72 and 73, she recaps the group discussion by summarizing members' input and listing the items in order: "I think that, I think that the compass is good and then should we do the canvas as second?" which elicits an affirmative confirmation by other speakers. By then, this all-inclusive style establishes Speaker 1 as a leader. She takes on a more vocal leadership role in the remaining part of the transcript.

Analysis of links between speaker turns: In contrast to the group leader in Excerpt 1 who does not show any linkage to the previous speaker's turn, Speaker 1 acknowledges the contribution of the previous speaker on a several occasions. In line 46, for example, she acknowledges S6's contribution and elaborates on the topic that he introduced: "Oh really? To stay warm." Similarly, in line 62 and 65, she continues on a topic that had been previously introduced by latching and overlapping with S5:

```
61  S5   Have you ever stayed in the middle of snow? You have no idea where you are.
62  S1:                          z you don't
63       even know w[hat's] up or down.
64  S5:            [with]      z pu[re snow, complete snow] you have no
65  S1:                        [everything looks the same]
```

Analysis of topic shifts: Speaker 1 uses elaboration and continuity as opposed to the sudden topic shifts demonstrated by Speaker 1 in Excerpt 1. Even when she changes the topic in line 73, her talk is linked to the previous speaker's contribution, creating a smooth transition that guides the team in its discussion:

```
72  S5:  z I'm I'm I'm just saying that we agree on [the com]pass
73  S1:                              [yeahhhh]    z I think that, I think that
         the compass is good and then [should we do the canvass] as second?
```

Analysis of listening: Although Speaker 1 uses just a few minimal responses (line 72) in this excerpt, her participation is marked with active listening. In lines 41–46, she is actively participating in the conversation by using repetition (line 41) and validating and elaborating on the previous speaker's turn (line 46):

```
36  S1:  z what did you guys put as the number one?
38  S4:          z what'd you get?
39  S3:                  z I put, I put canvass [not xxxxx]
40  S5:                          [oh canvass] is uh tent, the tent
41  S1:                          z oh canvass
```

```
43 S4:        z oh canvass
44 S6:    uh canvass, I put sleeping bag
45 S5:                      z ye[ah]
46 S1:                          [oh really? To stay warm. ]
```

She uses frequent latching, which because of the content, is supportive of the previous contribution made by an Asian speaker. Rather than introducing her own agenda, Speaker 1's latching is not perceived as intrusive by Asian group members; it does not cause them to exhibit discomfort or create a silencing effect.

Analysis of simultaneous speech: Speaker 1 overlaps rarely, and when she does, her overlaps are cooperative as shown in line 46

```
45 S5:                  z okay
46 S1:                      z mine's two as[well]
47 S3:                              [you] know, I think this, we have a lot of
        xxx how fast to to fi, figure out the the directions
```

and line 65

```
64 S5:  z I'm I'm I'm just saying that we agree on [the com]pass
65 S1:                          [eahhhh]    z I think that, I think that the com-
        pass is good and then [should we do the canvass] as second?
```

She does not use simultaneous speech to interrupt a previous speaker as was often the case with a male S1 in Excerpt 1. On one occasion, in line 72, she uses backchanneling "yeahhh," to show solidarity with S5.

As the analysis above suggests, the emergent group leader in Excerpt #1 exhibits a more directive leadership style organized on a competitive basis that is characteristic of Western leadership style. In comparison, more balanced discussion is evident in Excerpt #2 where an American female group leader exhibits a leadership style that is organized more cooperatively. In this particular interaction, the participation rates are comparable between Asian speakers and American speaker working in a mixed group (See Table 2 below).

TABLE 2 Contribution to decision-making meetings by cultural group, Excerpt #2

Cultural group	Average number of turns	Average number of words	Average words per turn
Asian speakers	105.7	843.7	4.6
American speakers	152.5	870.5	5.7

Excerpt #3

The group in Excerpt 3 consists of six group members, two Asian participants (one male and one female) and four American participants (two males and two females). In this excerpt, a female Asian participant (S6) attempts unsuccessfully to establish herself as an active participant in the decision-making process using discursive moves characteristic of a cooperative style. However, unlike Speaker 2 in Excerpt #2 above, her voice is silenced by the more aggressive discourse style exhibited by speakers from the US, who hold a majority in the group.

The first time S6 tries to take the floor she overlaps, acknowledging the contribution of the previous speaker at that point, and tries to elaborate on the topic initiated by S4.

> S4: Alright. See the thing is, I, I think it's more important to survive first before you start mov-
> ing, cause 50 miles, no matter how fast you walk will still take you like about, um, if you're
> with all that stuff maybe 5, 6 days. So you have to make sure you can survive first cause no
> matter what you're gonna have to stop and rest. [So] [I figured it would be more important
> to...]
> S3: [XX]
> S6: [Ya, especially it's, uh...   ] close to arctic.
> S4: [Ya.]
> S3: [Ya.]

S6 does not speak again until line 25 when she talks on the topic directly connected to with what has been said before, "[I think,   ] so it's October, close to Arctic, cause I've been to Alaska in the August, uh, the, uh in August the day, there, the day is really long..."

Just like the first time, she uses a cooperative overlap and contributes additional content relevant to the topic. She received validation from S3 in line 30, at which point she overlaps again in line 32:

```
29
30  S3:                          z Ya that's true.
31      [I was thinking of that] too.
31  S6:  [You have to          ]
32                               z take it into consideration.
```

In line 38, S5 challenges S6 by noting "September is the fall, um, is the end of September is the equinox. So you're getting about a 12 to 12. At, by October 5th." S6 at first defends her statement in line 40, "October the day should be much longer than the night," but after S5 continues to pursue her point in line 47, S6 concedes in line 49, "Oh, right." At this point S3 takes the leadership role again and changes the topic in line 50, "Maybe, maybe we should determine what is most useless before what's most important" and S6 overlaps again in agreement, "right."

Of importance in this excerpt is the strategies that S6 uses and the fact that she does not make another substantive contribution throughout the entire meeting. She only engages in conversation at the end of the recording when team members start chitchatting after they complete the task.

S6 uses a cooperative rather than directive style. Instead of talking on the topic directly without acknowledging the contribution of the previous speaker, she connects to the previous speaker on all occasions. Her contributions are directly linked to the topic at hand and build on what the previous speaker had said. S3 in line 50 provides a good example of an opposite style when he quite freely switches the topic and takes control of the conversation. S6 often overlaps cooperatively, building on the previous contribution, instead of competitively, interrupting a previous speaker without a transition. S6 also uses minimal responses in the form of *"yeah"* and *"mhm"* to signal listening. The cumulative effect of her interaction style puts her in a "powerless" position because of the lack of strategies associated with leadership in the Western culture. It is quite possible that S6 does not offer another substantive contribution for the remainder of the meeting because she is overpowered by a more aggressive conversational style exhibited by other speakers.

Excerpt #3 serves as an example of how a more cooperative discourse style exhibited by an Asian speaker may not be recognized and valued, and be "drowned" out when it is surrounded by a more aggressive and competitive style used by American team participants. As we have seen in Excerpt #2, S1 is successful in establishing a cooperative leadership style in an intercultural group that does not have a directive masculine style traditionally associated with the Western concept of leadership competing for the floor. In contrast, S6 in Excerpt #3 stops participating altogether in the discussion after she tries to enter unsuccessfully on a number of occasions. An examination of the contribution rates in both Excerpts #1 and #3 (See Table 3 below) shows that American team members are producing significantly more words and taking significantly more turns than Asian speakers. The contribution rates in Excerpt #2, on the other hand, show a much more balanced distribution of talk, which can be explained by a more cooperative leadership style that allows for multiple voices to be heard. The different contribution rates demonstrate that language proficiency alone cannot account for low participation rates among East Asian speakers. In fact, the data in Excerpt #2, when compared to Excerpt #1 and Excerpt #3, underscores the importance of communication styles and the different types of leadership that gets constructed in talk in intercultural settings.

TABLE 3   Contribution to decision-making meetings by cultural group, Excerpt #3

Cultural group	Average number of turns	Average number of words	Average words per turn
Asian speakers	26	119	3.2
American speakers	161	1202	7.2

5. Conclusion

The analysis illustrates two styles of leadership—directive and cooperative—and their effects on other team members, particularly in terms of whether they come from individualist or collectivist cultures. As shown in Except #2, a more cooperative leadership style leads to more balanced contribution and participation of all members in intercultural groups.

The study also illustrates how context, including cultural backgrounds of team members, affects which leadership style may be recognized and adapted by group members, as shown in Excerpt #3 in which a female Asian participant was unsuccessful at emerging as a leader with her cooperative style. The discourse style of each of the participating actors is influenced by cultural norms that may not be shared by group members from a different culture. As such, specific discursive strategies, such as those exhibited by Speaker 1 in Excerpt #2, if recognized and used by leaders from different cultural backgrounds, can create a more collaborative discussion space that can potentially produce more collaborative solutions and decisions.

Although Coates' original model was also applied to gendered talk, we believe the cooperative and competitive conversational styles described by Coates can be successfully mapped to the cultural dimensions of individualism and collectivism that have been described by Hui and Triandis (1986) as the most salient of cultural dimensions. Among other things, individualistic cultures tend to value competition over cooperation, while collectivist cultures value cooperation over competition because of the valuing of the group over the individual. As demonstrated by our data, a more cooperative style (usually associated with a more feminine discourse style), when used in intercultural teams consisting of members of East Asian origin, produced more balanced participation rates among all team members. By contrast, a more competitive, autocratic style, characteristic of male interactions, produced a greater discrepancy between American and Asian participants with Americans dominating the decision-making meeting.

One of the limitations of our study is a relatively small data sample. A larger data set is needed to be able to make stronger claims. In a related vein, some researchers have criticized the use of simulated data, suggesting it may not result in "authentic" encounters. Consequently, it would be useful to test our initial results in an actual workplace setting. Nevertheless, this case study produces interesting results that are derived using descriptive and interpretative modes and a close text analysis. It underscores the necessity and value of studies that focus on naturally occurring data and interaction between interlocutors and what they can contribute to our understanding of intercultural teams.

The case study has implications for those engaged in managing, training, or teaching heterogeneous groups composed of members from the US and East Asian countries. The key focus for instructors and trainers is to teach future leaders the value of a cooperative leadership style in supporting greater contribution and participation from members of collectivist cultures. The awareness of leadership as a dialogic skill can empower any group not only to deepen trust and understanding of the "Other" (Witteborn 2011), but to enable better joint decision-making.

References

Alversson M., & Karreman, D. (2000). Varieties of discourse. On the study of organizations through discourse analysis. *Human Relations, 53* (9), 1125–1149.

Aritz, J., & Walker, R. C. (2009). Multicultural groups in decision-making meetings: Language proficiency and group performance. *Journal of Asian Pacific Communication, 20*(2), 307–321.

Aritz J., & Walker R. C. (2010). Cognitive organization and identity maintenance in cross-cultural teams: A discourse analysis of decision-making meetings. *Journal of Business Communication, 47*(1), 20–42.

Ayman, R., & Korabik, K. (2010). Leadership: Why gender and culture matter. *American Psychologist, 65*(3) 157–170.

Bakhtin, M. (1981). The dialogic imagination. (C. Emerson & M. Holquist, Trans.). In M. Holquist (Ed.), *The dialogic imagination: Four essays*. Austin, TX: University of Texas Press.

Baraldi, C. (2013). Forms of decision-making: Gatekeeping and dialogic coordination in CISV meetings. *Journal of Business Communication, 45*(4), 339–361

Bargiela-Chiappini, F. (2004). Introduction: Reflections on a new research paradigm. *International Journal of the Sociology of Language, 166*(1), 1–18.

Bellah, R. N., Madsen, R., Sullivan, W. M., Swindler, A., and Tipton, S. M. (1985). *Habits of the Heart: Individualism and Commitment in American Life*. Berkeley, CA: University of California Press.

Carbaugh, D. (2007). Cultural discourse analysis: Communication practices and intercultural encounters. *Journal of Intercultural Communication Research, 36*(3), 167–182.

Cheng, W. (2003). *Intercultural conversation*. Amsterdam: John Benjamins.

Clyne, Michael. (1994). *Inter-Cultural Communication at Work: Discourse Structures across Cultures*. Cambridge: Cambridge University Press.

Coates, Jennifer 1993. *Women, men and language* (2nd ed.). London & New York: Longman.

Collard, J. (2007). Constructing theory for leadership in intercultural contexts. *Journal of Educational Administration, 45*(6), 740–755.

Earley, C. P., & Gibson, C. B. (2002). *Multinational work teams: A new perspective*. Mahwah, NJ: Lawrence Erlbaum Associates, Publishers.

Earley, C. P., & Mosakoski E. (2000). Creating hybrid team cultures: An empirical test of transnational team functioning. *Academy of Management Journal, 43*, 26–49.

Fairhurst, G. (2008). Discursive leadership. A communication alternative to leadership psychology. *Management Communication Quarterly, 24*, 510–521.

Fairhurst, G. (2010). The Social construction of leadership: A sailing guide. *Management Communication Quarterly, 24*(2), 171–210.

Fairhurst, G. & Cooren, F. (2004). Organizational language in use: Interaction analysis, conversation analysis and speech acts schematics. In David Grant, Cynthia Hardy, Clifford Oswick, Linda Putnam (Eds), *The Sage Handbook of Organizational Discourse* (pp. 131–152). Thousand Oaks, CA: Sage.

Foster, G. M. (1962). *Traditional cultures and the impact of technological change.* New York: Harper and Row.

Ganesh, S., & Holmes, P. (2011). Positioning intercultural dialogue—Theories, pragmatics, and agenda. *Journal of International and Intercultural Communication 4*(2), 81–86.

Gumperz, J. J. (1996). The linguistic and conversational relativity of conversational inference, in J. J. Gumperz & S. Levinson (Eds), *Rethinking linguistic relativity* (pp. 374–406). Cambridge: Cambridge University Press.

Hofstede, G. (1980). *Culture's consequences: International differences in work-related values.* Beverly Hills, CA: Sage.

Hui, C. H. / Triandis, H. C. 1986. Individualism-Collectivism: A Study of Cross-cultural Research. *Journal of Cross-cultural Psychology, 17,* 225–248.

Jehn, K. A., Northcraft, G. B., & Neale, M. A. (1999). Why differences make a difference: A field study of diversity, conflict, and performance in workgroups. *Administrative Science Quarterly, 44*(4), 741–763.

Lam, S., Lau, I., Chiu, C., Hong, Y., and Peng, S. (1999). Differential emphases on modernity and traditional values in social categorization. *International Journal of Intercultural Relations 23,* 237–256.

Marra, M., Jackson, B., Vine, B., Holmes, J., Pfeifer, D. (2008). Exploring co-leadership talk through interactional sociolinguistics. *Leadership, 4*(3), 339–360.

Pilkington, H., and Johnson, R. (2003). Relations of identity and power in global/local context. *Cultural Studies, 6,* 259–283.

Ravlin, E. C., Thomas, D. C., & Ilsev, A. (2000). Beliefs about values, status, and legitimacy in multicultural groups: Influences on intra-group conflict. In P. C. Earley & H. Singh (Eds.), *Innovations in international and cross-cultural management* (pp. 58–83). Thousand Oaks, CA: Sage Publications.

Sacks, H., Schegloff, E. A., & Jefferson, G. (1974). A simplest systematics for the organization of turn-taking for conversation. *Language, 50,* 696–735.

Tannen, Deborah. (1990). *You Just Don't Understand: Women and Men in Conversation.* New York: Ballantine Books.

Westwood, R. (2001). Appropriating the other in the discourses of comparative management. In R. Westwood and S. Linstead (Eds.), *The Language of Organization* (pp. 241–282). London: Sage Publications.

Witteborn, S. (2011). Discursive grouping in a virtual forum: Dialogue, difference, and the "Intercultural." *Journal of International and Intercultural Communication, 4*(2), 109–126.

Wodak, R., Kwon, W., & Clarke, I. (2011). "Getting people on board": Discursive leadership for consensus building in team meetings. *Discourse and Society, 22*(2), 592–644.

Endnote

1. The notation [xxx] in all transcripts indicates inaudible utterances.

PART VIII

Building Dialogue Through
New Information Technologies

15

Le Français en (Première) Ligne: Creating Contexts for Intercultural Dialogue in the Classroom

**Christine Develotte and
Wendy Leeds-Hurwitz**

Key Words

- ► Language learning
- ► Online teaching
- ► International collaboration
- ► Multimodal communication
- ► Synchronous communication

1. Introduction

This case study draws upon nearly a decade of Develotte's experience teaching language online, first through collaboration between a classroom in France and one in Australia, and then a separate cooperative effort between a classroom in France and one in the USA.[1] This project meets three goals simultaneously:

1. Supplementing French language learning for undergraduate students (in either Australia or the US);
2. Providing experience teaching French as a foreign language for Masters' students in France; and
3. Facilitating intercultural dialogue through synchronous online communication between the two populations of students.

One substantial aim of this project is to connect students from different countries who do not share the same language and culture. Students establish links based on the principle of mutual aid; the expected benefit varied by cohort. The French graduate students, in their fifth university year and in a vocational course, acquired professional experience as tutors, whereas the Australian, and later American, students, in their first year at university and beginners in French, gained support in learning about a new language and culture, as well as motivational enhancement. The central question for the professors designing the course assignments involved how to construct conditions under which an intercultural dialogue between students and tutors in different countries can occur. A variety of different technological tools were incorporated, including written chat, the video of interlocutor's image (to provide nonverbal cues), and the oral discussion, all of which will be considered below.

The initial idea for the project was introduced by Develotte, when she was Lecturer at the University of Sydney from 2000 to 2002. At that point, the goal was to use the Internet to put Australian students into direct contact with French culture through interactions with French students training to be teachers. The more formal action research project entitled "Le français en (première) ligne" debuted in 2002–2003 between France and Australia and, since then, the number of participants has increased each year. Beginning in 2006, a partnership between the University of Lyon 2 and the University of California, Berkeley, was established using synchronous online communication (specifically, desktop video conferencing, or DVC).

In the variation described here, second year French students at Berkeley meet four times each week with their local language instructors, and once each week with their Lyon tutors. The Lyon tutors work in pairs with typically two undergraduates. Tutors receive a full semester of technical and pedagogical training prior to the start of the course, and meet weekly with their professor in Lyon (Develotte) to analyze what has occurred in past online sessions, then meet with their students at Berkeley, and then again with their professor to prepare the next lesson. In addition to documenting all interactions between students on videotape, data collection has included videotaping debriefing sessions, as well as interviews and questionnaires. Each "debriefing session" includes the following steps: one week after the online interactions, the tutor pairs each choose three video clips taken from their own fifty-minute interactions with their students: one extract showing a good teaching moment, another a problematic one, and finally, an interaction which puzzles them. The debriefing session focuses on these extracts, shown to the entire group. The two tutors responsible for the interactions describe what occurred, after which the rest of the class holds discussion. This debriefing session provides concrete aid to pre-service teachers, improving their teaching skills through sharing their ideas with others. In addition, a number of graduate students have used all elements of data collected in order to write their Masters' theses or Doctoral dissertations under Develotte's direction, thus providing an opportunity for further detailed analysis and learning.

Additional data have been collected although not yet analyzed. In both France and the US, students answer questionnaires at the beginning of the semester regarding their preconceptions (their expectations for the course, their technical level, linguistic skills, pedagogical experience, etc.). Then, at the end of the semester, interviews of pairs of students (in the US) or focus groups (France) are conducted to determine their perceptions at that stage (whether the course was useful and in what ways, and what aspects could be improved).

This action research project had three goals: (1) helping Masters' students in *Teaching French as a Foreign Language* practice creating multimedia tasks for distant learners; (2) improving not only language learning but also knowledge of a foreign culture for students taking French; and (3) eliciting online dialogue between these two groups around these tasks. Each of these goals has been mentioned previously, but will be discussed at greater length below.

(1) The Masters' students in France (not all of whom are, in fact, French) enroll in a course entitled *Teaching French as a Foreign Language*. As they will become future teachers, they interact with actual students in order to test their ideas about appropriate multimedia tasks and online communication. The project permits them to practice the pedagogy of French as a Foreign Language, to create contextualized tasks for a specific population, as well as to reflect on the technologically-assisted distance-learning process. As a result, they not only learn specific, concrete techniques that work, but also become better, more reflective teachers who take for granted the appropriateness of discussing pedagogical issues with peers. When these students become teachers, they will need to facilitate group work among their students, demonstrate sensitivity to cultural aspects linked to the creation of multimedia tasks, and create a multimedia environment in order to develop a situated and contextualized approach to learning (also called "situated learning"). This project provided good practice for these objectives. Develotte wants the graduate student tutors to be fully aware of the cultural dimension of their pedagogical creations, so she explicitly asks to think about cultural aspects of their target audience (their students), and especially to emphasize aspects of French culture that would most likely interest the undergraduates. The tutors often choose to personalize their creations through thematic choices related to youth culture, including popular music and films, as well as through sharing their own subjective experience of life in France, so that a friendly bond develops between them and the Australian or American undergraduate students.

(2) For the language learners enrolled in a French course in either Australia or the United States, the project substantially supplements their instruction by permitting them to interact with native French speakers, to link their language learning experience to an authentic communication context, to undertake tasks that have an authentic cultural dimension, and thus to reduce the distance between their country and France.

(3) For both populations of students, the project uses current technology to create an opportunity for intercultural dialogue. These intercultural dialogues permit the language students to learn much more than either grammatical structure or discourse conventions, including a variety of cultural learning (about France generally and Lyon specifically), both formal (that is, planned, intentional) and informal (unplanned conversations resulting in discussions about such topics as immigration, or leisure activities). In addition to the undergraduates learning French, and the graduate student tutors learning to teach French, both populations learn a great deal about one another's cultures, as well as how to hold intercultural dialogues in future. The students thus come close to the goal of acquiring "communicative competence"—that is, a complex understanding of how to appropriately use the language they are learning in a wide variety of contexts (Hymes 1972, 1984). By creating a safe space for discussion, as well as supplying a clear task and agenda, this project provides all of the students the opportunity to expand their knowledge about another culture specifically, as well as learning about some of the distinctions between cultures generally.

2. Logistics of Establishing the Project

The project environment for the latest iteration (France/US) is briefly described from a pedagogical and technological point of view so that others who may wish to attempt a similar project will know what to do.

2.1. Establishing a Partnership

The first bond was made at the University of Sydney through Develotte's colleagues in the French department. Then personal links with the other partners were created, often through friends of friends. Archiving the project online (http://fle-1-ligne.u-grenoble3.fr/) permitted additional partners to spontaneously volunteer to join the project. A few years ago Develotte recommended that the Agence Universitaire de la Francophonie (AUF) create an online resource matching learners with future teachers in partnerships through their website, and they agreed. As a result, a French language teacher now can ask AUF to be connected to a partner training future French teachers (or the reverse).[2]

Collaborative projects such as this one require considerable time spent before the beginning of the project in negotiations between the two partners. In order to equally benefit both cohorts, each instructor must anticipate how activities can be appropriately embedded within an existing course. For example, instead of leaving the language learners to integrate conversations with their tutors on their own, knowing the outline of what occurred, the language professor tries to incorporate these dialogues into the following lesson by asking students to reflect on what they have learned, sharing their insights with the entire class.

A second point relates to pre-consideration of the levels of preparation of the students involved. The tutors in France are typically Master's students learning how to teach French as a foreign language. The course is optional in both Grenoble (using asynchronous communication) and in Lyon (using synchronous communication).[3] Both formats have advantages, and deliberate choices should be made by the instructors concerned. Asynchronous communication provides time to think carefully about the right thing to say, especially when coming up with correct grammatical forms as well as coping with divergent intercultural expectations. Synchronous communication provides realistic practice for real-world interaction. Only eighteen total students can participate in the online teaching component due to the small size of the computer laboratory.

2.2. Pedagogical Aspects

The different organization of the academic year across countries has led to a typical schedule of two successive one-semester stages. The following describes the latest US-France model.

Stage 1 (October–January): The French tutors, working in pairs, create multimedia online activities intended for the American students. They know that the Americans are second-year language students, intermediate level, and that they are using a textbook covering seven units in one semester. This work constitutes the main task for a 24-hour course (part of their Master's degree of French as a Foreign Language) called *Learning to Teach Language Online*.

Stage 2 (January–March): the American language learners, who have enrolled in five hours of French class every week, complete the activities created by the French teacher trainees who act as tutors for one hour each week (specifically, they answer questions proposed by the tutors during their online synchronous tutoring session). In addition, they meet four hours per week with their Berkeley instructor, completing the same amount of homework as other students enrolled in this level of French instruction. Experience shows that taking time to coordinate academic schedules between countries and universities is critical—otherwise incorrect assumptions about starting and ending dates, or holidays, could prove disastrous in a cooperative venture of this sort.

2.3. Technical Aspects

Widely available instructional technologies can provide a rich online environment encouraging the establishment of intercultural dialogues between students at various stages and in different countries. Specifically, participants in this project used a desktop video conferencing system (DVC) for both video and chat, supplemented by a variety of documents related to the course used in either electronic form or in hard copy. Various iterations of the project have used MSN Messenger, Skype, or Adobe Connect. The goal has been to choose the simplest communication tool for both partners. The computer laboratory in which the course takes place must have appropriate hardware and software installed. The screenshot in Figure 1 demonstrates resources available to participants in the project.

FIGURE 1 Student Perspective

To explain: Each of the Berkeley students sits in a lab with other students, on a computer with one window showing the lesson for the day, another showing a video image of the tutor in Lyon, and a third available for written exchanges (chat) with their tutors. They wear headphones and a microphone so they can hear the audio aspect of the videotape interaction with their tutors, and respond orally. Typically two tutors sit together in Lyon, having all of the above equipment, plus a detailed lesson plan to guide them, and prepared materials for activities. They also have pencil and paper to note corrections that the students should practice before their next session. For further details on technical aspects, see Develotte, Guichon, and Vincent (2010); Develotte, Mangenot, and Zourou (2005, 2007).

2.4. Communication Tools and Modalities

Choices must be made about both the technologies utilized (Instant Messaging, blogs) and modalities (visible text, audio, webcam image, still image). In the most recent iteration discussed here, and as documented in Figure 2, Skype was chosen as the primary platform for social communication, with a collective blog used to present information about the two cohorts of participants (students in Berkeley and tutors in Lyon), as well as to store documents (pictures or weblinks to online videos).

FIGURE 2   Close up of screen

The workspace is divided into three main areas. Area A (on the left) shows a written file in which tutors can provide different types of information relevant to the pedagogical interaction, including:

▶   A link to the blog where various resources available to serve as a basis for interaction are stored, as well as the password necessary for access; and

▶   Detailed information about each task planned for the teaching session (with instructions, major issues, lexical, and grammatical items).

Area B (in the middle) is composed of written words: a Skype chat presenting vocabulary designed to complement interaction between the tutor and student. Finally, area C (on the right) shows the Skype webcam images of the student (top) and the tutor (bottom). Skype and the blog are only two of the technologies used, those limited to what appears on the computer screen. Additional offline tools, including books, papers, and pens, surround the computer, providing resources that permit the performance of additional tasks (a dictionary to look up a word's definition, or the textbook to consult over questions of what will be included in the next lesson). Articulating two spaces in the same work environment enables participants to pay equal attention to simultaneous ongoing operations. To use Goffman's

(1959) terms, tutors must learn to gracefully move between front stage (what the students and tutors see and hear) and back stage (what only tutors can see and hear). For example, when there are two tutors on the same computer, they regulate interaction either by whispering (e.g., "write it down!" to suggest using chat to convey information to the students) or by gestures made beyond the area visible to the screen (e.g., bumping knees).

3. Constructing Intercultural Dialogues

Rather than attempt to create a new definition for our own purposes, we will use the definition of intercultural dialogue proposed by the Council of Europe, widely used internationally: "Intercultural dialogue is an open and respectful exchange of views between individuals and groups belonging to different cultures that leads to a deeper understanding of the other's global perception" (http://www.coe.int/t/dg4/intercultural/concept_EN.asp-P30_3374). Using this definition, the conversations generated by the project "Le français en (première) ligne" constitute examples of intercultural dialogue: they involve individuals and groups belonging to different cultures, they entail open and respectful exchanges of views, and they lead to a deeper understanding of others' global perceptions. This sort of international pedagogical exchange has particular value in serving as a way to establish dialogues between residents of different countries. The question for the professor designing the course assignments will be how to construct conditions under which a dialogue between students in different countries can occur. Informal dialogues emerge in conversations between the student/tutor pairs even during formal lessons, but also around the edges of official business. These generalizations will be demonstrated through the analysis of a series of examples demonstrating a wide variety of ways in which intercultural dialogues operate, including movement between formal and informal topics, metacommunication, multimodality, the gradual nature of revelations, reflexivity, explicit cross-cultural comparison, and multiple levels of understanding.

3.1. Movement from Formal to Informal

Research on this project shows that it is primarily during non-instructional times, e.g., in moments of authentic dialogues, that opportunities for improving the language and linguistic learning are the most abundant (Nicolaev, 2012; Vincent, 2012). Each week a specific discussion topic, chosen to match Berkeley's French curriculum, guides the activities offered by the Lyon tutors. Among these themes we find, for example, means of transport. This topic of conversation allows students to dialogue by comparing details drawn from their everyday experiences (thus something all students can be expected to easily discuss). The result allows some surprises to emerge during the online interactions, as in the following exchange:

Example 1

Tutor	(Dans ta famille) combien vous avez de voitures ?
	How many of the people in your family have cars?
Student	Quatre
	Four
Tutor	Wouah !!
	Wow!!

Later during this exchange, the student explains that cars are less expensive in the US. The transition between a question asked by a tutor of a language learner to a question by a young French student of a slightly younger American student occurs easily as a result of the degree of investment and engagement in topics such as students' lives. It is when the American students answer questions regarding their personal context (in this example, "people in your family") that the dialogue takes the form of an authentic exchange between interactants. Dialogues co-constructed during the sessions result from the degree of involvement induced by the platform and technological tool(s).

3.2.   Movement from Informal to Formal

However, occasionally the opposite occurs. That is, what appears to be a casual conversation about topics of mutual interest to students and/or tutors is interrupted for a grammar lesson. This can either occur at the request of the students (who may ask for clarification about a confusing grammatical issue) or the tutors (who may correct what they hear). The following example includes both methods of turning a casual conversation into a grammar lesson, demonstrating that even when students and tutors are engaged in learning new information about one another's cultures, they never completely set aside their primary purpose of language learning/teaching.

Example 2

Student:	Je suis surpris par le partie des gens qui va au campagne, campagne est masculin ou féminin
	I am surprised by some of the people who go to the country, country is masculine or feminine?
Tutor:	Qui va à la campagne ouais
	Who go to the country [in feminine form], yeah

Student: Ah il y a beaucoup de gens qui va à la campagne, ici beaucoup de gens qui va à la campagne pour les vacances

Ah, there are many people who go to the country, here many people go to the country for vacation

Tutor: Pas aux états-unis ?

Not in the United States?

Student: Il y a des arbres et des légumes ((rire))

There are trees and vegetables ((laughs))

Tutor: ((laughs))

Student: Je ne sais pas il n'est pas les places qui fait du vin vigne.

I don't know, it's not the place where wine is made

Tutor: L'endroit ce n'est pas l'endroit tu as dit la place, c'est ca, ce n'est pas l'endroit préféré des américains pour les vacances, tu dis

The destination, it wasn't "the destination," you said "the location," that's it, so you're saying it's not the preferred vacation destination for Americans

Student: Oui

yes

Tutor: okay

3.3.   Metacommunicative Comments

Since the beginning of the project, data have been used for research into language learning; thus all students typically have been interviewed at the end of March to learn their impression of their lived experience, and what impact the technological tools have had on them. Specifically, the goal is to learn what benefit comes from the DVC platform and the use of each different interactional tool used: the written chat, the video of interlocutor's image (for nonverbal cues), and the oral discussion.

   In the following example drawn from interview data, a Berkeley student discusses issues that may arise during an online conversation.

Example 3

Student: There's so much to talk about because it's probably like anything we'd mention to her [the tutor], she would have something to say about that would be different than what we would have expected. And like a lot of times, we'd say, oh we've done such and such, and she'd say like, "Really, you do that?" She was talking about fraternities. "We don't have fraternities in France" and it sparks a whole other conversation level. Why is that? There's a whole lot to talk about.

This student's words convey an enthusiasm representative of other interview comments. The substantial value of the project lies in the fact that it introduces "real life" into the classroom by allowing students to interact with each other in real time through technology. This student expresses the openness of the online conversations and questions the international differences (that there are no fraternities in France, in this example) as preliminary evidence from which participants can engage in dialogue to better understand a world differently organized elsewhere.

During interviews, at least some of the students were quite explicit about the benefit of interactions with their French tutors. The fact that they recognized the multiple types of learning occurring during their lessons means they will have a more complex understanding in future learning opportunities.

Example 4

Student: I mean it wasn't as much the exercises that we did, that stuff, that was cool, but I don't think that was the most important thing to us during the sessions. I think we most enjoyed being able to talk to her and like when we talked about what was going on in Lyon, if there's a protest happening that day like what it was about, we just kind of talked about just everyday stuff that you talk about with another student you know. I think that was the coolest thing just to be able to have the chance to just kind of have a normal conversation with somebody in French you know that didn't have to be structured around ok, let's walk through this exercise.

Similarly, tutors could also be explicit about what they gained during their own interviews.

Example 5

Tutor: Apports au niveau culturel : on a l'impression de plus apprendre qu'eux, ça pouvait être les journées sécurité routière organisées là-bas, les annonceurs TV les plus marrants en ce moment aux Etats Unis, c'était surtout les assureurs, vraiment chaque jour j'ai appris de trucs sur Berkeley, les colloques dépendant de la TV, non franchement l'échange interculturel il était vraiment bilatéral.

[On] contributions to the cultural level: It seems like the more we learn, it could be about road safety days held there, or which TV announcers are the funniest right now in the US, it was mainly insurers, really each day I learned things about Berkeley, online TV seminars, no, frankly the intercultural exchange was truly bilateral.

Part of what is important here is the increased ability of participants to learn to talk explicitly about what (and how) they are learning, as with the students. But for the tutors there was a second level: in keeping with the fact that they were learning to become teachers, understanding how learning occurs, and how to establish contexts in which learning could easily occur, were equally critical.

3.4.   Multimodal Communication

Using a DVC platform allows participants to have access to their interlocutor's image, and more, to have access to nonverbal elements of the communication system used by another culture. Hence, synchronous online exchanges directly confront each speaker's norms of politeness and the socio-affective expressions of interlocutors, and their expectations about what is typical and appropriate behavior. It is possible to test the reactions they may have to otherness, as in the following example.

Example 6

At one point, a tutor ended a lesson by sending kisses to her students in three modes: via chat and audio and video.

TDP		TEMPS			MODALITÉS		
		DEBUT ACTIVITE	FIN ACTIVITE	DUREE	AUDIO	CLAVARDAGE	VIDÉO
840	CEL CLA	39:12,9	39:16,1	00:03,2		gros bisous !!!	
841	CEL	39:16,5	39:20,0	00:03,5	gros bisous (bruits bisous)		
842	CAI	39:18,5	39:24,6	00:06,1	(rires) merci (rires)		
843	CEL	39:20,2	39:23,0	00:02,8	(rires)		
844	CEL CLA	39:24,5	39:32,1	00:07,6		💋 💋	
845	CEL	39:25,0	39:29,0	00:04,0	on va faire des bisous hop		
846	CAI	39:31,3	39:31,9	00:00,6	(rires)		
847	JAI CLA	39:32,2	39:32,5	00:00,3		😊	
848	SIL			00:00,0			
849	CEL	39:33,7	39:34,8	00:01,1	oh (rires)		

Extrait 48 : Dernières salutations de clôture intimidantes (séance 8*)

FIGURE 3   Leave-taking Exchange

In reaction, one of her two students returned a smiley face representing shyness. In this case, differences in language and cultural norms need to be accommodated as well as differences in social status between student and tutor. In discussing this, the two (male) students participating in this exchange said about the interaction with their two (female) tutors:

Student 1:   One thing I noticed as we became more friendly toward the end like when they'd say goodbye to us, when leaving, they'd say "Kisses!" and, like, what else? [laughter] and that would kind of throw me off guard because that's not something we usually say when we're saying goodbye to someone [laughter].

Student 2:   I remember the last day, they're like "bisous!" [kisses] and I'm like "I'm not going to throw them a kiss!"

In her doctoral dissertation analyzing this data, Samira Drissi shows that

> through the study of affective behavior of tutors a tacit consent appears through the online sessions. Tutors, by expressing many emotions, especially laughter, and lots of humor, have created an affective atmosphere conducive to exchanges, at the risk of making the learners uncomfortable. We [tutors] were also able to identify the chemistry between the participants during greetings and salutation closing. These salutations are warm or too warm for learners (2011, 300)

Drissi refers to the precise sequence mentioned above. In regard to the French tutors, such an extract of online interactions can be used effectively when preparing for future online sessions. The following are some of the questions that this exercise has prompted: How should tutors show themselves to foreign learners? What degree of friendship/fellowship should they show? To what extent? Through discussions of authentic interactions with their students, tutors become aware of the impact their own words and actions as teachers have on their students.

3.5.   Successive Revelations over Time

Understanding of another cultural reality is often constructed gradually through the slow accretion of detail. In the following example, the tutor begins with the French context, a known quantity, gradually making sense of the new reality through clarification of common education-related concepts such as large lecture classes versus small discussion sections.

Example 7

Tutor: Puisque tu as passé une année à Bordeaux, que penses-tu des études en France?

Given that you spent a year in Bordeaux, what do you think of studying in France?

Student: Il y a une grosse différence entre les universités françaises et américaines. Il y a moins d'interactions dans les universités françaises.

There is a big difference between French and American universities. There is less interaction in French universities.

Tutor: Tu veux dire qu'il y a plus de cours magistraux ?

You mean there are more large lectures?

Student: Oui, ici pour chaque cours magistral il y a un autre plus petit dans lequel on discute.

Yes, here for each large lecture course there is a smaller discussion section.

Tutor: Plus petit comment ?

Smaller how?

Student: Dans une classe où on est moins nombreux

In a class where there are fewer students.

Tutor: Ah, comme des travaux dirigés ?

Oh, like tutorials?

Student: Oui, et c'est des étudiants-doctorants qui enseignent dans les petits cours alors c'est plus facile de parler avec eux.

Yes, doctoral students teach the smaller sections so it's easier to talk with them.

3.6.   Self-reflection

Often students are able to demonstrate reflexivity as a result of their efforts to discuss their own past behavior and understandings with their tutors (and other students). In such cases, they may show comprehension of what they did not adequately understand in the interactional moment. This process of re-consideration of past inappropriate behavior permits students to demonstrate their increased knowledge over time.

Example 8

Student: Je me souviens quand j'étais à Bordeaux c'était une fête et on commençait à boire et un garçon a levé son verre et à dit : « santé » et moi j'ai compris « sentez ! » et j'ai senti mon verre et j'ai vu que le garçon a pensé que j'étais folle !

I remember when I was in Bordeaux, it was a party and they began to drink and one guy raised his glass and said "cheers" and I understood "smell!" And I smelled my glass, and the guy thought I was crazy!

Participants typically only tell stories about their own incompetence to friends so, although it is an apparent contradiction, this sort of exchange of personal stories about embarrassing moments both demonstrates trust and builds it.

3.7.   Cross-cultural Comparison

One key element of intercultural dialogues occurs when participants explicitly compare their assumptions, their past experiences, and their cultures, learning the ways in which others make different assumptions based on different experiences in different cultures. Given the context of a language course, often the issues described relate to methods of language teaching and learning, as in the following.

Example 9

Tutor: Les conjugaisons en français sont différentes et plus complexes en français qu'en anglais.

French conjugations are different and more complex in French than in English.

Student: Moi j'ai appris les conjugaisons en anglais quand je les ai apprises en français.

I learned conjugations in English when I learned them in French.

Tutor: Nous, on nous fait apprendre tous les verbes irréguliers en anglais par liste. Il faut les apprendre par cœur, ce n'est pas amusant. Et toi c'était pareil ?

We learn all the irregular verbs in English as a list. We have to memorize them, and it's not fun. Is it the same for you?

Student: Non, c'est très difficile pour moi d'apprendre par cœur, c'est quand j'entends les mots que je les retiens sinon je n'arrive pas les apprendre toute seule, je les oublie vite.

No, it's very difficult for me to memorize by heart. It's when I hear the words that I remember them, because if I don't have the chance to learn them one at a time I forget them quickly.

Partly due to the metacommunicative nature of this conversation (since it is about ways of learning the language that is the subject of the course), the student and tutor each learn something new from the other. Each knows only their own method, and so is surprised by that of the other. In France, typically primary school students learn explicit grammatical terms as they learn their first language, and then have an easier time learning the parallel constructions in their second language. But in the US many primary school students are no longer explicitly taught grammatical terms, and so they are faced with triple work when learning a second language: they need to learn the grammatical categories, then learn how these are used in their first language, and then learn how to use them in a second language. At the same time, the tutor and student each gain knowledge about multiple techniques for acquiring new knowledge: both straight memorization and more gradual learning in context exist as alternatives.

3.8. Multiple Levels of Understanding

The American students expressed considerable curiosity about the private lives of their tutors, and sometimes asked explicit questions in order to increase their understanding of French culture. And of course, sometimes the French tutors did the same with their American students. Both cases indicate the safe context constructed for the asking of personal questions, and a willingness to answer such questions in this context, even though they might be deemed inappropriate in other contexts.

Example 10

Student: Je suis curieux.

I'm curious.

Tutor: Oui oui je vois ça.

Yes, yes, I can see that.

Student: J'ai une question : où est ce que tu voyages ?

I have a question: where have you traveled?

[The tutor tells a story about traveling to Spain, and how she loves this country where she taught French. At the end of the conversation, the student sums up.]

Student: J'ai appris un peu les habitudes des Français. Je pense que c'est toujours intéressant nous avons appris quelque chose de ta vie en Espagne.

I've learned a little about French habits. I think it's always interesting, we've learned something about your life in Spain.

The student's question uses an opening marker that, at least in English, indicates politeness, and a warning that something potentially inappropriate is about to be asked. The student learns that this works equally well in French by virtue of the fact that the tutor both acknowledges understanding the curiosity, and answers the question explicitly posed. As a result, the student learns not only the answer to the explicit question (about where the French travel) but also about how to ask potentially delicate personal questions of the French.

4. Conclusions

Creating contexts and opportunities for intercultural dialogue in the classroom no longer requires being confined to the classroom space. Technological advances have opened the classroom to the world existing outside of an educational institution, and students can now easily cross the borders between countries. The whole point of live contact, as documented in this study, involving young speakers (the Berkeley undergraduates average twenty-two years old, while the Lyon graduate students average twenty-four) lies in the fact that, even if they are all in front of their computer screen, students see themselves as interacting as if they were in the same country and in the presence of students of the target language (in this case, French), without the usual intermediary of their teacher. In the absence of the opportunity to take advantage of a study abroad program, this online exchange helps to bring some authenticity to the language learning process. In addition, students acquire the opportunity to ask the same sorts of questions, regarding topics such as age, knowledge of languages, where they live, family, activities, etc., as would be asked during a study abroad experience. This is not to suggest that technology has outdated study abroad, only that technology now permits lesser but similar experiences for those who do not have the time or money available for the full immersion experience. Online discussions compare with study abroad in the way they permit language learners to interact in real time with native speakers, and learn unexpected details about the structure of interaction as well as vocabulary and grammar. However, using technology rather than being face-to-face obviously means that students miss some channels of communication with their tutors, as well as the entire larger context of living abroad, which typically would result in a wide variety of supplementary conversations with additional native speakers, rather than only their tutors.

Current technology readily permits the construction of many similar intercultural dialogues across international borders, and globalization requires that such dialogues occur because they are an excellent resource for learning about other cultures, and far less superficial than many alternatives. This chapter has provided explanation of the benefits in order to encourage other faculty members to begin similar projects, as well as sufficient details to make comparable projects possible. Language learning and intercultural communication courses are the most obvious beginning points, but similar intercultural dialogues using current instructional technologies could be established for a wide variety of courses and disciplines, from history to area studies to the arts. In addition, creation of online resources to aid in finding an appropriate partner in a foreign country, as already exists in France, would significantly increase the number of future projects. The key elements to establishing a successful collaboration are:

1. Having a shared, necessary task that brings about and then frames the interaction (in this case, either language learning or language teaching);
2. Repeated opportunities for interaction with the same conversational partner so that participants become comfortable with one another and begin asking more personal questions (in this case, pairs of undergraduate/graduate students);

3. Sufficient flexibility to permit informal learning to occur (in this case, through time and structural flexibility permitting students (and tutors) to ask questions and expand on the formal conversational topics); and

4. Continued analysis of recent interactions matched to guidance for the next steps (in this case, through faculty instruction during graduate courses in France, and faculty instruction during undergraduate courses in the US).

Together these components assist in creating the appropriate context for stimulating intercultural dialogues through synchronous exchanges within language learning contexts by encouraging and permitting an open exchange of views between individuals coming from different cultures, leading to increased understanding of the other's global perception (to paraphrase the original Council of Europe definition previously presented). By definition, language courses have as their primary goal the teaching of a new language; the fact that students gain functional communicative and intercultural competence through their intercultural dialogues with their foreign tutors appropriately and substantially expands this goal, as demonstrated by much foreign language education research.

Courses in other topics could easily incorporate similar intercultural dialogues, only substituting expanded global knowledge of their primary subjects, whether history, political science, geography, or something else, as the initial spark for interaction. In any of these cases, the specific elements of intercultural dialogue presented here, including movement between formal and informal topics, metacommunication, multimodality, the gradual nature of revelations, reflexivity, explicit cross-cultural comparison, and multiple levels of understanding, are all likely to occur. These essential elements to holding intercultural dialogues are part of what is learned as a result of them, and why gaining intercultural understanding of members of any one group makes it a little easier to understand members of any other group.

References

Develotte, C., Guichon, N., & Kern, R. (2008). "Allo Berkeley? Ici Lyon… Vous nous voyez bien?" Étude d'un dispositif d'enseignement-apprentissage en ligne synchrone franco-américain à travers les discours de ses usagers. *ALSIC: Apprentissage des Langues et Systèmes d'Information et de Communication, 11*(2), 129–156.

Develotte, C., Guichon, N., & Vincent, C. (2010). The use of the webcam for teaching a foreign language in a desktop videoconferencing environment. *ReCALL, 23*(3), 293–312. Retrieved from http://halshs.archives-ouvertes.fr/halshs-00806433

Develotte, C., Mangenot, F., & Zourou, K. (2005). Situated creation of multimedia activities for distance learners: Motivational and cultural issues. ReCALL, *17,* 229–244. Retrieved from http://halshs.archives-ouvertes.fr/halshs-00151847

Develotte, C., Mangenot, F., & Zourou, K. (2007). Learning to teach online: 'Le français en (première) ligne' project. In R. O'Dowd (Ed.), *Online intercultural exchange* (pp. 276–280). Clevedon: Multilingual Matters.

Drissi, S. (2011). *Apprendre à enseigner par visioconférence: Étude d'interactions pédagogiques entre futures enseignants et apprenants de FLE.* (Unpublished doctoral dissertation). École Normale Supérieure de Lyon, France.

Goffman, E. (1959). *The presentation of self in everyday life.* Garden City, NY: Doubleday.

Hymes, D. H. (1972). On communicative competence. In J. B. Pride & J. Holmes (Eds.), *Sociolinguistics* (pp. 269–293). London: Penguin.

Hymes, D. H. (1984). *Vers la compétence de communication.* (Trans. F. Mugler). Paris: Hatier.

Nicolaev, V. (2012). *L'apprentissage du FLE dans un dispositifi vidéographique synchrone : etude des sequences métalinguistiques.* (doctoral dissertation). École Normale Supérieure de Lyon, http://tel.archives-ouvertes.fr/docs/00/79/31/85/PDF/NICOLAEV_Viorica_2012_These.pdf.

Vincent, C. (2012). *Interactions pédagogiques "fortement multimodales"en ligne : le cas de tuteurs en formation.* (doctoral dissertation). École Normale Supérieure de Lyon, http://tel.archives-ouvertes.fr/docs/00/76/59/86/PDF/VINCENT_Caroline_2012_these.pdf.

Endnotes

1. There have been numerous partner sets over the past decade between several different universities in France and other countries, including partners not only in the US and Australia, but also Latvia, Brazil, Japan, Luxembourg, and Spain. This analysis relies primarily upon data drawn from the iteration of the project between the Université de Lyon 2 (Christine Develotte and Nicolas Guichon) and the University of California, Berkeley (Richard Kern and Désirée Pries), but makes generalizations as a result of the entire decade of collaborations. Further information on earlier iterations may be found in Develotte, Guichon, and Vincent (2010); Develotte, Mangenot, and Zourou (2005, 2007).

2. See http://www.aidenligne-francais universite.auf.org/spip.php?page=sommaire_appui_ens_fr

3. The course in Grenoble is taught by François Mangenot; the one in Lyon by Develotte, with a colleague, Nicolas Guichon.

16

Potential of Diasporic Discussion Forums for Inter- and Transcultural Dialogue: Case Studies of Moroccan and Turkish Diaspora in Germany

Çigdem Bozdağ

Key Words

- ▶ Transcultural communication
- ▶ Moroccan and Turkish diaspora
- ▶ Online discussion forum
- ▶ Contact zone
- ▶ New communication technologies

1. Introduction

The issue of dialogue between cultures is today discussed more than ever through increasing globalization, migration flows, and developing information and communication technologies (ICTs). While intercultural encounters become a part of people's daily lives, ICTs contribute to the emergence of new "contact zones," where cultures meet (Pratt 1991). Among these technologies, the Internet, especially, enables different forms of contact zones by creating a potential space for inter- and transcultural dialogue through its participatory and open structure. This paper deals with the potential of the Internet for dialogue between different migrant groups and other people in their country of settlement by looking at the cases of Moroccan and Turkish diasporic discussion forums.

The paper primarily relies on the transcultural perspective, alongside the intercultural paradigm, for the discussion of dialogue on the Internet. The concept of intercultural dialogue deals with communication processes "between" cultures. Nevertheless, culture is not something pre-given with clear boundaries, but is continuously (re)articulated through the interactions of people. We can still speak of intercultural communication, when people imagine cultures as distinct entities and communicate with 'others' on the basis of the perceived cultural differences. But it is also crucial to look at communication situations, in which no such cultural boundaries are articulated. Hence, transcultural communication can be a useful concept to understand transgressions between cultures and hybrid forms, especially in the case of diaspora, which are marked by these.

Moreover, in order to understand the potential of the Internet for inter- and transcultural dialogue, we need to move beyond techno-deterministic perspectives, which consider technologies as the driving forces behind socio-cultural change. The media, in this case the media of diaspora, have a potential to change migrants' and other groups' perspectives of each other by providing a space not only for dialogue between them. (Diasporic) media production becomes even cheaper and easier through the Internet. This paves the way for emergence of new forms of contact zones, in which users of different cultural backgrounds meet and enter into dialogue as in the example of diasporic discussion forums. However, this technological capability of the Internet should be considered in relation to its social use (Ang & Pothen 2009, 6).

On the basis of user interviews, observation protocols and forum threads, this paper analyzes the social use of four diasporic discussion forums in Germany: Dimadima (DD) and MarocZone (MZ) (Moroccan Diaspora) as well as Turkish-Talk (TT) and Vaybee (VB) (Turkish diaspora) in order to understand if and how dialogue between cultures takes place on the Internet. The discussion revolves around the following questions: How is a communication space for dialogue being established through the implication of formal and informal rules on the forums? How do users reflect on cultural differences that they encounter in their everyday lives? And how do users of different cultural backgrounds on the forums engage in inter- and transcultural dialogue? I argue that through intercultural dialogue on the diasporic discussion forums, cultural differences can be articulated, reinforced, recognized, and accepted. We also observe the processes of transcultural dialogue on the forums, through which a common horizon of meaning production beyond cultural differences emerges.

2. Inter- and Transcultural Dialogue on the Internet: Emerging Contact Zones

Intercultural communication in general refers to communication processes between people of diverse cultures. In contrast to more essentialist conceptualizations of relations between cultures, which suppose a necessary tension between them because of their differences, the intercultural paradigm seeks ways through which cultures might communicate beyond conflicts (Welsch 1999; Jandt 2010). However, most popular definitions of intercultural communication still consider cultures as clearly bounded entities "spheres" or "islands" and do not consider "cultures beyond contraposition of ownness and foreignness" (Welsch 1999, 2–3).

Perceived cultural boundaries still play an important role in the everyday lives of people. Nevertheless, these boundaries are continuously being renegotiated through communication, and the research on communication between cultures should focus on such communicative construction processes of cultures. For the diaspora, as well as for other cultural groups, the boundary-making processes are marked by the "transculturation"; transgressions of cultural boundaries which cannot be understood through the lenses of cultures as enclosed 'spheres' (Robins 2006, 29–31; Hepp & Couldry 2009, 40). We can speak of intercultural communication when the communication takes place between people who imagine cultures as separate entities during their communication and perceive themselves as members of culturally different groups (Conti 2010, 185; Witteborn 2011, 123). However, we should also consider the transcultural communication processes between people, in which they deconstruct such perceived differences. Through transcultural communication, a potential for a common horizon for interpretations of reality beyond cultural differences emerges because cultural boundaries are being transgressed. This paper refers to both intercultural and transcultural communication.

Dialogue, as a specific form of communication, can also be intercultural or transcultural depending on the perceptions of people involved. Dialogue is a useful concept for analyzing communication between cultures. The concept is mostly used normatively and influenced by the policies of different institutions. For example, the Council of Europe defines "intercultural dialogue" as "an open and respectful exchange of views between individuals and groups belonging to different cultures that leads to a deeper understanding of the other's global perception" (Council of Europe 2008). In this definition, dialogue is directed toward certain goals perceived as a way to increase empathy between people and groups. Other definitions emphasize openness or equal opportunities for active participation during dialogue, and mutual understanding and cross-cultural adaptation as outcomes of the process (see Baraldi 2006, 62). Such definitions presume that processes of dialogue will have certain outcomes. However, even if people are engaged in an "open and respectful" dialogue, it is not guaranteed that they will foster broader participation, equality, or mutual understanding. Dialoguing is itself an open-ended process of meaning-making, in which users encounter, negotiate, deconstruct or (re)create difference, and also exclusions (Witteborn 2011, 111–112). Still, dialogue is not to be equated with any kind of communication; it rather refers to a specific form as I argue.

This paper defines dialogue also as an 'open' and 'respectful' form of communication between people with different backgrounds, who enter into a reciprocal, verbal interaction and produce meanings, yet does not specifically presume any outcomes. If people are excluded from the communication or just fight, flame, and insult each other, we cannot speak of a reciprocal communication situation. Therefore, the process of communication should be inclusive regardless of the political, ethnic, or religious backgrounds of the users, and promote respect for each other. Dialogue does not always change people's views of others, but in order to make a difference about the perceptions of cultural differences, it should be a process of "self-reflection" and "reflection on others" and go beyond rhetoric as a practice of persuasion or a non-oppositional discourse (McPhail 2004, 215).

Dialogue between cultures takes place in different forms of 'contact zones'; "social spaces where cultures meet, clash and grapple with each other, often in contexts of highly asymmetrical power relations" (Pratt 1991, 34). In this paper, the 'contact zone' refers to the spaces of the Internet, such as diasporic websites, where people of different cultural backgrounds meet, communicate, and change their perspectives of each other by reflecting on differences, and entering into inter- and transcultural dialogue. However, online contact zones involve unequal power relations, conflict, or sheer indifference and do not necessarily entitle dialogue (Ang & Pothen 2009, 6). Therefore, technological capabilities of the Internet lead to socio-cultural change and dialogue only through a process of appropriation by the users. The following section discusses such processes of appropriation of online contact zones that emerge through the diasporic discussion forums.

3. Online Discussion Forums of the Moroccan and Turkish Diaspora in Germany

Through increasing global migration, the questions of dialogue and living together with cultural differences become even more crucial than before. This study undertakes a comparative analysis of discussion forums of Moroccan and Turkish migrants in Germany, who began arriving in Germany in the 1960s through the bilateral recruitment agreements and an increasing educational migration after the 1990s (Karakasoglu 2007; de Haas 2009). A comparison between these groups is promising since they have a similar migration history, similar religious backgrounds, and similar experiences with Germans as well as other Non-Muslims in Germany. The Moroccan diaspora in Germany, with a population of 108,000 (de Haas 2009, 4), is much smaller than the Turkish diaspora, which has a population over 2 million (Rühl 2009, 34). This difference in size also influences their relationships with people from other cultures. Furthermore, in the Turkish case, very diverse and contradicting cultural positions are to be found in terms of relations to other cultural (Muslim and Non-Muslim) groups, whereas in the Moroccan case, the religious identity is a strong uniting factor with other ethnic groups with Muslim backgrounds.

Arguments presented here are based on a media-ethnographic analysis of German-speaking discussion forums of the Moroccan and Turkish diaspora: MarocZone (MZ), Dimadima (DD), Vaybee! (VB) and Turkish-Talk (TT). As the ethnographer in this study, I am a migrant with Turkish background living in Germany, which helped the entrance in the field as well as understanding the cultural contexts. The empirical material consists of individual, semi-structured interviews with seventy people from the Turkish and Moroccan diaspora on their media use[1], observation protocols of the forums and selected forum threads. The quotes from forum threads are translated from German to English by the author and the names of the posters are changed with fictional names. The chosen forums define themselves as migrant forums implicitly or explicitly (for example, VB as "The Website of the New Generation," or DD as "Arab Community Forum"). These forums provide migrants with their "own" space, where they do not feel as a minority and they can interpret their experiences and negotiate identity discourses in this "safe" space (Mitra 2005, 375); the forums also provide a communication space for dialogue among people of different cultural backgrounds. The four forums are similar in their structure with pre-given thematic areas about politics in Germany and the homeland, questions of identity, cooking, sports, finances, etc. However, they differ in terms of the diversity of their users. For example, MZ consists mostly of Moroccan users from Germany and users who identify themselves as Germans. DD, on the other hand, has many users from different Arabic countries and German users, who mostly have an Islamic religious background. In the Turkish case, TT-users constitute a mixture of Germans and Turkish migrants in Germany, whereas VB has a majority of Turkish users. Through these different compositions of user profiles, each website has a different potential for dialogue. On the basis of these cases, firstly, I discuss how an open and respectful communication space is being established through formal and informal rules on the forums. Secondly, I look at the ways users reflect on cultural differences they experience in their everyday lives, and interpret these experiences. Lastly, I develop a discussion on the ways users articulate cultural differences on the forums.

3.1. Establishing a Space for Dialogue

An open and respectful communication maintained through formal and informal rules is the prerequisite of dialogue on the discussion forums. Formal rules are implemented by the administrators of the forums through sanctions like public warnings, deletion of postings or threads, and blocking or banning of the users. Informal rules are negotiated and implemented by the users also through sanctions such as public accusations, and ignoring or excluding from discussions.

The *formal rules* of the communication are presented transparently on all forums and include banning of insulting words, off-topics, and illegal, defaming, racist, or pornographic content. As they are applying the formal rules, the administrators are influenced by their social, cultural, political, and religious backgrounds. This sometimes leads to conflicts between the administrators and users and raises questions about the fairness of administrators' decisions. In the following exchange Lina complains about the administrator of the website DD because of her deleted posts:

> **Lina:** The truth is painful, isn't it!!! My postings were deleted, you couldn't bear the truth [. . .]

> **Tamar:** I couldn't bear my truth either so I also deleted my own postings. Your and my postings didn't have anything to do with the subject, everyone can take a look at it in the recycle bin [. . .]

> **Faithless:** But Toufik also deleted my postings as well as other users'. On top of that you can still read them. [. . .] (DD, My postings were deleted, 1)[2]

In cases of dispute, the administrators have the right to decide, which creates a hierarchical communication situation on the forums. However, in the case above, the forum administrator Tamar is defending his decision by arguing that he acted fairly by also deleting his own posts as well and points out that the deleted postings can still be read in the "recycle bin" of the forum. Such transparency of rules is appreciated by the users, like Faithless, whose postings were also deleted from the same thread, but he is still defending Tamar's decision to Lina.

The intensity of the formal rules varies on the analyzed forums. Tight control and frequent interventions in MZ, DD, and TT are perceived as a constraint on communication and freedom of speech by some of the users. However, absence of the formal regulations, might easily lead to insult, flame, or hate speech by discouraging any form of dialogue. For example, VB-user Fossil complains in a thread about the lack of regulations and the arbitrary implementation of rules by the moderators of VB: "Woow . . . First, leave the unchivalrous postings of Wowwow [a user] here for days, then delete them altogether with the honest-meant and good-written reaction-postings to it! What a dull policy . . .". Compared to the other three forums, the postings on VB are loosely controlled. This situation sometimes results in the hostility of the users.

The communication on the forums is also shaped by usually tacitly implemented *informal rules*. These emerge through discussions about the communication style on the forums when there is a change in the communication infrastructure or when some users break the rules. For example, in a discussion about the banning of the burka in France, a conflict emerges and TT-users start to discuss the norms of debating:

> **Kinik:** [. . .] At the beginning you are good and to the point but you disqualify yourself with this [quote from above], in the developing "dialogue" with Lale, which blots your fame definitely!!!!

Hs-again: Good, I am ridiculous with my polemic. I see this as a chevalier act from your side and from people like you. But I find it sad that you can't enrich this discussion with arguments or examples or even with polemic. [. . .] For me, the discussion was over with the last posting of Pit. He has his way of things and I have mine. But still, I think that we will engage in a rational discussion again and exchange arguments like irony and polemic (TT, Burka-Ban in France, 91).

Whereas Kinik criticizes the polemic in the thread above, Hs-again believes that polemic is part of dialogue and can even enrich the discussion. Through such discussions the users interpret what is considered a good and acceptable form of dialogue and these negotiations are crucial for shaping the communication style on the forums. Besides the formal ones, such negotiated informal rules also contribute to an 'open' and 'respectful' communication environment.

3.2. Reflections on Cultural Differences in Everyday Life

On the forums, dialogue takes place about cultural differences that users face in their everyday lives, and their experiences gain a meaning. These reflections on the forums often contribute to the reconstruction of perceived differences because cultural boundaries in people's minds are not deconstructed easily. However, they might also be important moments of transcultural dialogue, through which these boundaries are deconstructed in debates between different positions.

Because many users, as members of diasporas, are constantly confronted with tensions between various cultural contexts in their everyday lives, questions of belonging and being in-between two cultures, as well as issues and reflections about themselves and other cultures, constitute an important part of discussions taking place on the forums. This can be seen in the exchange between ak and unusual:

ak: I am a Turk! I will always remain to be a Turk!
I hate Germany and the Germans!
They hate us too but they can't do anything [. . .]
BUT I know that germanized Turkish youth who forgot their own identity and disdain their own people are the majority! [. . .]

Unusual: That is not true. The people, who are integrated, who are germanized in your opinion, are much less. Many are just among themselves and cannot even speak German accurately. They don't think with a wide horizon and that is because of the family and the environment. To be with people from different countries broadens one's perspective. It does not mean that you would lose your Turkishness.

Try not to hate everybody and be tolerant to all despite all that happens so that they also treat you the same way. Until now, I never had the feeling that the Germans or the others hate me. [. . .] (VB, Participation in a research from Turkey]

The exchange above provides a good example of the articulation of different cultural identification patterns in the diaspora. Whereas ak sees a clear difference and hatred between "Germans" and "Turks," for Unusual the difference lies between the "integrated" Turks and the people "who are among themselves." Unusual is still trying to convince ak to open up to "people from other countries" to have a "wide horizon," but she is also talking about "Germans" or "others" as separated groups. Whereas the differences in the Turkish diaspora are often articulated along ethnic lines between "Turkish" and "German" people, in the Moroccan diaspora differences are mostly perceived between "Muslims" and "Non-Muslims." Processes of dialogue like the above might even reinforce these differences because users tend to defend their own positions, but they also bring encountering positions together, and open up a discursive space to question and relativize their opinions.

As members of minority groups in national contexts, the experiences of difference in diaspora are also related to questions of power and exclusion. Forum users especially discuss situations in the country of migration in which they felt discriminated because of their cultural backgrounds. For example, in the MZ-Thread "wearing a head scarf," Marocgirl describes how her manager reacted after she started to wear a headscarf by stating that she was employed as she was not wearing a headscarf and asks her to remove it. In this thread, Morocgirl receives support from other users about her decision to wear it. Both Moroccan and Turkish migrants are often addressed in Germany as the more problematical migrant groups in comparison to Non-Muslim migrant groups. Having their 'own' communication space like the diasporic websites, in which they are not 'the problematical minority,' but the majority, is important for them to exchange their experiences and build self-confidence as minority groups. Sharing their experiences of discrimination among a public that has similar experiences can help the users to cope with these experiences as in the case above. However, reciprocal approval might also contribute to the reinforcement of one's own perception of differences through a shared position and this might lead to avoidance of contact with 'others.'

Users not only share negative experiences on the forums, but also negotiate the framework of their relations with the perceived 'others' in their everyday lives. For example, the user Elif explains in the MZ-forum that she/he is willing to invite a colleague to dinner to thank her for a favor. However, she/he is not sure how to behave during the dinner as a Muslim and asks for advice from other users (MZ, inviting Non-Muslims to dinner). Many of the users agree that he/she should never pay for pork or alcohol, but should still invite her to a halal restaurant. Elif indicates that she/he has not thought about this aspect before and thanks the other users for their advice. This exchange shows how users discuss on the basis of pre-assumed differences between Muslims and Non-Muslims on the forums, but still look for and negotiate ways to relate to them in their everyday lives.

The discussions about the experiences of cultural differences in everyday life might end with a re-approval of one's own position and a distinction from that 'other' culture, sometimes even with disdain. However, when different positions within the diaspora are juxtaposed, users might also rethink their perceptions and open up toward other cultures through a process of transcultural dialogue. This could in turn influence their practices in everyday life situations.

3.3. Articulations of Cultural Differences on the Discussion Forums

When forum users act on the basis of claimed cultural differences, conflicts and segregation might emerge, especially in the cases of unequal power relations as can be seen in the following example. In MZ, a discussion about the naked pictures of a Moroccan television host escalates into a fight. The user Lets-see criticizes the "German" user Stubborn because she is complaining about "Morocs" on a "Moroccan" forum:

> **Stubborn:** Hold your breath, girl, and think about it first before you insult me!
>
> **Lets-see:** when did I insult YOU then. Read it right first. It is still sassiness to complain like this about Morocs in a Morocc. Forum. I see this also after reading it twentieth time and thinking it over 30 times
>
> I don't find it bad if sentences like that come from Moroccans or when Muslims are mad about Muslims, or blacks rail against each other as "nigger", you know exactly what I mean . . . (MZ, Moroccan naked on the first page, 3)

As can be seen, the question about what can be said by whom on the forums also leads to discussions about cultural differences. The user Lets-see argues that since Stubborn is not Moroccan, she should not complain about "Morocs" on a Moroccan forum. She then refers to the example of "black" people calling themselves a "nigger" and implies that a cultural group's criticizing and defining itself as something is different than another cultural group doing the same thing. This is an important point for relations between groups with unequal power, like between migrant groups who are often perceived as "foreigners" and the local group in the country of migration. However, to argue only 'Morocs' can criticize 'Morocs' creates new forms of discrimination and exclusions on the forums, reproduces cultural boundaries and might delimit the potentials of the forums for dialogue between people of different cultural backgrounds.

Communication between users of different cultural backgrounds does not always result in segregation on the forums. Communication in the form of intercultural dialogue can also lead to reciprocal recognition and offer a ground for dialogue despite differences, or through transcultural communication, cultural boundaries can be deconstructed and a common ground for dialogue beyond differences can emerge. Processes of inter- and transcultural dialogue on the forums intertwine with each other in different communication situations. This can be seen in the following TT-thread, in which one of the users posts a Friday preachment and another user asks if it would also be adequate to post a Catholic preachment. With this question, a discussion about religion and differences among the users starts:

BuKa: hm, am I also allowed to post a catholic Sunday sermon?
I don't mean this ironically. Such preachments always have something that inspires to think—also for people who don't believe in God or people from other religions [. . .]
Are we here a friendly-moderate forum to deal with this respectfully? [. . .]

Fajita: [. . .] the religion simply belongs to a German-Turkish forum, I think. If we exclude this, we will be staying on the surface of agreement.

Even if it is difficult for some of the users without a migration background to realize that most of our Turkish friends are committed Muslims.

It can't be the purpose of such a forum to try to dissuade them—it would never succeed. (TT, Friday preachment, 2)

In the exchange above, the users enter into intercultural dialogue since they assume, but also accept the differences between "users without a migration background" and the "Turkish" users. There is a process of negotiation among the Muslim and Non-Muslim users about how to deal with religious differences on the forums since they meet in the online contact zone created by discussion forums and are in a sense forced to face each others' (religious) differences. As in TT, feelings of belonging to the online community also provide a common ground for transcultural dialogue beyond differences. In TT-forum, many users see themselves as a part of the online community with common norms like reciprocal tolerance beyond cultural and religious differences as it is articulated in expressions like "we," "our," or "a German-Turkish forum."

In the Moroccan forums, we can also speak of a transcultural horizon among the users, which, however, rather emerges on the basis of a shared religious identity. Especially in DD, users engage in transcultural dialogue without articulating ethnic differences based on their common Muslim backgrounds. For example, in a thread, users talk about the brotherhood among "Turks" and "Moroccans" because they are both Muslims. Thereupon, the user Sarah asks "what about the Germans? . . . or are they stepbrothers?" The answer of SMT_mild is that "all Muslims are brothers and sisters." In this sense, we can speak of a common horizon among Muslim users with different cultural backgrounds, through which transcultural dialogue between them takes place. But cultural differences are rearticulated in relation to Non-Muslims, who are excluded from this transcultural dialogue.

4.   Potentials of Diasporic Discussion Forums for Inter- and Transcultural Dialogue

Online communication can foster dialogue between cultures by giving different (ethnic) minorities their 'own' communication space, in which they are not perceived as a minority and by reducing the social barriers of entering into communication with others through anonymity. At the same time, due to the lack of strong social sanctions, it is also easier to segregate, flame, or insult others. In order to enable dialogue on the forums, having formal and informal rules on the forums that guarantee an inclusive and peaceful communication environment is crucial.

Through the diasporic discussion forums, on the one hand, the users in the Moroccan and Turkish diaspora have a chance to represent themselves in a communication space without being addressed as the (problematical) Muslim minority group. On the other hand, users of different cultural backgrounds meet and engage in inter- and transcultural dialogue on the forums. However, dialogue as a form of 'open' and 'respectful' communication is a process of meaning-making and not to be thought of per se in a positive sense. Yet, only through dialogue are differences between cultures articulated, mutually recognized, or deconstructed. Assumed differences, without any type of contact zone between cultures, might lead to stronger feelings of estrangement or to conservatism and confinement within the cultural groups' boundaries.

As demonstrated through the cases of discussion forums of the Moroccan and Turkish diaspora in Germany, the Internet broadens the space for dialogue between cultures and new forms of contact zones. This space for dialogue is appropriated differently by the users depending on the communication rules of the websites as well as the social and cultural contexts. In the Moroccan case, both forums foster dialogue among different cultural groups with Muslim backgrounds in Germany. In the Turkish case, dialogue occurs less often in VB because of continuous fights among the users, whereas TT serves as a base for inter- and transcultural dialogue between users of different cultural and religious backgrounds. Furthermore, both Turkish and Moroccan migrants living in Germany as a minority find their 'own' communication space on the Internet. In this online communication context existing power relations are challenged or even reversed since migrants are the majority and Germans or Non-Muslims are the minority. Thus, through these forums in particular, diasporic websites in general have the potential to enable new forms of dialogue between these groups.

References

Ang, I., & Pothen, N. (2009). Between promise and practice: Web 2.0, Intercultural dialogue and digital scholarship. *fibreculture, 14*, 1–9. Retrieved from http://journal.fibreculture.org/issue14/issue14_ang_pothen.html

Baraldi, C. (2006). New forms of intercultural communication in a globalized world. *International Communication Gazette, 68*(1), 53–69.

Conti, L. (2010). Vom interkulturellen zum transkulturellen dialog: Ein perspektivenwechsel. Hühn, M. Hühn, D. Lerp, K. Petzold, & M. Stock (Eds.), *Transkulturalität, transnationalität, transstaatlichkeit* (pp. 173–89). Berlin: Lit.

Council of Europe. (2008). *White paper on intercultural dialogue: "Living together as equals in dignity."* Retrieved from http://www.coe.int/t/dg4/intercultural/concept_EN.asp

de Haas, H. (2009). Country profile: Morocco. *Focus Migration, 16*, 1–11. Retrieved from http://focus-migration.hwwi.de/Morocco.5987.0.html?&L=1

Hepp, A., & Couldry, N. (2009). What should comparative media research be comparing? Towards a transcultural approach to 'media cultures.' D. K. Thussu & M. Park (Eds.), *Internationalizing media studies* (pp. 32–47). New York, Routledge.

Jandt, F. E. (2010). *An introduction to intercultural communication identities in a global community.* Los Angeles [et al.]: Sage.

Karakasoglu, Y. (2007). Türkische arbeitswanderer in West-, Mittel- und Nordeuropa seit der Mitte der 1950er jahre. K. J. Bade (Ed.), Enzyklopädie migration in Europa: vom 17. jahrhundert bis zur gegenwart (pp. 1054–61). Paderborn [et. al]: Schöningh [et. al].

McPhail, M. L. (2004). Race and the (im) possibility of dialogue. L. A. Baxter & R. Anderson & K. N. Cissna (Eds.), *Dialogue: theorizing difference in communication studies* (pp. 209–224). Thousand Oaks [et al.]: Sage.

Mitra, A. (2005). Creating immigrant identities in cybernetic space: Examples from a non-resident immigrant web-site. *Media, Culture and Society, 27*(3), 371–90.

Pratt, M. L. (1991). Arts of the contact zone. *Profession, 91*, 33–40.

Robins, K. (2006). *The challenge of transcultural diversities transversal study on the theme of cultural policy and cultural diversity.* Strasbourg: Council of Europe Publ.

Rühl, S. (2009). "Grunddaten der zuwandererbevölkerung in Deutschland". Working Paper No. 27, Bundesamt für migration und flüchtlinge, Nurnberg, Germany. http://www.integrationskompass.de/global/show_document.asp?id=aaaaaaaaaaaadfpa

Welsch, W. (1999). Transculturality—The Puzzling form of cultures today. M. Featherstone & S. Lash (Eds.), *Spaces of culture: City, nation, world*, (194–213). London: Sage.

Witteborn, S. (2011). Discursive grouping in a virtual Forum: Dialogue, difference, and the "intercultural". *Journal of International and Intercultural Communication, 4*(2), 109–126. doi: 10.1080/17513057.2011.556827.

Endnotes

1. The interviews were conducted (60 of them by me) within the context of the project "Communicative Networks of Ethnic Minorities" (Chaired by Prof. Dr. Andreas Hepp, 2008–2011, ZeMKI, University of Bremen) and re-analyzed for the presented project in relation to the use of diaproric websites. The length of the interviews varied from 45 minutes to 120 minutes.

2. All quotes are translated from German by the author.

INDEX